WHAT HAPPENS WHEN WE PRACTICE RELIGION?

What Happens When We Practice Religion?

TEXTURES OF DEVOTION
IN ORDINARY LIFE

ROBERT WUTHNOW

PRINCETON UNIVERSITY PRESS
PRINCETON & OXFORD

Copyright © 2020 by Princeton University Press

Requests for permission to reproduce material from this work should be sent to permissions@press.princeton.edu

Published by Princeton University Press
41 William Street, Princeton, New Jersey 08540
6 Oxford Street, Woodstock, Oxfordshire OX20 1TR

press.princeton.edu

All Rights Reserved

Library of Congress Cataloging-in-Publication Data

Names: Wuthnow, Robert, author.
Title: What happens when we practice religion? : textures of devotion in everyday life / Robert Wuthnow.
Description: Princeton : Princeton University Press, 2020. | Includes bibliographical references and index.
Identifiers: LCCN 2019024278 (print) | LCCN 2019024279 (ebook) | ISBN 9780691198583 (hardcover) | ISBN 9780691198590 (paperback) | ISBN 9780691201276 (epub)
Subjects: LCSH: Religious life. | Spirituality.
Classification: LCC BL624 .W88 2020 (print) | LCC BL624 (ebook) | DDC 204/.4—dc23
LC record available at https://lccn.loc.gov/2019024278
LC ebook record available at https://lccn.loc.gov/2019024279

British Library Cataloging-in-Publication Data is available

Editorial: Fred Appel and Jenny Tan
Production Editorial: Debbie Tegarden
Jacket/Cover Design: C. Alvarez-Gaffin
Production: Erin Suydam
Publicity: Nathalie Levine and Kathryn Stevens
Copyeditor: Karen Verde

Jacket/Cover Credit: the cover art is from iStock

This book has been composed in Classic Arno

Printed on acid-free paper. ∞

Printed in the United States of America

10 9 8 7 6 5 4 3 2 1

CONTENTS

Preface vii

	Introduction	1
1	Theories	14
2	Situations	42
3	Intentions	77
4	Feelings	105
5	Bodies	146
	Conclusion	193

Bibliography 197

Index 229

PREFACE

IN THE MID-1980S, I had the privilege of being asked to co-direct an interdisciplinary seminar tasked with bringing together faculty and graduate students interested in the intersections of religion and culture—scholars from anthropology, history, religious studies, sociology, and several related programs. The seminar evolved into a center that eventually became the Princeton University Center for the Study of Religion, and under the center's auspices the seminar continued to meet weekly, engaging scholars in sustained cross-departmental conversations and serving as an extraordinary space for critical discussions of research papers, dissertations, and books in progress. The present volume is an outgrowth of those conversations and is an attempt to address one of the recurring questions that inhabited those discussions.

That question can be simply stated even though it cannot be simply answered: What do we mean when we say that people *practice* religion? What do we look at? What do we need to think about, not to discern some essential universal feature of religion or to advance yet another grand theory, and certainly not to revisit thoroughly trod ground about how religion functions or what it causes people to do, but to piece together the intricate textures of how it is present in ordinary life? What takes place in the immediate moment that illuminates, not the consequences of religion or what people hope to get out of it, but what they do? In brief, what happens? And what do we scholars do as we seek to understand the diverse manifestations of religious practice? What provisional concepts do we have at our disposal? What insights are there in the existing literature? What promises to be of continuing benefit? From week to week and from year to year, these were the topics that kept appearing in the background of the seminar's discussions.

The discussions turned, without anyone quite being able to say precisely when or why, in two decisive directions. The first was a shift from descriptive generalizations about American religion toward approaches offering greater capacity to take account of the vast variety of religious expression in wider contexts as well as the remarkable diversity within American religion itself. To converse constructively about monastic Buddhism in China and hospice care in Japan and Pentecostal worship in a Brazilian *favela*, or even about yoga practice and choir practice and prayer in the United States, the point of research has to shift. Important as it is for scholarship about religion to examine the intricate details of these vastly diverse practices and to depict them in their distinctive social and historical contexts, it must also be reflexive about its aims. It has to quit searching for the underlying empirical commonalities and start looking for the heuristic devices that equip the investigations to better understand the richness of the topics at hand. It has to plunge more deeply into the webs of significance in which we are suspended, as Clifford Geertz described them, not by seeking only to discern the meanings present but also by examining how the webs are constructed. The second was a shift toward an epistemological framework that foregrounded the inevitably messy habit-driven but also improvisational character of action in the unfolding events of day-to-day life while including sufficient attention to the inequities of power that inevitably constrain those activities. Attentiveness to these situated agentic processes further underscores the importance of bringing multiple analytic tools to bear as opposed to ambitiously parsimonious explanations.

The conversations that form the back story of what I have attempted to do here operated at several levels. There was the topic of the day, which posed familiar graduate seminar questions about clarity of argument and credibility of evidence. Many of these draft presentations became journal articles and chapters in books. They contributed immensely to my own thinking, as is evidenced in the frequent references I make to them in the pages that follow. Besides the publications themselves, the seminar discussions brought to the group and to me insights from the latest developments in the various disciplines from which the participants came, thus significantly broadening the range of ideas, concepts, and considerations beyond what generally happens within single departments. Those connections were furthered in opportunities the Center provided for personal interaction with scholars in the various humanities and social science departments at Princeton and with guest speakers, panelists, conference participants, postdoctoral fellows, and visiting scholars from numerous other universities.

Any seminar worth its time leaves far more questions unanswered than it answers. The questions I was left with range far too widely to have ever been given sufficient attention. Many of them nevertheless concern the micro details of what happens when people say they practice religion, whether in mumbling a prayer they learned in childhood, embarking on an exhausting pilgrimage, arranging the items on display at a home altar, wearing a hijab, viewing an icon, or walking the dog. The questions I've tried to address here have been with me for a long time and I do not claim to have found the best ways of thinking about them. My approach has been mostly to ask what a concept, such as "practice," that appears frequently in discussions of religion is taken to mean in treatments that have little to do with religion and then to move back and forth among those discussions to see what is of greatest interest and why. As a sociologist drawn to empirical research, my approach is also to seek insights from the numerous empirical studies that have been conducted by scholars of religion in various disciplines and to interrogate those as examples of the approaches and concepts that have been of interest.

Just as my students and colleagues have done for me, I hope that what I offer here will contribute to an ongoing conversation about the tools that can be brought to bear from multiple disciplines and approaches on the study of religion. The task is not to keep asking what religion is or what its future may be but to *see* what people do and say and to understand how they make sense of those acts and utterances when they practice religion. The task, moreover, is to quit thinking about religion as if it is unlike everything else that people do, and rather to make full use of the tools we have at our disposal in the human sciences.

My gratitude to the dozens and dozens of scholars from whose work I have benefited directly and indirectly through the interdisciplinary seminar is beyond measure. The origins of the seminar have mostly faded into the dim mists of time, but it would not have happened without the significant input and counsel of my colleagues John Wilson and Albert Raboteau. I am also deeply grateful to Princeton University for its support of the seminar and the Center for the Study of Religion, to the skilled hand of Katherine Rohrer in guiding its development, and to Jenny Wiley Legath and Anita Kline for their faithfulness in administering the Center. I am indebted to my colleagues in the sociology department for their forbearance and support, and my editor at Princeton University Press, Fred Appel, for suggesting some years ago that I consider putting together a book of this kind and for his gracious colleagueship.

WHAT HAPPENS WHEN WE PRACTICE RELIGION?

Introduction

PRACTICING RELIGION FOCUSES on what people do and say rather than only on what they think and believe. Practices are the interconnected strings of activity that constitute our personal lives and the social relationships that shape the contours of our collective existence. They are what we do to get things done. Some take hardly any time at all; others unfold over months and years. Many of them become so routine that we rarely think about them; others require extensive deliberation and discipline. All practices are an interplay of habit and improvisation, of choice and constraint.

Emphasis on practice in the study of religion is an emerging and yet insufficiently elaborated development. It valuably directs attention to how religion is enacted within the everyday settings of our personal lives and in the public discourse and power arrangements that govern our lives together. It boldly challenges the notion that religion can be understood in terms of predefined categories of affiliation and belief or that religion is too subjective, too idiosyncratic, to be a focus of academic inquiry at all. Practicing is observable. It is observable in gestures, demeanor, speech, social arrangements, and public policies. Practicing religion occurs not only in ashrams and churches and mosques. It happens in homes and hospitals, on the street, at work, and in art galleries, concert halls, government offices, and prisons. Understanding religion as a practice necessitates delving deeply into what happens in these situations. It requires paying attention to how the social interaction there unfolds through time, how people express their intentions and feelings, and what they do with their bodies as they devise the routines and rituals that give their lives spiritual meaning.

This approach represents a continuation but also a departure. The study of religion has long been fraught with divisions that reflected its origins in multiple disciplines. Sociological, anthropological, psychological, and historical studies of religion have differed in how they approached the topic. The literature has also been divided between hermeneutic and positivistic epistemologies. The interpretive literature has drawn heavily from qualitative studies while the positivistic literature has favored quantitative research. The various studies have differed greatly in levels of analysis, ranging from micro-level studies in which individuals' beliefs and actions were taken as the unit of analysis, to macro-level comparative historical studies focusing on modernity and secularization. Within disciplines, the literature has also been fragmented in terms of favored theoretical arguments and counterarguments emphasizing rational choice, social psychological assumptions, cognitive evolution, and cultural influences. Much of the literature has dealt only with Christianity in the United States.

Many of these divisions persist and, if anything, have deepened in recent years as work on religion has proliferated. Research interests have significantly expanded to take greater account of race, gender, and sexual orientation. Theoretical approaches pay closer attention to feminist, queer theory, anti-racist, and anti-colonial arguments about domination and resistance. Considerably greater numbers of studies focus on Buddhism, Hinduism, Islam, and Judaism. More of the research published in English-language venues has been conducted in Africa, East Asia, South Asia, and Latin America, and US-focused studies pay greater attention to the diverse religions of immigrants. Suggestive cross-fertilization also continues within disciplines: work on religion draws variously from phenomenology, relational sociology, ritual studies, cognitive science, and evolutionary psychology. Surveys of the literature in handbooks, edited compendia, and review essays underscore the proliferation of topics and approaches.

A growing body of work nevertheless has developed concepts that have mobilized new research spanning disciplinary boundaries. The "lived religion" approach that emerged in the 1980s encouraged scholarship in history, religious studies, and eventually in ethnographic sociology to focus on grassroots activities outside of religious organizations rather than the formal theological teachings of those organizations. Lived religion provided a broad umbrella under which to study street festivals, prayer groups, home altars, gifts, holidays, and burials, among other manifestations of religion that engaged people in ordinary life. A second development focused on "materiality," as featured in studies of religious art and architecture, icons, portraiture, and photographs. A third development emphasized the discursive structures evident in sermons, testimonials, conversion narratives, music, prayer, and stories about spiritual journeys. Together, these developments broadened the scope of religion scholarship beyond its Protestant-centric traditions to pay greater attention to other religions and to the intersection of multiple traditions. Epistemological assumptions about structure and agency, gender, power, and mind-body distinctions also commanded greater interest.

The "practice turn," as it is called, has proven attractive as an approach that embraces much of this work. Practice theory is a collection of ideas in the social sciences about the importance of situating the study of human behavior in the ordinary contexts in which it occurs. As it pertains to religion, practice theory builds on Émile Durkheim's well-known discussion of sacred ritual and Max Weber's work on meanings and theodicies. It borrows from a rich lineage of anthropological work evident, for instance, in Clifford Geertz's definitional essay on religion and in sociological contributions such as Peter Berger and Thomas Luckmann's discussion of the social construction of reality. It draws from Pierre Bourdieu's emphasis on the situational dispositions that shape and are shaped by processes of reflectively and bodily engaged social interaction. It embraces Michel Foucault's and Talal Asad's focus on status distinctions and power. It is situated in epistemological discussions oriented toward the structured but agentic actions of persons and collectivities and in discussions of the embodied characteristics of thought, intentions, discourse, and emotions.[1]

The late-twentieth-century literature on social practices focused on how best to make sense of human behavior while acknowledging its complexities and enormous variations. In contrast with positivistic approaches that objectified human behavior in an effort to generate theoretically parsimonious law-like generalizations, practice theory emphasized research truer to the diversity and complexity of social life and sought less to produce empirical generalizations

---

1. Practice theory is discussed in chapter 1; for introductory essays and overviews, see Joseph Rouse, "Practice Theory," in *Philosophy of Anthropology and Sociology*, edited by Stephen P. Turner and Mark W. Risjord (New York: Elsevier, 2007), 499–540; Theodore R. Schatzki, Karin Knorr Cetina, and Eike von Savigny, eds., *The Practice Turn in Contemporary Theory* (New York: Routledge, 2001); and Davide Nicolini, *Practice Theory, Work, and Organization: An Introduction* (New York: Oxford University Press, 2012); and for a valuable discussion of practice theory's roots in American pragmatism and influence in sociological theory, see Neil Gross, "A Pragmatist Theory of Social Mechanisms," *American Sociological Review* 74, 3 (2009), 358–79.

than to identify sensitizing concepts. The key points that emerged in this period were these:

- The thoughts and actions of human persons take place in lived and imagined situations, which are concrete in the sense of being emplaced and providing the situational cues and material affordances that shape and are shaped by the ensuing social interaction that occurs within them.
- Human action and interaction is purposive, less in the sense posited traditionally of being driven teleologically by long-term goals, but more in the sense of being guided by provisional prior intentions, plans, and decisions, and by immediate intentions in action that provide feedback and alternatives during the temporal unfolding of purposive action.
- Human behavior is best understood through consideration not only of the causes and consequences of action but also of the feelings, bodily kinesthetics, and interpretive discourses that render it meaningful.
- The situated character of human behavior does not occur in a spatial or temporal vacuum but is conducted by persons who bring relatively stable selves grounded in previous interaction and memory, and thus including dispositions and gendered, racial, ethnic, sexual, and religious identities in their social interaction.
- The situated action of individuals pertains to communities as well, which necessitate investigation in terms of space, temporality, identity, and their competitors and environments.
- Power dynamics—interpersonal, institutional, and societal—play a significant role in structuring the action and interaction within practices engaged in by individuals and communities.

The practice approach is thus concerned with understanding the details of situated temporal action and is interpretive, though not in terms of time-ordered unidirectional causality, but in examining the structuring processes through which situational, dispositional, and unequally distributed power arrangements affect the agentic activities of individuals and collectivities.

In the years since these emphases emerged, practice theory has again shifted. What might be termed its "second generation" has focused less on epistemological orientations, especially in moving beyond a phenomenological emphasis on the perspectives and experiences of the individual to embrace ideas of social structure and the decentering of the self in discourse, and more on substantive studies. Voluminous work has been done on religious practices. Much of this work has been ethnographic, conducted through close participant observation in settings that illuminate in greater detail how practices are influenced by the situations in which they occur. Studies of pilgrimages, dietary rituals, speaking in tongues, devotional practices, and political rallies are among the many investigations that shed new light on practitioners' intentions, feelings, and narratives, and on the roles of bodies and material affordances. The second-generation literature is also informed increasingly by experimental studies of situational cues, habits, improvisation, and cognitive processes.

Studies of religious practice take for granted the arguments advanced in social constructivism; namely, that religion is not an essentialized category that can be identified in terms of a few defining core components, but is a culturally constructed category, the construction of which has developed over time, varies according to context, and is held in place by power as much as by conviction. Second-generation practice-oriented research has been less concerned with why religion exists at all than with how its various manifestations are constructed and maintained. Large questions about what counts as religion at all are mostly answered by the fact that religion is well-institutionalized and that even terms such as "secular" and "spiritual" occur in relation to these institutionalized designations. Religion in these institutional manifestations is maintained by the devotion of adherents and by persons in positions of authority but also by the resistance of persons who disavow being religious.

The constructivist perspective underlying practice approaches to religion has evolved from suggesting that religion can be identified functionally as a source of sacred experience and meaning toward asking what all may be involved when a person prays, bows, kneels, worships, testifies, visits a shrine, views an icon, feels divinely inspired, or practices something deemed religious in a hundred other ways. The vast diversity of these practices means shifting from earlier efforts concerned with categorizing them and seeking generalizations about them toward a focus on the *how to* of observation and analysis. Knowing that whatever the topic under consideration may be, it will be different in a year's time and in another context, the task is for researchers to learn and sharpen the analytic tools that are likely to prove useful in the next time and place.

In the chapters that follow I describe the central concepts and arguments now advancing the study of religious practice. I foreground studies both of religion and of related topics that serve as empirical examples. These concepts and studies are located in a variety of disciplines and subfields and draw on disparate analytic traditions that can be furthered in subsequent interdisciplinary research. The literature on religious practice developed initially along two lines that largely made separate contributions: discussions that advanced the approach in terms of epistemological arguments, on the one hand, and empirical studies that offered insightful descriptive evidence, on the other hand. Epistemological contributions drew from Maurice Merleau-Ponty, Michel de Certeau, Pierre Bourdieu, Henri Lefebvre, Michel Foucault, Talal Asad, and others who challenged decontextualized positivistic approaches to knowledge. Notable empirical contributions included studies of prayer groups, street festivals, and religious experiences by Robert Orsi, Thomas Csordas, Saba Mahmood, and Lila Abu-Lughod, among others. In the decades since these contributions were made, theoretically informed empirical studies have expanded through the work of anthropologists, historians, religion scholars, social and cognitive psychologists, and sociologists into a wide range of topics that illuminate significant aspects of religious practice such as its role in the construction of sacred space, in gendered social relationships, and in somatic learning, affordances, the visual and performing arts, meditation, and ritual. These contributions are rich with suggestive insights for further exploration.

The historical moment in which we live makes it imperative to better understand the role of religious practices in our world. The frequency with which religion dominates national and international events testifies to that imperative, as does the vast number of study groups, worship places, meditation centers, college courses, and scholarly books and articles about religion. The diversity of religious practices and the contextual variation in how the sacred is understood and experienced falsifies the assumptions of earlier scholarship suggesting that religion could be essentialized under simple generalizations about its core components and societal functions. Its diverse manifestations further demonstrate the necessity of locating religious practice amid the convergences of mental, emotional, and bodily experience and the social interaction that shapes that experience. Interesting as it may be to read about a poll or political speech or pilgrimage or act of violence that invokes religion, the take-home will be disappointing—and not only because the news cycle reboots minute by minute—unless greater care is taken to understand these events.[2]

---

2. Practice theory does not argue that beliefs are unimportant, but seeks to embed the discussion of beliefs in the situations in which beliefs are enacted and embodied and in which they are constituted as dispositions and intentions. As Danièle Hervieu-Léger observes, following de Certeau, "belief is lived." Danièle Hervieu-Léger, "Religion as Memory: Reference to Tradition and the Constitution of a Heritage of Belief in Modern Societies," in *Religion: Beyond a*

If the current practice turn is to inspire new research that provides new insights about religion, we need to take stock of what has been learned, not in terms of demographic and attitudinal generalizations, but about the repertoire of concepts and questions that can serve usefully in the conduct of this research. I have organized the discussion that follows under the following headings: theories, situations, intentions, feelings, and bodies. Studies have illuminated one or another of these, but students of religious practice must be aware of the potential influence and interaction among all of them. Whether the topic under consideration is a festival, religious art, private devotional routines, or a worship service, these are all relevant to the investigation.

The need to start by discussing theory is that the practice approach represents a departure from how the study of religion has been theoretically grounded in the past. Social science discussions of religion typically reference the work of Émile Durkheim and Max Weber in the late nineteenth and early twentieth centuries, turn next to mid-twentieth-century conceptual contributions by writers such as Clifford Geertz and Peter Berger, and then discuss recent studies in these lineages. The unifying thread in standard interpretations of that work has been an emphasis on *classificatory concepts*, such as Durkheim's concepts of sacred and profane, Weber's ideal types, Geertz's definitional essay on religion, and Berger's idea of a sacred canopy. Classifications of these kinds seek to describe the conceptual categories in which people in ordinary life organize their worlds and at the same time identify the characteristics that facilitate scholarly investigations to advance. Classification contributes importantly to grassroots and scientific knowledge, but has proven repeatedly to be less stable and more diverse than earlier generalizations allowed.

The practice approach locates itself within much the same theoretical tradition but emphasizes different aspects of these influential contributions, particularly the meta-concepts that provided analytic tools, rather than the culturally circumscribed applications to which they were put. For instance, instead of taking Durkheim's categories of sacred and profane as fundamentally different aspects of reality, the practice approach emphasizes Durkheim's discussion of the rituals in which people engage to create, maintain, and empower these divisions. And instead of favoring Weber's categories of inner- and other-worldly asceticism, the insights to be drawn from Weber focus on the status relations and disciplines that lend themselves more to certain practices than to others.

Concept, edited by Hent de Vries (New York: Fordham University Press, 2008), 245–58, quote on page 253.

As a rule, the practice approach emphasizes *structuring processes* instead of classificatory concepts. Structuring processes refer to series of actions that unfold over time and do so within the constraints of circumstances, resources, and previous activities. Structuring processes take account of the reality that outcomes are shaped by multiple converging conditions. I discuss the theoretical contributions associated with this shift from classificatory concepts to structuring processes in chapter 1.

Chapter 2 discusses the characteristics of *situations* that shape the way religious activities and experiences take place. Practices are influenced by the discrete physical and temporal spaces in which social action occurs. They are constructed by the actors involved and in interaction with the other people who may be present as well as physical objects such as rooms, furniture, and food. Whether a study is conducted using ethnographic methods that directly take account of these interactions or is a survey or is based on archival research, the point to understand is that religious practices make use of and bear the imprint of the situations in which they occur.

I discuss *intentions* in chapter 3. Although some research has focused on intentions, these are admittedly difficult to study effectively because they are for the most part subjective. A person who intends to pray but does not, for instance, is hard to think about because the intention may be known only to the person. Nevertheless, religions so frequently emphasize intentions—stating, for instance, that what a person intends by helping the poor may be as important as helping itself—that the topic bears consideration. As it happens, advances in the philosophical and linguistic study of intentions offer useful insights.

Feelings are the focus of chapter 4. Feelings have been emphasized especially in studies of religious experience and ritual. The argument in many of these studies is that powerful feelings are a significant reason for these experiences and rituals being deemed sacred. However, these arguments warrant critical scrutiny in relation to religious practices, some of which may not include powerful feelings at all. The two broad questions that merit consideration are: under what conditions do certain religious practices prompt kinds of feelings, and what are the rules in various situations that govern the public expression of those feelings?

The role of *bodies*, which has been the focus of increasing interest in studies of religion, is addressed in chapter 5. Insofar as religious practice is conducted by people in concrete situations, it goes without saying that bodies are involved. However, the extent and ways they are involved varies considerably, as evident for instance in comparisons of Muslim prayers, the clothing of Orthodox Jews, and the postures involved in Buddhist meditation. Important questions include the kinds of somatic and kinesthetic imprint these activities may have on the body and how people learn or unlearn these bodily sensations.

Many of the studies conducted with an interest in the practice approach have been ethnographic and historical, taking advantage of opportunities for in-depth exploration of the situations involved and people's negotiations of the constraints and opportunities present. Ethnographic and historical studies are well-disposed toward observing social relationships as they unfold and the language and emotions and interactions that result as well as such matters as ritual events, food, clothing, and spatial arrangements. Quantitative research has also contributed significantly to understandings of practices. Controlled experimental-design studies, for instance, have examined how people respond to situational cues and how they learn skills through practice. Surveys offer opportunities for closer examination of the role of childhood practices, responses to artifacts and hypothetical situations, and the stability or instability of practices. Beyond their empirical implications, such studies also suggest the value of what Karin Knorr Cetina has termed "methodological situationism," which examines situational variations and biases that may challenge generalizations based on large population studies. Insofar as knowledge is situational, derived from our many situated experiences, social science is enriched by investigating the practices that occur within them.[3]

Practices, unlike classifications, are messy, fluid, and dynamic, extending from situation to situation and taking place over time. Indeed, developments in practice theory itself have increasingly emphasized the tension that characterizes them in everyday life between stable routine behavior that requires little conscious thought and the small or large adjustments that people make to accommodate changing circumstances and desires. Practices are characterized by a fundamental *plasticity*, João Biehl and Peter Locke write in *Unfinished*, by the "figuring out, disfiguring, and refiguring of lifeworlds."[4] As relatively

---

3. Karin D. Knorr Cetina, "Introduction: The Micro-Sociological Challenge of Macro-Sociology: Towards a Reconstruction of Social Theory and Methodology," in *Advances in Social Theory and Methodology*, edited by Karin Knorr Cetina and Aaron Cicourel (Boston and London: Routledge and Kegan Paul, 1981); and on suggestions about examining practices in surveys, Michael Burawoy, "The Extended Case Method," *Sociological Theory* 16, 1 (1998), 4–33.

4. João Biehl and Peter Locke, "Foreword," in *Unfinished: The Anthropology of Becoming*, edited by João Biehl and Peter Locke (Durham, NC: Duke University Press, 2017), x.

patterned sequences of activities, practices thus necessitate paying close attention to how regular or irregular they are and the conditions under which routines remain stable or change. The dynamics that run through the constitutive aspects of practices and that shape them in these significant ways include in various forms *habit, improvisation,* and *power.* These are the aspects that yield "know-how," the information that draws on past experience to make sense of present conditions and thus to shape responses and agendas. Each is implied in the situations, intentions, feelings, discourses, and embodied practices in which individuals and communities engage.[5]

Studies of habit have brought together recent interests in cognitive processing with earlier theoretical emphases in the literature on American pragmatism that identified habit as a central feature of human problem solving. John Dewey's work has been particularly relevant in this regard. Dewey characterized habit as the inseparable mental and bodily means of accomplishing tasks. It was socially derived and reinforced not only through specific routines but also as dispositions that reflected the impact of interdependent activities. Habit, which operated below the seat of consciousness, he argued, provided moral conduct its essential grounding and durability in contrast with spontaneous impulses.[6] Habit in recent research is understood as both situationally and dispositionally cued, which locates it within practice theory as the inclination that guides action in terms of experiences in similar situations and the memory of those experiences.

Habit is the practice that is (or should be) impossible to ignore in discussions of religion. The significance of habit in Jewish and Christian traditions is summarized in the biblical statement, "Train up a child in the way he should go and when he is old he will not depart from it."[7] The training suggested includes cultivating good habits through such repetitive behavior as daily prayers, memorization of scripture, and worship attendance. The deadening

---

5. Archer's treatment of habitus and reflexivity provides helpful ontological background for the distinction between habit and improvisation; see Margaret S. Archer, "Routine, Reflexivity, and Realism," *Sociological Theory* 28, 3 (2010), 272–303.

6. John Dewey, *Human Nature and Conduct: An Introduction to Social Psychology* (New York: Henry Holt and Company, 1922); the sources and impact of Dewey's work on habit are discussed in Serena J. Woolf, "The Nature of Habit: F. M. Alexander and John Dewey," *AmSAT Journal* 9 (Spring 2016), 46–56; Gross, "A Pragmatist Theory of Social Mechanisms"; and Larry A. Hickman, *Pragmatism as Post-Postmodernism: Lessons from John Dewey* (New York: Fordham University Press, 2007), 241–54.

7. Proverbs 22:6 KJV.

possibilities of habit have been recognized as well. As William James observed, "Standing, walking, buttoning and unbuttoning, piano-playing, talking, even saying one's prayers, may be done when the mind is absorbed in other things."[8] Recent psychological research distinguishes habit in terms of the repetitiveness with which people give the same responses in a given context, the frequency and durability of these responses, the apparent automaticity or lack of immediate awareness and intention with which they occur, their efficiency, and in many instances the seeming inability of persons to exercise control over them. Neuropsychological studies suggest that human cognition operates as a dual processing system in which habit is typified by fast spontaneous processes rather than slow deliberative processes. The study of habit holds far-reaching and largely unexamined implications for research on religion, whether in inquiries of routine religious practices or in considerations about the circumstances under which people may be held responsible based on their intentions for the consequences of their behavior.[9]

Improvisation is the concept that best captures the cognitive and behavioral aspects of human conduct, which in Dewey's terms differed from habit in terms of greater spontaneity and impulsiveness but also thoughtfulness and innovation. Whereas habit implies continuities and conformity, improvisation evokes connotations of novelty, curiosity, malleability, adaptation, and deliberation. It is the emergent aspect of practices that gives them their agentic quality. Studies of improvisation in music, theater, sports, and organizational management distinguish it in terms of individuals' ability to adapt on short notice to new and unusual situations by creatively processing a range of choices. Improvisation is "slow" compared with habit in the deliberative cognitive processing and heavy reliance on memory it requires. The growing focus of research on improvisation stems from practice theory's insistence on the indeterminate character of action when considered in relation to the processing of situational cues and social interaction. While improvisation differs from habit in terms of its relation to the dual processing model of cognition, the two overlap and indeed are shown in research to be switched from one to the other as situations require. For the

8. William James, *Principles of Psychology* (New York: Henry Holt & Co., 1890), 5.
9. Valuable summaries of the literature on habit include Ann M. Graybiel, "Habits, Rituals, and the Evaluative Brain," *Annual Review of Neuroscience* 31 (2008), 359–87; Tom Sparrow and Adam Hutchinson, eds., *A History of Habit: From Aristotle to Bourdieu* (New York: Lexington Books, 2013); and Wendy Wood and Dennis Rünger, "Psychology of Habit," *Annual Review of Psychology* 67 (2016), 289–314.

study of religion, improvisation underscores the extent to which religious practice is pragmatic, deliberative, and often constituted as much by ad hoc behavior as by habit.[10]

Power in the form of facilitation and constraint is present both in general terms in situations and more specifically in the habits and improvisations of which practices are comprised. The role of state, institutional, and interpersonal power in religious practice has been recognized in anthropological, historical, and of course political science research, but has been surprisingly neglected in sociological investigations in which growth and decline of membership and free market assumptions about religion's separation from the state have been emphasized. But power at all levels shapes the activities that are possible and is shaped in turn by these activities. Its presence is evident in the force that habits exercise in daily life, the institutional power through which habits are learned, the social interaction that maintains them, and the political authorities that legitimate them. It is evident in the circumstances under which improvisation is or is not deemed desirable and the constraints that govern how much improvisation is possible. In Bourdieu's suggestive phrase, practice is "regulated improvisation."[11] In religion it is the organizational imprimatur that encourages parents to "train up" children's religious activities and the authority determining that certain innovations in doctrines and rituals are acceptable and others are not. Moreover, it is the power exercised in trade relations and working conditions and through information technology to embrace certain religious practices in preference to others. These regimes of power are the past and present macrostructures that influence what happens in local situations.

A focus on regulated improvisation posits that religion can be usefully understood in terms of the practices that take shape as habits and as ad hoc adaptations and innovations in the daily circumstances in which we live.

---

10. On improvisation, see Aaron L. Berkowitz, *The Improvising Mind: Cognition and Creativity in the Musical Moment* (New York: Oxford University Press, 2010); David Hargreaves, Dorothy Miell, and Raymond MacDonald, eds., *Musical Imaginations: Multidisciplinary Perspectives on Creativity, Performance and Perception* (New York: Oxford University Press, 2011); George E. Lewis and Benjamin Piekut, eds., *The Oxford Handbook of Critical Improvisation Studies*, 2 vols. (New York: Oxford University Press, 2016); Jeff Pressing, "Improvisation: Methods and Models," in *Generative Processes in Music: The Psychology of Performance, Improvisation, and Composition*, edited by John Sloboda, 130–79 (New York: Oxford University Press, 2001); and Eitan Wilf, "Semiotic Dimensions of Creativity," *Annual Review of Anthropology* 43 (2014), 397–412.

11. Pierre Bourdieu, *Outline of a Theory of Practice* (New York: Cambridge University Press, 1977), 21.

Regulated improvisation emphasizes the indeterminacy of human behavior, the reality we know from personal experience if not from religion that life is uncertain, events are unpredictable, and circumstances necessitate adapting and innovating. The habits and the adaptations and the implicit regulations that constrain them offer constructs with which to organize the discussion of religious practice, both in terms of personal circumstances and societal conditions. They serve as reference points for the situated interactive processes that practice entails. These conceptual emphases necessitate focusing on the temporal unfolding of learned sequences of behavior through which habits are acquired and in which improvisation occurs. The sequences take place in settings that include power dynamics, social interactions, and discursive formations that cue and constrain the emerging practices. The formation of habits and the improvisation in which individuals engage focus analytic attention on the repetition that is present, the idiomatic templates through which it is represented, the situational cues that prompt and disrupt familiarity, and the choices for adaptation and innovation on which individuals and collectivities deliberate and act.

1

Theories

SOCIAL SCIENCE DISCUSSIONS of the sacred have been exceptionally rich, extending beyond the study of religion into sociological and anthropological theory, phenomenology, semiotics, psychology, and cultural analysis. The starting place for most of these inquiries nevertheless is religion. In religious settings and through religious teachings people not only hear about the sacred and are encouraged to believe in it; they also *practice* it. They do things—worship, sing, pray, meditate. They speak in idiomatic ways in places of worship and carry these idioms into the experiences of daily life. Practicing religion in these ways is shaped by where we live and how we were raised. They are thus manifestly social both in how they are shaped and in how we structure our lives.

This chapter traces the theoretical contributions that have influenced how the social shaping of the sacred in religion has been understood. The logic that runs through much of this literature emphasizes *classificatory concepts*; that is, concepts that state what the sacred is and what religion is by identifying its essential defining features as a social category and by distinguishing that category from other categories. After discussing the various ambiguities and criticisms that theorists have made of this approach, I show how a focus on *structuring processes* can be developed from much the same literature but with the result being an emphasis on how religion is *practiced*.

Sacred and Profane

Émile Durkheim's *Elementary Forms of Religious Life* is the place to begin in thinking about the social role of the sacred. Durkheim's underlying concern was with problems of symbolism and social order. Its expression in the *Elementary Forms* lay principally with the potential of things and people deemed "sacred" to symbolize and thus reinforce people's moral conviction to the society in which they lived. The sacred could be a symbol of power that drew its ritual adherents toward a commitment to something they shared that was greater than any of their divergent self-interests. Its defining feature was that it was *set apart*. It differed from the mundane realities in which people lived most of the time. It did so cognitively in the language with which its set-apart-ness was described and especially in the dramatic rituals and taboos that evoked a sense of collective effervescence about it that was not present in everyday life.[1]

Durkheim's approach to the sacred resembled his earlier efforts to classify kinds of solidarity ("mechanical" and "organic") and kinds of suicide ("egoistic" and "altruistic"). Theoretical conceptualization in his view required progressing beyond an indiscriminate collection of facts toward a typological classification based on principles of comparison such as morphological complexity. Each construct identified "a category of facts with very distinctive characteristics," as he put it, making sense of observed realities by simplifying them.[2] The distinction between "sacred" and "profane" included the important feature that it was not only an analytic classification but also an empirical one.[3] Whereas people in the real world would likely not have distinguished kinds of solidarity or suicide, they did, as Durkheim and Marcel Mauss argued in *Primitive Classification*, sharply separate the sacred from the profane.[4] Being a "thing set apart" was one of the defining criteria for calling something "sacred." The sacred was further distinguished, Durkheim argued, by being set aside in a way that evoked intense emotion. The "setting aside" was observable because it involved carefully orchestrated rituals in which people physically participated in one another's presence. And the sacred was to be understood as a symbol of the collectivity's power. It was thus an absolute distinction that expressed

---

1. Émile Durkheim, *The Elementary Forms of Religious Life*, trans. Karen E. Fields (New York: Free Press, 1995 [1912]).

2. Émile Durkheim, *The Rules of Sociological Method* (New York: Free Press, 1964, originally published in 1895), 3; Robert N. Bellah, "Durkheim and History," *American Sociological Review* 24, 4 (1959), 447–61; for a critique of Durkheim's approach to classification, see also Kieran Allen and Brian O'Boyle, *Durkheim: A Critical Introduction* (London: Pluto Press, 2017), 57–79.

3. Anthony Giddens, *New Rules of Sociological Method: A Positive Critique of Interpretative Sociologies* (London: Hutchinson, 1976), 162, refers to the "dual hermeneutic" present in such theoretical and empirical classifications.

4. Émile Durkheim and Marcel Mauss, *Primitive Classification*, trans. Rodney Needham (London: Taylor and Francis, 2009 [1903]), especially pages 50 and 52.

something about "totality" because the society's power that it symbolized was all-encompassing.⁵

In these respects, Durkheim's approach to the sacred and profane as distinct categories of social life was consistent with the way other conceptual representations in the social sciences were made. "To classify the phenomena of a given kind it is necessary to recognize the important resemblances and differences by which they are characterized," a 1911 *American Journal of Sociology* essay advised, adding: "The ideal criterion of a class would be a difference in *kind*, a quality possessed by the members of a class and entirely absent from all cases outside the class."⁶ In contributions as diverse as August Comte's influential theological-metaphysical-positive division of evolutionary stages, Herbert Spencer's classification of societies as militant or industrial, Gabriel Tarde's sixfold classification of societal elements, Ferdinand Tönnies's *gemeinschaft-gesellschaft* distinction, and, for that matter, Sigmund Freud's id-ego-superego conceptualization, as well as in later examples such as Ruth Benedict's Apollonian and Dionysian cultures, Claude Levi-Strauss's raw and cooked representations, and Talcott Parsons's numerous fourfold categorizations, the preferred practice was clarification through the "classification of social facts."⁷ Interest in classification was evident not only in attempts to group entire societies and epochs into conceptual categories but also in efforts, of which Durkheim's focus on the sacred was an example, to distinguish kinds of social relations. The task required identifying regularities in social life and examining as best one could which ones clustered together and where those clusters formed patterns that differed from other patterns.⁸

---

5. Durkheim, *Elementary Forms*, 35–36.

6. Edward Cary Hayes, "The Classification of Social Phenomena," *American Journal of Sociology* 17, 5 (1911), 90–118, quote on page 90.

7. Franklin H. Giddings, "The Concepts and Methods of Sociology," *American Journal of Sociology* 10, 2 (1904), 161–76, illustrates another effort at the classification of social facts; and several decades later, Howard Becker, "Constructive Typology in the Social Sciences," *American Sociological Review* 5 (February 1940), 40–55; John C. McKinney, "The Role of Constructive Typology in Scientific Sociological Analysis," *Social Forces* 28, 3 (1950), 235–40. Among recent discussions of the uses and limitations of typological concepts, one of the most valuable is Richard Swedberg, *The Art of Social Theory* (Princeton, NJ: Princeton University Press, 2014), 52–79.

8. Robert N. Bellah, "Introduction," in *Émile Durkheim on Morality and Society*, edited by Robert N. Bellah (Chicago: University of Chicago Press, 1973), ix–lv, notes Comte's influence on Durkheim and the similarities with Tönnies's *gemeinschaft/gesellschaft* distinction.

The sacred was identifiable as a category based on not one thing but several things that together were its constituent attributes. These properties, Durkheim insisted, were not intrinsic to it. The sacred could not be identified because of the objects associated with it having intrinsically special or surprising features or because it referred to nature or the gods or high-ranking persons. Its properties were social. The sacred was defined socially, meaning that its identity was constructed in a group or community or society. The things set apart and not set apart were distinguished *mentally*—"two kinds of mental state"—in radical opposition to one another. They constituted "two distinct sorts of reality with a clear line of demarcation between them: the world of profane things on one side, the world of sacred things on the other." The mental distinction, Durkheim argued, was sufficiently sharp that "they repel and contradict one another so forcefully that the mind refuses to think of them at the same time."[9]

Besides this mental distinction, the sacred was distinguished from the profane *emotionally*: "a collective feeling of respect," which could be expressed in fear or awe or adulation, and in any case was "especially intense," which made it eminently contagious, "like an oil slick."[10] These mental and emotional characteristics above all were produced and maintained *ritually* in "assembled groups" as people came together at special times and in special places to define the sacred by setting it apart and protecting it by enacting certain prohibitions.[11] The ritual in turn reinforced a transformative separation in participants' *self-perceptions*: "In one world he languidly carries on his daily life; the other is one that he cannot enter without abruptly entering into relations with extraordinary powers that excite him to the point of frenzy [such that he] feels he is no longer himself."[12] The sacred was thus experienced as *power* and the force it symbolized was a *collective representation* in two senses of the word: the result of interaction in a collectivity and an expression of the constraining reality of that collectivity.[13]

In brief, the sacred was set apart as a ritually shielded object or event and protected from the contamination of profane life, it was held in emotionally rich regard that generated a kind of contagious excitement that differed from the drudgery of everyday life, and it was a symbolic expression of the

9. Durkheim, *Elementary Forms*, 214.
10. Ibid., 269, 328.
11. Ibid., 303, 350.
12. Ibid., 220.
13. Ibid., 9.

absolute power of the totality people inhabited. The sacred was an analytic construct that referred to potentially observable aspects of social life and was thus a tool for understanding social arrangements. In its ritual manifestations, it was identifiable as a set of ingredients "put together in requisite combinations and intensities."[14]

Durkheim's logic in contrasting the sacred and profane was one of *conceptual classification*. In that respect, it was like Max Weber's classificatory logic in identifying types of asceticism and types of authority, a logic based on establishing, as Weber wrote in another context, "knowledge of what is essential."[15] It was a binary conceptual scheme similar in form—though not in substance—to Ernst Troeltsch's binary distinction between "churches" and "sects" and William James's categorization of religious experience as "healthy-minded" or "sick-soul."[16] The sacred in its various contexts and interpretations represented the holy, the pure, and the ideal, while the profane signified the ordinary, the impure, and the real.

Durkheim's discussion of the sacred was enormously influential in the study of religion. It emphasized ritual and suggested that religious rites and myths were rooted in the societal power people felt constraining them but that they naïvely attributed to the gods. It posed opportunities for thinking about the social role of collective representations and it prompted inquiries into the classification systems that people constructed to impose order in their social relations. Its emphasis on rituals was one to which scholars would return repeatedly in considering formulaic social interaction and its emotional aspects in quite different contexts. The distinction between sacred and profane itself became a way of classifying whole societies and activities within societies. Indeed, one of its earliest adaptations in American sociology was to classify personality types and occupations as sacred or profane; another was to categorize societies as sacred or secular and thus to consider the evolution of one to the other. Apart from such direct applications, the distinction gained lasting attention in discussions

---

14. Randall Collins, "The Classical Tradition in Sociology of Religion," in *The Sage Handbook of the Sociology of Religion*, edited by James A. Beckford and N. Jay Demerath (Thousand Oaks, CA: Sage, 2007), 19–38, quote on page 28.

15. Max Weber, *Roscher and Knies: The Logical Problems of Historical Economics*, trans. Guy Oakes (New York: Free Press, 1975), 213.

16. Ernst Troeltsch, *The Social Teachings of the Christian Churches* (New York: Free Press, 1931); William James, *The Varieties of Religious Experience: A Study in Human Nature* (Adelaide, South Australia: University of Adelaide Library, 2005, originally published 1902), 62–144.

of cultural logics that separated the pure and impure and in other ways imposed categories and classificatory schemes on social life.[17]

In *Elementary Forms*, though, tensions were evident that revealed Durkheim's discomfort with considering the sacred-profane distinction strictly as a mode of classification. One was whether the complete cluster of beliefs and activities had to be present or whether some held conceptual primacy over the others. Durkheim was ambivalent as to whether the sacred's symbolization of totality was more important than the objects, rites, and emotions that might be involved. Another was whether sacred and profane should be considered as a continuum, as Durkheim conceded other categories should be, or whether they were truly opposites—and if they were, whether the one could penetrate the other—as Durkheim's discussion of the impure sacred suggested. By extension, was it better to think of the two as static side-by-side categories or as dynamic relational categories constructed by crossings, transgressions, and ambiguities? There was also the question of how observable the distinction was in view of Durkheim's acknowledgment that the sacred was necessarily constructed differently in different societies and his insistence that the sacred nevertheless stood for something universal. In short, the sacred in both its theoretical and empirical manifestations was fraught, as Tomoku Masuzawa observes, by the "precariousness of typological demarcation."[18]

---

17. Everett Cherrington Hughes, "Personality Types and the Division of Labor," *American Journal of Sociology* 33 (March 1928), 754–68; Howard Becker and Robert C. Myers, "Sacred and Secular Aspects of Human Sociation," *Sociometry* 5 (August 1942), 207–29; Howard Becker, "Sacred and Secular Societies: Considered with Reference to Folk-State and Similar Classifications," *Social Forces* 28 (May 1950), 361–76. Jeffrey Alexander, "Citizen and Enemy as Symbolic Classification," in *Cultivating Differences: Symbolic Boundaries and the Making of Inequality*, edited by Michele Lamont and Marcel Fournier (Chicago: University of Chicago Press, 1992), 290, for example, emphasizes symbolic codes that "supply the structured categories of pure and impure into which every member, or potential member of civil society is made to fit." Mustafa Emirbayer, "Useful Durkheim," *Sociological Theory* 14 (July 1996), 109–30, describes "cultural logics" as "structuring the very categories and classificatory schemes through which social life itself is ordered" (p. 116).

18. Warren Schmaus, *Rethinking Durkheim and His Tradition* (Cambridge, UK: Cambridge University Press, 2004) offers a valuable discussion of the ambiguities in Durkheim's and subsequent Durkheimian treatments of the social construction of categories and their representation of variations in social structure. Dmitry Kurakin, "Reassembling the Ambiguity of the Sacred: A Neglected Inconsistency in Readings of Durkheim," *Journal of Classical Sociology* 15 (November 2015), 377–95, argues that sacred and profane as categories are hard to tell apart and thus are better regarded in terms of dynamic border violations. Tomoko Masuzawa's thoughtful

These tensions were particularly evident in Durkheim's concluding reflections on how the sacred might differ in industrial societies from its aboriginal manifestations. On the one hand, Durkheim's emphasis on ritual participation suggested that powerful collective effervescence representing an entire society required physical co-presence in local contexts, which was hard to enact on a large scale, but, on the other hand, the idea of collective representations seemed to be a way of promoting social cohesion even in these large-scale settings. Which was most important?[19] Another question was whether it was possible that the sacred or something like it could be lodged in the legitimacy modern societies granted to the individual? Durkheim entertained the possibility that the sacred could continue "by incarnating itself in individual consciousness," leaving unspecified how that might happen, and at the same time suggested it would no longer be a collective representation: "A philosophy can very well be worked out in the silence of inward meditation," he wrote, "but not a faith."[20]

Even if collectivities such as occupational groups and voluntary associations were involved, were the sacred rites and symbols associated with them like or fundamentally different from ones pertaining to the universe in toto? Another question was whether complex societies needed unifying symbols and rituals at all? Should these symbols and rituals be considered collective *representations* that closely resembled specific social arrangements, or could *any* symbol serve just as well? Was it the observer who decided that something was sacred based on what it did, even if people themselves didn't see it that way, and if so how was that decision to be made? Above all, if the distinction between sacred and profane was socially constructed, was it satisfactory in complex societies to imagine that invisible norms and values absorbed mentally through a kind of cultural contagion were all that mattered, or was it necessary to investigate in greater detail what Ann Warfield Rawls has termed the "enacted practices" of

---

reading of *Elementary Forms* ("The Sacred Difference in the *Elementary Forms*: On Durkheim's Last Quest," *Representations* 23, Summer 1988, 25–50, quote on page 40) emphasizes the tension between the sacred as totality and the sacred as its constituent parts and argues that Durkheim presented conflicting theses regarding the sacred as a universal and as a variable construct.

19. Stephen R. Marks, "Durkheim's Theory of Anomie," *American Journal of Sociology* 80 (September 1974), 329–63, is still one of the most insightful discussions of this tension.

20. Durkheim, *Elementary Forms*, 427; Bellah, "Introduction," stresses Durkheim's apparent despair both toward the end of *Elementary Forms* and in subsequent essays about the difficulties of reinstituting a sense of collective effervescence.

social construction?[21] These were questions that animated discussions among Durkheim's many academic followers. There were, to be sure, valuable insights about how to think about religion and the sacred. And yet, it wasn't workable simply to import Durkheimian arguments into studies of modern religion without further explication.

The Cultural Turn

The cultural turn of the 1960s in contributions by Clifford Geertz, Peter Berger and Thomas Luckmann, and Robert Bellah worked within the inherited emphasis on conceptual classification and at the same time extended it in ways that demonstrated its limits. Geertz's influential contribution in the much cited 1966 essay on religion treated the topic as culture rather than as an institution and was thus less about religion per se than about sacred symbols. Geertz held that the sacred could best be identified not only in contrast with the profane but also in terms of the confluence of its several component attributes. The sacred was, as Durkheim had claimed, set apart from everyday life and it was so, Geertz argued, through its association with the defining conjuncture of long-lasting moods and motivations, powerful emotions, a compelling sense of factuality, and symbolization of a generalized order of existence or, as he termed it, "an envisaged cosmic order." In advancing this formulation, Geertz drew from Durkheim but benefited more explicitly from Weber. The vague notion of what a general order of existence might be took form in repeated references to the "problem of meaning," which Geertz found in Weber's discussions of meaninglessness and theodicy and, more specifically, as problems of suffering, evil, and injustice. For Geertz, as for Weber, these were universal concerns not only for

---

21. Ann Warfield Rawls, "Durkheim's Epistemology: The Neglected Argument," *American Journal of Sociology* 102 (September 1996), 430–82; Ann Warfield Rawls, "Durkheim's Epistemology: The Initial Critique, 1915–1924," *Sociological Quarterly* 38 (Winter 1997), 111–45; the philosophical subtleties of the relationship of enacted practices to the formation of categories are further examined in the exchange between Schmaus and Rawls (Warren Schmaus, "Rawls, Durkheim, and Causality: A Critical Discussion," *American Journal of Sociology* 104, November 1998, 872–86, and Ann Warfield Rawls, "Durkheim's Challenge to Philosophy: Human Reason Explained as a Product of Enacted Social Practice," *American Journal of Sociology* 104, November 1998, 887–901).

individuals but also for societies and thus necessitated a system of symbols with which to make sense of them.[22]

Geertz's approach was explicitly semiotic, "the whole point" of which, he said, was "gaining access to the conceptual world in which our subjects live so that we can, in some extended sense of the term, converse with them."[23] Geertz drew extensively from Suzanne Langer as well as from Kenneth Burke and Ludwig Wittgenstein in defining this approach.[24] Langer was interested in understanding how language signified, structured, and communicated meaning not only in common daily activities but also in providing a general orientation to life.[25] Like Langer, Geertz disagreed with philosophical approaches that abstracted symbol systems from the lived world of experience and that focused only on those systems' elements and their internal relationships. Symbol systems had to be investigated in the context of behavior, which was the reason for engaging as Geertz did in ethnographic research. It was in this sense that symbol systems were representational. They corresponded with and thus were "models for" and "models of" the classifications in which social life occurred.[26]

Although Geertz was centrally concerned with what sacred symbols *did*, his discussion resembled the classificatory approach—"a repertoire of very general, made-in-the-academy concepts and systems of concepts"—in Durkheim's work and in that of Geertz's mentor, Talcott Parsons.[27] Parsons argued that symbols should be understood analytically as the "expressive" or communicative aspect of all social action, but he also believed symbols were organized into broad analytically distinct patterns or systems that served to integrate and legitimate

---

22. Clifford Geertz, "Religion as a Cultural System," in *Anthropological Approaches to the Study of Religion*, edited by Michael Banton (London: Tavistock Publications, 1966), 1–46; reprinted in Clifford Geertz, *The Interpretation of Cultures: Selected Essays* (New York: Basic Books, 1973), 87–125, quote on page 90.

23. Geertz, *Interpretation*, 24.

24. Jason A. Springs, "What Cultural Theorists of Religion Have to Learn from Wittgenstein; Or, How to Read Geertz as a Practice Theorist," *Journal of the American Academy of Religion* 76, 4 (2008), 934–69, emphasizes congruence between arguments in Wittgenstein and Geertz and points to Geertz's own acknowledgment of Wittgenstein's influence in Clifford Geertz, *Available Light* (Princeton, NJ: Princeton University Press, 2000), 948.

25. Suzanne K. Langer, *Philosophy in a New Key: A Study in the Symbolism of Reason, Rite, and Art* (New York: New American Library, 1948).

26. Geertz, *Interpretation*, 93.

27. Ibid., 28.

whole societies. A "cultural system" could thus be identified that included a "religious sphere" in which Durkheim's notion of ritualized expressions of group solidarity was a principal component.[28] Geertz not only agreed that sacred symbols were indeed a cultural system and could be distinguished by its content and functions from other cultural systems such as art, ideology, science, aesthetic values, and common sense, but also devoted considerable attention to describing and identifying the broader concept of cultural systems. He recognized that the specific symbols of which a cultural system was composed were highly variable but argued that symbols expressing the sacred could be identified anywhere by the cluster of moods and motivations they produced, the positive and negative values they dramatized, and their identification with a general order of existence. To know what the sacred was and to understand what it did, it was thus necessary to identify the symbols that portrayed a kind of cosmic or metaphysical grounding of values.[29]

Writing at the same time as Geertz, Berger and Luckmann's 1966 *Social Construction of Reality* and Berger's *Sacred Canopy* a year later situated the sacred in concerns about the intersubjective experience of everyday life, drawing on George Herbert Mead as well as Durkheim and Weber and grounding the discussion in Alfred Schutz's phenomenological sociology, which emphasized perceptions of phenomena from the actor's perspective. Schutz argued that everyday life was internally segmented into distinct zones of relevance and differed from such "finite provinces" of meaning as dreams and hallucinations, making it the "paramount reality" in which wide-awake goal-oriented activities took place and in which shared assumptions about space and time were taken for granted. Berger and Luckmann considered everyday reality in these respects to be meaningfully sustained through social interaction but incapable of providing the kind of overarching symbolically integrative meaning that pertained to the cosmos and that addressed the inevitabilities of death, suffering, and inexplicable mysteries. The sacred served in this capacity as a "symbolic universe." It was set apart from everyday life, as Durkheim argued, but in agreement with Geertz it was also understood to be functionally related to everyday life through the all-encompassing meaning it provided.[30]

28. Talcott Parsons, *The Social System* (London: Routledge, 1991 [1951]), 267.
29. Geertz, *Interpretation*, 131–32.
30. Peter L. Berger and Thomas Luckmann, *The Social Construction of Reality: A Treatise in the Sociology of Knowledge* (Garden City, NY: Doubleday, 1966); Peter L. Berger, *The Sacred Canopy: Elements of a Sociological Theory of Religion* (Garden City, NY: Doubleday, 1967).

Bellah's contributions to the cultural turn of the 1960s approached the topic as Berger and Luckmann did by grounding it in a phenomenological emphasis on everyday reality and as Geertz did in treating the sacred as a cultural system. Informed by Weber and Parsons, Bellah borrowed heavily from Durkheim but also incorporated ideas from sources as varied as Paul Tillich, Abraham Maslow, Wilfred Cantwell Smith, and Wallace Stevens. In a 1968 essay on transcendence, Bellah described the "unsatisfied desires and longings" that drive people toward something "wholly other" that is then expressed in "symbols that attempt to grasp reality as a whole." The symbols that did this in "the modern situation" necessarily differed from the aboriginal ones Durkheim identified, which made it of interest to describe them. The sacred was thus experienced as a "felt whole" that gave life a coherent meaning but at the same time was ambiguous and mysterious in its representation of life itself and the universe.[31] These were themes Bellah had introduced in a previous essay on religious evolution and to which his attention would return in subsequent writing.[32] The symbol systems expressing the sacred were, as Durkheim had suggested, absolute and yet were in a process of "constant revision and alteration," which produced the fundamental "dualism" separating the transcendent realm from the natural world that characterized historic and early modern religion and was then subject to renegotiation in the post-traditional world.[33]

Although Geertz, Berger and Luckmann, and Bellah diverged on particulars, there was striking convergence in their depictions of the sacred. A first point of agreement was that symbols should be the primary focus of inquiry and should be taken as real. They were real in that they mediated experience and shaped consciousness, thus constituting the perceived world in which we live. This was crucial to the argument that culture was a significant influence in social life and not to be reduced to or explained away by material structures. Geertz emphasized the "factuality" of symbol systems, Berger and Luckmann's dialectic stressed its "objectification," and Bellah coined the phrase "symbolic realism" to underscore the epistemological reality of symbols. None of the

---

31. Robert N. Bellah, "Transcendence in Contemporary Piety," in *Transcendence*, edited by Herbert W. Richardson and Donald R. Cutler (Boston: Beacon Press, 1969), 85–97, reprinted in Robert N. Bellah, *Beyond Belief: Essays on Religion in a Post-Traditional World* (New York: Harper & Row, 1970), 196–208, quotes on pages 202 and 204.

32. Robert N. Bellah, *Religion in Human Evolution* (Cambridge, MA: Harvard University Press, 2011).

33. Robert N. Bellah, "Religious Evolution," *American Sociological Review* 29 (June 1964), 358–74; reprinted in Bellah, *Beyond Belief*, 20–50.

discussions neglected mentioning ritual, but ritual was now a symbol more than an actual set of activities. Moreover, the symbols expressing the sacred were especially real, if that were possible, "really real," as Geertz put it, creating an "aura of utter actuality," because they constituted the unique facticity of the universe.[34] This was of key significance, at least for Bellah and Berger, for theological as well as sociological reasons.[35] If the literal existence of supernatural deities was no longer believable, their existence in symbolic representations arguably served significant social and psychological functions.

A related claim held that humans everywhere needed special symbols with which to make sense of the whole, as in the whole of life and the totality of the cosmos. This was Weber's argument about "meaning making" but with a semiotic twist. Transcendent symbols dealt not only with the mysteries of life that shattered the comforting order of everyday life. They also bridged the separate spheres of relevance into which everyday life was compartmentalized, providing meaning to the small details of daily life by placing them in ever larger frames of reference. It was this need for everything to be interpreted within an expanding system of symbols that explained why the sacred existed and what role it played in social life.

Symbols of wholeness were classificatory constructs in two respects: as popular references to God, spirits, the wholly other, life, the ground of being, transcendence, ultimate reality, and so on, to designate a special sacred realm, and in academic discourse to identify a comparable topic for cultural investigation. The latter was meant to correspond with the former, as Schutz explained in another context: "The thought objects constructed by the social scientists refer to and are founded upon the thought objects constructed by the common-sense thought of man living his everyday life among his fellowmen."[36] Whatever the sacred's functional role was in fulfilling needs for an all-encompassing meaning, its substantive location was predefined: it rarely appeared except in discussions of religion. Schutz's influential essay on multiple realities in which he

---

34. Geertz, *Interpretation*, 112.

35. Bellah, *Beyond Belief*, xi–xxi; Peter Berger, *Adventures of an Accidental Sociologist: How to Explain the World Without Becoming a Bore* (Amherst, NY: Prometheus Books, 2011), 20–24.

36. Alfred Schutz, "Common-Sense and Scientific Interpretation of Human Action," *Philosophy and Phenomenological Research* 14 (September 1953), 1–38, quote on page 3; see also William Outhwaite, "Hermeneutic and Phenomenological Approaches," in *Philosophy of Anthropology and Sociology*, edited by Stephen P. Turner and Mark W. Risjord (New York: Elsevier, 2007), 459–84, especially page 462, who relates this comment to Schutz's criticism of Weber for too readily imposing ideal types on lived realities.

identified the world of religious experience, the world of scientific theorizing, and the world of childhood fantasy as finite provinces of meaning set apart from everyday reality, for instance, drew the idea of separate realities from William James's discussion of "sub-universes," of which mythology and religion ("the various supernatural worlds"), along with science, abstract truths, individual opinions, and madness, were examples.[37] Geertz's, Berger's, and Bellah's discussions of course focused on religion as well. In short, the preferred way to think about the sacred was to locate it within a category of cultural symbolism called religion and then ask how it functioned in that context.

The connection with Durkheim in all this was its interest in symbolism, which included collective representations and the classification system inherent in separating the sacred and profane. A stronger philosophical basis in semiotics gave a clearer sense of the social significance of symbols. They were constitutive of reality itself, shaping what could be perceived because words for it existed. The half-century since *Elementary Forms*, however, placed the cultural turn in a radically different setting. The heavily psychologized version of American individualism that blossomed in the 1960s shifted the discussion toward questions of personal well-being. The sacred instantiated itself in fulfillment, self-esteem, and, in Abraham Maslow's well-known phrase, as "peak experiences." Transcendence was a feeling, a transforming power, which even in conveying a sense of sacredness on an entire society did so by helping its citizens clarify their personal identity.[38]

These formulations offered several attractive features, not the least of which was a reason to think that religion in some form (whether it was called that or not) was essential to the human condition and that it would prevail against the onslaught of secularity. Defined in terms of the functions it served, the sacred became, as Durkheim had argued, less specifically tethered to the specific objects that fulfilled these functions. A tree or stone as much as a story of divine redemption could symbolize a transcendent order of existence, which was of enormous consequence to investigations into the manifold ways in which the sacred was symbolized in different religions, societies, and historical periods. Insofar as the goal of social science was to formulate generalizations that

---

37. Alfred Schutz, "On Multiple Realities," *Philosophy and Phenomenological Research* 5 (June 1945), 533–76; William James, *The Principles of Psychology* (London: Macmillan, 1890), II, 290–93.

38. Herbert W. Richardson, "Three Myths of Transcendence," in *Transcendence*, edited by Herbert W. Richardson and Donald R. Cutler (Boston: Beacon Press, 1969), 98–113.

pertained to societies everywhere, this was a significant contribution. Furthermore, the sacred was more elaborately grounded in the logic of social constructionism than it had been for Durkheim. Its existence as an identifiable cultural category depended less on a vaguely perceived sense of societal constraint than on the universal human need for order, integration, and reassurance. To be sure, it fulfilled a psychological need, but it was not reducible to the psychological projections of individuals. Its concern with subjective meaning was balanced by the insight that symbols were externalized and thus observable. As Geertz said, they were "as public as marriage and as observable as agriculture."[39]

But there were ambiguities and weaknesses in how the sacred was theorized. While the main argument of these approaches was that the sacred was socially constructed, relatively little was said about how that happened, a lack compounded by the fact that these were theoretical perspectives concerned with bridging the gap between objective reality and subjectivities, and yet, as most evident in Berger's treatment of objectification and internalization, had little to say about the dynamic processes involved other than projections of thoughts onto the external world and reabsorption of those ideas through socialization. In keeping with constructivism's larger interest in "reality," the sacred was especially interesting because it was *not* observable, as nature arguably was, but had to be the result of social construction. The question was why that which could not be observed was nevertheless taken to be real, rather than what people did with this reality in their ordinary lives. The sacred was simply externalized, projected, and evoked, apparently at some time in the past that was long since clouded in memory. Sacred symbols were like language, the example best illustrating that symbols were simply out there to be absorbed and taken for granted. Insofar as the sacred existed in the present, its reality as a plausible interpretation of the universe was more at issue than anything about its specific forms. A further difficulty was that references to universes and the cosmos and general orders of existence implied grand systems composed by theologians and philosophers but with dubious connections to the lived experiences of ordinary people. The symbols representing them were arguably a distinct conceptual category, but whether they existed apart from organized religion was unclear, as was how they related to the enacted set-apart-ness of the sacred that interested Durkheim. Above all, defining the sacred in terms of its functions instead of substantively still required that some classificatory construct be identified to say what that function was. The sacred need not have been identified

39. Geertz, *Interpretation*, 91.

with a conception of the supernatural because it referred to something called the cosmos, the universe, or a general order of existence. Yet somehow the scholar interested in the sacred had to know what these terms meant.

The ambiguity—if it could be called that—between the symbols that conceptualized the sacred, on the one hand, and the activities, on the other hand, through which these symbols were instantiated ran through all the major contributions of the period. Symbols were produced and articulated in rituals and in ordinary behavior. Yet the symbols were powerful, compelling thought itself and conveying meanings that shaped action. The intense emotion evoked by the gods, Langer observed, is "brought forth" as "someone leads the shouting and makes a demonstration of joy" and "delight seizes the congregation." But the activity was not crucial: "Their joy is not in an event, but in a presented idea."[40] "Repetitive chants," "ritual manipulations," kneeling, singing, and rites of bodily purification, Geertz considered important, but less so than the "problem of human suffering" that these symbols placed "in a meaningful context."[41] Berger and Luckmann regarded conversation as the foundation on which reality was constructed, but conversation's interesting feature was the "language" that "typifies experiences" and allows them to be subsumed under "broad meaning in terms of which they have meaning."[42] Surely the point was simply that action *and* ideas worked in concert to evoke the sacred. But that was not the argument. It was rather that the activities were themselves to be understood as symbols and that the interesting facts about symbols were the conceptions they signified—conceptions in the case of the sacred of basic ideas about life and death and humans and the world.

Toward Practice

Talal Asad's 1983 critical examination of Geertz's work on religion brought several of its ambiguities into sharp relief. Asad argued that at least four aspects of Geertz's approach were problematic. First, it attempted to classify religion too much in terms of cognitive representations, beliefs, attitudes, and perspectives and not enough in terms of the institutional forms in which dispositions are created and sustained. Second, the emphasis on humans' need for symbol

---

40. Langer, *Philosophy in a New Key*, 122; Langer's discussion of the sacred drew insights from Durkheim, who she said considered religion first and foremost a "form of ideation" (p. 134).
41. Geertz, *Interpretation*, 105.
42. Berger and Luckmann, *Social Construction*, 52–53.

systems to deal with ignorance, pain, and injustice fails to specify why those symbols take different forms that sometimes become institutionalized as religion and in other instances do not. Third, the relationship between the sacred and the commonsense perspective of everyday life is problematic insofar as crossing the line separating the two is said to be hugely dramatic to the point of being self-transforming and yet the reality a person experiences in everyday life somehow remains unchanged; indeed, the distinction separating the two is further complicated by the fact that sacred pursuits cannot be distinguished a priori from activities that have instrumental, aesthetic, and political objectives. And fourth, too little attention is given to the processes of elaboration and modification and especially the power dynamics present as competing discourses vie to authenticate definitions of reality and authorize moods and motivations.[43]

It was the last of these—the concern about power dynamics—to which Asad devoted greatest attention, offering a reading of Christianity's history of ecclesial reckonings, sanctions against heresy, and disciplinary activities as a case in point. Not surprisingly, the role of power dynamics also figured prominently elsewhere in Asad's work and in subsequent studies it inspired. Without referencing them explicitly, these were arguments firmly grounded in the work of Michel Foucault and others commonly grouped under the headings of critical theory and cultural Marxism. However, it was less the raw assertion of power that was of concern in any of this work than the processes through which it was produced and reproduced. The sacred was a category to which certain significations could be assigned only because there were hearings, tribunals, church councils, and trials to do the assigning.

In an article on medieval heresy Asad devoted further attention to the *processes* through which truth and falsehood were classified, not in terms of a "fitting cosmology" (as Geertz might have argued), but as institutional practices. "The formation of orthodoxy and of heresy," he wrote, "were dependent on the institutional processes of judging, teaching and administering Christian

---

43. Talal Asad, "Anthropological Conceptions of Religion: Reflections on Geertz," *Man* 18 (June 1983), 237–59; expanded in Talal Asad, *Genealogies of Religion: Discipline and Reasons of Power in Christianity* (Baltimore: Johns Hopkins University Press, 1993), 27–54; Asad's concerns about classification are previewed somewhat more explicitly in an earlier essay about marriage: Talal Asad, "The Definition of Marriage," *Man* 98 (May 1960), 73–74; on Asad's contributions to the "turn to power" in religious studies, see Stephen S. Bush, *Visions of Religion: Experience, Meaning, and Power* (New York: Oxford University Press, 2014).

subjects." Specifically, as the church's power expanded and became more centralized, new practices and new roles were instituted to formulate more differentiated rules and regulations, to refine doctrinal discourses, and to discover and attack dangers threatening the church.[44]

Asad's criticisms prompted a flurry of discussions as to whether or not they had misinterpreted Geertz. There was general agreement nevertheless that the conceptual categories in which the sacred was placed or not placed needed to be understood as socially constructed and that closer attention should be paid to the *practices* through which social construction occurred. While representational concepts (such as "sacred," "profane," "religion," and "common sense") identified topics for investigation, they objectified them, giving them a fixed, ideational, disembodied, decontextualized quality based on similarities and differences among their elements as contrasted with dynamic, action-oriented processes characterized by mutually interacting elements.[45]

Bringing processes into the foreground meant emphasizing that moods and motivations not only were meaningful but were *made meaningful*, including the bafflement and moral paradoxes that the sacred was said to address. It meant that symbols representing the sacred could not be understood simply by saying that they evoked something about a general order of existence; utterances, arguments, and practices needed to be examined in terms of contestation, exclusion, and denunciation. That was true at least in the modern world where competing interpretations of the sacred co-existed. It could hardly be ignored historically, either, at least if theological disputes, religious wars, and the persecution of heretics were acknowledged. The point, then, was to think about the sacred in the more dynamic sense of something that emerged and was contested, elaborated, and constituted as a practice.[46]

The concerns Asad articulated about Geertz's understanding of religion corresponded with similar discussions in other contexts about the drawbacks of taxonomies, typologies, and categorical concepts. Catherine Bell in an

---

44. Talal Asad, "Medieval Heresy: An Anthropological View," *Social History* 11 (October 1986), 345–62, quote on page 360.

45. On these characteristics of representational concepts, see Gunther Kress and Theo van Leeuwen, *Reading Images: The Grammar of Visual Design* (New York: Routledge, 2006).

46. William H. Sewell Jr., "Geertz, Cultural Systems, and History: From Synchrony to Transformation," *Representations* 59 (Summer 1997), 35–55, observes that Geertz's brief discussion of the confusion of tongues in the encounter among Jews, Berbers, and the French could be extended to include more of the "cultural misunderstandings, conflicts, and negotiations" that occur because of differences in status, gender, and class (p. 51).

impressive review of the literature on ritual, for example, observed that "categorization develops a dizzying momentum" as each generation of scholars produced additional evidence, which necessitated new debates about what fit and what did not fit into the previous generation's categories and prompted ever more exacting quests for distinctions and subdistinctions. As with religion, categorization in ritual studies focused on identifying the properties that distinguished it from other activities, debating whether it truly was different or not, and seeking ways to further divide it into subtypes. Besides the conceptual difficulties involved, the resulting categories tended to "override and undermine" the distinctions people in the real world made. The more useful questions to ask, she suggested, dealt with the circumstances and activities involved in the process of ritualization.[47]

In an influential essay on language and learning, Maurice Bloch advanced an argument that could be interpreted as a similarly critical view of categorization, albeit for a different reason. Bloch did not dispute that "classificatory concepts" were evident in indigenous language but questioned whether social scientists were correct in focusing on them and assuming that people made sense of the world by locating things within conceptual categories. He agreed that reality became knowable in "chunks," as cognitive psychologists suggested, but the seemingly instantaneous process by which that happened probably did not involve linear thinking or thoughts formulated in language. What needed to be investigated, he argued, were the non-cognitive practices—the ways things "look, sound, feel, smell, taste and so on—drawing on the realm of bodily experience."[48]

Interest in practices was also attracting greater attention at the time of Asad's critique in the theoretical contributions of Michel de Certeau and Pierre Bourdieu as well as in the field research of several social scientists who found inspiration from an alternative reading of Geertz. The principal emphasis in what from various strands became known as practice theory was the indeterminacy of action, symbols, and their meanings as they were negotiated in social interaction through the choices and adaptations of participants and the constraints with which they were confronted. Attention shifted from symbols as linguistic

---

47. Catherine Bell, *Ritual Theory, Ritual Practice* (New York: Oxford University Press, 1992), 69–70.

48. Maurice Bloch, "Language, Anthropology and Cognitive Science," *Man* 26, 2 (1991), 183–198, quote on page 193.

codes to the practical strategies guiding action among embodied agents.[49] Interest in ontological questions about the reality or unreality of religious objects diminished relative to the unobjectionable claim that what people *do* in ordinary life is patently real. To be sure, perceptions and symbols continued to be of interest, not in support of contentions that *only* they were real, but in sharpening understandings of the *emergent* qualities of action and experience. In this view, categories such as sacred, profane, religion, transcendence, or for that matter work, play, and everyday reality were not stable categories that external observers could investigate through abstract concepts. They were instead constituted by the interactive processes of engagement and interpretation that took place in specific situations and at the same time were subject to the influences of the larger contexts of those situations. Practices developed and changed over time and thus reflected the histories and dispositions participants brought to them but also the pragmatic rules they followed and decisions they made.[50]

Neither Bourdieu nor de Certeau directed much attention to religion or the sacred. Their contributions focused on practices in other settings, including everyday life, which of course had always been the contrasting case, the location of the profane, and thus was relevant in that regard. De Certeau's influential work on everyday life emphasized that it is a practice, by which he meant that it is composed of active, ongoing, and yet fluid social interaction in which meanings are negotiated and tasks are achieved.[51] While de Certeau's substantive

---

49. Gabrielle M. Spiegel, "Introduction," in *Practicing History: New Directions in Historical Writing after the Linguistic Turn*, edited by Gabrielle M. Spiegel (New York: Routledge, 2005), 1–31, who valuably traces the emergence of practice theory among historians, writes (p. 22), practice theory "asserts the continuing relevance of semiotic insights proffered by the linguistic turn, yet reinterprets them in favor of a rehabilitation of social history by placing structure and practice, language and body into dialectical relation in systems construed as 'recursive,' 'thinly coherent,' 'weakly continuous,' and always 'at risk.'"

50. On these ontological grounds and emphases on emergence and the interplay of structure, power, and action, practice theory was in marked convergence with what was to become increasingly prominent under the heading of critical realism. See especially Jon Frauley and Frank Pearce, "Critical Realism and the Social Sciences: Methodological and Epistemological Preliminaries," in *Critical Realism and the Social Sciences: Heterodox Elaborations*, edited by. Jon Frauley and Frank Pearce (Toronto: University of Toronto Press, 2007), 3–29; and Philip S. Gorski, "What Is Critical Realism? And Why Should You Care?" *Contemporary Sociology* 42, 5 (2013), 658–70.

51. Michel de Certeau, *The Practice of Everyday Life*, trans. Steven Rendall (Berkeley and Los Angeles: University of California Press, 1984).

focus was the relations between consumers and the mechanisms of production, one of his important contributions to the broader discussion of everyday life was to argue that it is characterized by specific practices as well as by a more general mode of relationships or practice. Everyday life in this conception is highly variegated in terms of the spaces, agendas, actors, and activities of which it is composed even though certain dynamics of power and negotiation run through all of them. The practices of which everyday life is composed include such common and yet varied activities as taking a walk, talking with a friend, cooking a meal, going to work, shopping, arranging for a doctor's appointment, reading a story to a child, watching television, or attending religious services. The relative frequency with which such practices occur is at the same time not meant to exclude less common activities, such as voting, participating in a political protest, or tending to a dying loved one, but to set the context in which these activities occur—particularly important for considering sacred experiences and other exceptional moments that deviate from daily routines.

Bourdieu's contributions in *Outline of a Theory of Practice* and *The Logic of Practice* were concerned with shifting social science, especially ethnographic research, from an "objectivist" approach in which the topic of investigation was treated as an "object of observation and analysis, a representation," toward an approach that took greater account of the "knowing subject" and the "conditions of possibility" that generate practical knowledge and action. What counted as practices for Bourdieu ranged from examples mentioned in passing such as chess, dancing, and boxing to topics receiving more extended treatment such as marriage, law, and language. The questions Bourdieu wanted social scientists to emphasize included the generation and structuring of practices such as ones that evoked a sense of reasonableness or that involved strategies of demonstrating oneself to be a rule-regarding person. In simplest terms, the aim was to bring together the dispositions, structures, symbols, meanings, and improvisations that went into the practices in which people engaged, which was different from focusing on abstract categories. "Performing a rite," he observed, "presupposes something quite different from the conscious mastery of the sort of catalogue of oppositions that is drawn up by academic commentators."[52]

---

52. Pierre Bourdieu, *Outline of a Theory of Practice* (New York: Cambridge University Press, 1977), 2–3, 118. In some treatments of Bourdieu's work, *habitus* is emphasized as his principal contribution, leaving little room for considerations of practice except as a kind of outcome or dependent variable for which variation is explained with reference to the *habitus*. But that interpretation, in my view, misses Bourdieu's important claim about practices being bundles of

Bourdieu's philosophical reflections on the ontological status of practices took shape more concretely in his discussions of the genesis and structure of the "fields" of cultural production, including literature, art, and religion. In emphasizing the practices involved, Bourdieu directed attention away from classificatory schemes (such as genres) and toward the concrete processes through which cultural producers secured resources, developed their work, and dealt with hierarchies of consumption and commercialization. The more formalized and formally organized character of these processes contrasted with the routine practices of daily life but were similar insofar as power and status relationships were present in both. The monopolization, symbolization, and legitimation of power were prominent concerns in these contributions. It was here too that Bourdieu's focus shifted increasingly to the "structuring" of practices and the "structures" of practice, meaning the ways in which activities both took account of and reproduced the inequalities in which they were situated.[53]

The "practice turn" took up the challenge that phenomenological studies had posed, namely, of how objects of consciousness and experience—phenomena—came to be perceived as reality, and shifted attention from the objects and their consequences toward the conditions and processes that gave experiences that sense of reality. In this respect the emphasis on practices was a natural extension of the constructionist approach. Practices were the enablers, the contexts, and the blueprints that went into the outcomes that were experienced as objective realities. There was an important addition, however. The objectively experienced realities were not as readily identified in advance, certainly not by defining them in terms of a prespecified function. The approach was not, for example, to classify as vehicles any motorized object that transported people from one place to another. It was rather to acknowledge the varying realities of what people experienced, such as cars and motorcycles as modes of transportation but also as collectors' items and symbols of status, and ask what might be at work behind the scenes to produce these meanings.

---

activities and discourses that unfold over time, wrapped in histories and dispositions and emotions and responsive to immediate circumstances. In this preferred interpretation of Bourdieu, the concept of practice subsumes the elements of *habitus* and puts them into play as the embodied, emotive, intentional, and situational dynamics of everyday life.

53. Pierre Bourdieu, "Genesis and Structure of the Religious Field," *Comparative Social Research* 13, 1 (1991), 1–44; Pierre Bourdieu, *The Field of Cultural Production: Essays on Art and Literature*, edited by Randal Johnson (New York: Columbia University Press, 1993); Pierre Bourdieu, *The Rules of Art: Genesis and Structure of the Literary Field* (Stanford, CA: Stanford University Press, 1995).

Moreover, the meanings in this approach were to a significant degree intrinsic to the practices—constituted by them—rather than being extrinsic objects emanating from and standing apart from them.[54]

Practice theory, as such, was less of a theory (not a logically integrated system of empirically testable propositions) than it was a perspective, or better, a bundle of perspectives loosely united in privileging the role of social actors engaged in activities over time and confronted with having to negotiate their way through the limitations of social structures. Theory and research in several disciplines during the 1980s oriented themselves in these directions. Reflecting on the perspectives that began taking shape in anthropology, for example, Sherry Ortner wrote that practice theory "restored the actor to the social process without losing sight of the larger structures that constrain (but also enable) social action." It focused attention on the discourses, representations, and social relations of people "on the ground." The "larger structures" included economic arrangements, cultural patterns, and political processes, but in specific repudiation of the idea that they could be categorized as separate functionally differentiated institutions ("artificial chunks") were cast as intertwined formations of production and reproduction.[55]

Ann Swidler's influential essay on the sociology of culture, which drew on a wide range of recent theoretical and empirical contributions (including Bourdieu's), advanced an argument that was similar to practice theory (though not in name). Culture was more effectively understood, Swidler argued, not as discrete ultimate values toward which action was oriented, but as "strategies of action" in which repertoires of habits, rituals, stories, and idioms were selectively resorted to as ad hoc guides and justifications.[56] Insofar as actions and experiences might be deemed as sacred pursuits, the culture-in-action approach

---

54. Andreas Reckwitz, "Toward a Theory of Social Practices: A Development in Culturalist Theorizing," *European Journal of Social Theory* 5, 2 (2002), 243–63, writes, practice theory "does not invite the analysis of mental phenomena 'as such,' but the exploration of the embeddedness of the mental activities of understanding and knowing in a complex of doings" (p. 258).

55. Sherry B. Ortner, "Theory in Anthropology Since the Sixties," *Comparative Studies in Society and History* 26, 1 (1984), 126–66; and Sherry B. Ortner, *Anthropology and Social Theory: Culture, Power, and the Acting Subject* (Durham, NC: Duke University Press, 2006), 3.

56. Ann Swidler, "Culture in Action: Symbols and Strategies," *American Sociological Review* 51, 2 (1986), 273–86; the parallel development in psychology, which situated talk, memory, and experience as resources in social interaction, was suggested in Jonathan Potter and Margaret Wetherell, *Discourse and Social Psychology: Beyond Attitudes and Behavior* (London: Sage, 1987); and on the ensuing paradigm shift, see Jovan Byford and Cristian Tileaga, "Accounts of a

suggested a need to investigate the repertoires from which idioms might be selected in particular contexts and the self-referential meanings communicated in these idioms.[57]

In religious studies, what became known as the "lived religion" approach argued for a similar perspective. Religion, historian Robert Orsi wrote, "comes into being in an ongoing, dynamic relationship with the realities of everyday life." To study lived religion was to inquire into the non-institutional spaces in which it appeared in practice through real and imagined relationships, in idioms and bodies, and in tension with social structures.[58]

The practice turn's appeal was putting into play a multiplicity of interacting components including symbols, meanings, dispositions, habits, social interaction, discourse, rules, and constraints, which were not the objectified experience given priority in previous approaches but the operative negotiations through which those experiences became possible. It presented a distinct contrast with taxonomic approaches that identified, classified, and named the properties by which features of social life were to be conceptualized and their causes and effects investigated. It was an invitation to probe deeper into the relations among these various aspects of social construction.

Sorting out the indeterminate processes and the complex relations among them implied an epistemological hermeneutic of a different order than predictive hypotheses about relationships among relatively fixed conceptualized topics. Indeed, the difference constituted a profound acknowledgment that, whatever methodologies social scientists might employ, there was merit to looking more closely at the conjunctures, contingencies, and heuristic conditions that resulted in the great proliferation of human forms and actions in addition to concentrating on the uniformities that might also be observed in these variations. The reason for shifting perspectives had been anticipated in the difficulties present in previous approaches of which inquiries focusing on the sacred were a case in point. If the sacred was symbolized, experienced, and made meaningful in as many ways as it seemed to be, attention needed to shift from conceptualizing

---

Troubled Past: Psychology, History, and Texts of Experience," *Qualitative Psychology* 4, 1 (2017), 101–17.

57. This approach to some extent was adopted in the interpretation of qualitative interviews in Robert N. Bellah et al., *Habits of the Heart: Individualism and Commitment in American Life* (Berkeley: University of California Press, 1985).

58. Robert Orsi, "Everyday Miracles: The Study of Lived Religion," in *Lived Religion in America: Toward a History of Practice*, edited by David D. Hall (Princeton, NJ: Princeton University Press, 1997), 3–21, especially page 4.

it as a predefined category or, for that matter, locating it strictly within a category called religion. Practice theory suggested as an alternative focusing on the interactive processes through which it was popularly experienced.

It was particularly in anthropological studies of religion, ritual, and power in colonial and postcolonial settings that the epistemological shift from functionally determined classifications toward practices shaped by differentially distributed power arrangements became evident. Rejecting the functionalist interpretation of Durkheim in which power was mostly ignored, and the essentialist functionalism in Geertz's cultural approach, investigations turned toward what Sherry Ortner has termed "dark anthropology," drawing from Foucault, Bourdieu, Asad, Edward Said, Frederic Jameson, and others, to examine the extent to which practices reproduce power and mobilize acts of resistance.[59] These inquiries at the time had relatively little impact on sociological studies of religion in the United States, which focused on quantitative investigations of denominational growth and decline and ethnographic research on new religious movements, in most instances implicitly suggesting that diverse religious adherence and belief were voluntaristic contributions to the greater good. It was rather in sociological studies of religion and political upheaval outside the United States, such as Phillip Berryman's *Religious Roots of Rebellion: Christians in Central American Revolutions* and David Martin's *Forbidden Revolutions: Pentecostalism in Latin America and Catholicism in Eastern Europe*, that questions of power dynamics came to be emphasized.[60]

The further development of practice theory included a significant recasting of earlier work from which new ideas about practices could now be retrieved. Durkheim's work on ritual gained greater attention, relative to his interests in representations and classifications, thereby suggesting that the distinction between sacred and profane be examined chiefly as an enacted process of purification and consecration.[61] Structuralist applications of Durkheim's ideas receded in the face of arguments, particularly those put forth by Mary Douglas,

---

59. Sherry B. Ortner, "Dark Anthropology and Its Others: Theory Since the Eighties," *HAU: Journal of Ethnographic Theory* 6, 1 (2016), 47–73.

60. Phillip Berryman, *The Religious Roots of Rebellion: Christians in Central American Revolutions* (Maryknoll, NY: Orbis Books, 1984); David Martin, *Forbidden Revolutions: Pentecostalism in Latin America and Catholicism in Eastern Europe* (London: SPCK, 1996), religion's relationships with states in David Martin, *A General Theory of Secularization* (Oxford: Blackwell, 1978).

61. Robert N. Bellah, "Durkheim and Ritual," pp. 183–210 in *The Cambridge Companion to Durkheim*, edited by Jeffrey C. Alexander and Philip Smith (New York: Cambridge University Press, 2005).

that conceptual categories were better considered as products of transgressions and defilement.[62] Geertz's contributions underwent a similar transformation as discussions embraced more fully his ideas about rituals and his borrowing from Wittgenstein about the *uses* of language.[63] Berger's sacred canopy continued to be described as a source of transcendent meaning, but studies grounded in a constructionist perspective focused increasingly on the local plausibility structures, social networks, conversations, and rhetorical styles through which transcendence was objectified and affirmed.[64] Classification was thus redirected toward "categories in practice," such as race and gender, that were constructed, deployed, and often reified through social interaction, rather than as analytical categories ostensibly based on essentialized concepts.[65]

The renewed interest in pragmatism that occurred at roughly the same time and that sought to rediscover ideas from Charles Peirce, William James, John Dewey, and George Herbert Mead can be understood in part as a parallel acknowledgment of the indeterminacy of social action and necessity of linking the discussion of ideas with practice. Pragmatism offered a tradition in which to legitimate a focus on concrete locally situated practice and to emphasize the improvisational nature of problem-solving activities. In various efforts at

---

62. Mary Douglas, *Purity and Danger: An Analysis of Concepts of Pollution and Taboo* (London: Routledge, 1966).

63. C. Jason Throop, "Interpretation and the Limits of Interpretability: On Rethinking Clifford Geertz's Semiotics of Religious Experience," *Journal of North African Studies* 14, 3 (2009), 369–84, takes as given Geertz's emphasis on practice, which Throop finds deficient in being too anti-subjectivist; Springs, "What Cultural Theorists of Religion Have to Learn from Wittgenstein," reads Geertz as a practice theorist.

64. Ortner, "Theory in Anthropology," 159, offered the provocative observation toward the conclusion of her essay that the versions of practice theory she saw on the ascendancy in anthropology were quite consistent with Berger and Luckmann's approach; see also the brief discussion of Berger's work in relation to Asad and Bourdieu in Philip Gorski and Jeffrey Guhin, "The Ongoing Plausibility of Peter Berger: Sociological Thoughts on *The Sacred Canopy* at Fifty," *Journal of the American Academy of Religion* 85, 4 (December 2017), 1–14. Responding to Asad's critique of Geertz and linking Berger's concept of plausibility structures to the lived religion approach, Nancy Ammerman writes that the most fruitful work "has placed religion in a field of practice." Nancy Ammerman, "From Canopies to Conversations: The Continuing Significance of 'Plausibility Structures,'" in *Peter L. Berger and the Sociology of Religion: 50 Years after The Sacred Canopy*, edited by Titus Hjelm (London: Bloomsbury Academic, 2018), 58.

65. The distinction between "categories of practice" (following Bourdieu) and "categories of analysis" is developed in Rogers Brubaker and Frederick Cooper, "Beyond 'Identity,'" *Theory and Society* 29, 1 (2000), 1–47.

retrieval, it offered a critique of rational-choice theory, an argument for the moral basis of social action amid multiple and competing claims of normativity, an emphasis on discursive formations, a non-causal interpretation of social mechanisms, and an approach that included both the stabilizing role of habits and the situational conditions of improvisation.[66] The principal interest in pragmatism's philosophical implications for inquiries about religion occurred in religious studies while its empirical implications centered in cultural sociological work on aspirations, values, symbols, and ritual performance.[67]

Something akin to dark anthropology gradually emerged in other disciplines through work that addressed the negative cultural influences on religion if not of religion itself. Bellah's writing, while remaining grounded in Durkheimian theory, became increasingly critical of American culture and religion, first in *The Broken Covenant* and then in the co-authored *Habits of the Heart*. Orsi's emphasis on lived religion as social practice inspired studies of gendered power dynamics such as Carolyn Chen's *Getting Saved in America*, Marie Griffith's *God's Daughters*, and Pamela Klassen's *Blessed Events*. Another significant development was a rebirth of the earlier interest in religion's role in community power structures represented by Liston Pope's *Millhands and Preachers: A Study of Gastonia* and John Dollard's *Caste and Class in a Southern Town* and in such studies as David G. Hackett's *Rude Hand of Innovation: Religion and Social Order in Albany, New York, 1652–1836* and Albion M. Urdank's *Religion and Society in a Cotswold Vale: Nailsworth, Gloucestershire, 1780–1865*.

These and subsequent studies focusing on such varied topics as fundamentalism, the sanctuary movement, community-based organizing, sexuality, violence, and political activism reflected a widening interest in the distinctive

---

66. Albert Ogien and Toby Matthews, "Pragmatisms and Sociologies," *Revue française de sociologie* 55, 3 (2014), 414–28; Mustafa Emirbayer and Douglas W. Maynard, "Pragmatism and Ethnomethodology," *Qualitative Sociology* 34 (2011), 221–61; Neil Gross, "A Pragmatist Theory of Social Mechanisms," *American Sociological Review* 74, 3 (2009), 358–79; Neil Gross, "Pragmatism and the Study of Large-Scale Social Phenomena," *Theory and Society* 47, 1 (2018), 87–111; Antti Gronow, *From Habits to Social Structures: Pragmatism and Contemporary Social Theory* (Frankfurt: Peter Lang, 2011); and on Peirce, Aleksandar Feodorov, "Habit Beyond Psychology," *European Journal of Pragmatism and American Philosophy* 9, 1 (2017), 1–18.

67. For example, in religious studies, Jeffrey Stout, *Democracy and Tradition* (Princeton, NJ: Princeton University Press, 2004); and in cultural sociology, Margaret Frye, "Bright Futures in Malawi's New Dawn: Educational Aspirations as Assertions of Identity," *American Journal of Sociology* 117, 6 (2012), 1565–1624; and Jeffrey C. Alexander, "Cultural Pragmatics: Social Performance between Ritual and Strategy," *Sociological Theory* 22, 4 (2004), 527–73.

localized processes and structures through which religion and social life were mutually engaged, rather than a commitment to furthering a particular theory of religion or approach to the study of religion. The impetus nevertheless demonstrated the value of cross-disciplinary interaction and the possibilities of engaging with richer and more detailed aspects of religion as practiced in ordinary life. Unlike earlier approaches in which empirical generalizations about religion in national populations were sought, the manifestly greater diversity of religious practices in varied and dynamic situations posed challenges about the kinds of conceptual tools with which to conduct such research.[68]

While the practice turn valuably emphasized the situations and processes in which symbols, rituals, and social interaction are instantiated, the features of these situations and processes necessarily require disentangling for further refinement to proceed. Specifically, I suggest, any reasonable hope of utilizing practice approaches as a guide for conducting and interpreting research into the practice of religion must begin by separating and identifying the key components that the various literatures have described as characteristics of practice. At minimum, these characteristics include the contexts in which activities take place, the intentions and feelings of which they are constituted, the fact that they are embodied, the subjectivities they include, and their discursive manifestations.

Practicing religion, then, as conceived here, consists of doing things that provisionally draw a distinction between things constructed as sacred, special, or religious and the routine activities of everyday life but that work out religion's place in ordinary affairs through cues provided by the situation and dispositions

---

68. A significant exception to the shift from classification to practice was the continuing interest among sociologists of culture in categories that were predefined and publicly reinforced in ritual and discourse, such as racial and ethnic categories, partisan identities, and musical genres; however, studies of such categories also paid increasing attention to the processes (cognitive, social, and political) through which they were structured; examples include Marion Fourcade and Kieran Healy, "Categories All the Way Down," *Historical Social Research* 42, 1 (2017), 286–96; and Amir Goldberg, Michael T. Hannan, and Balázs Kovács, "What Does It Mean to Span Cultural Boundaries? Variety and Atypicality in Cultural Consumption," *American Sociological Review* 81, 2 (2016), 215–41. See also the provocative argument (that conceptual categories in ordinary life are sufficiently unstable that emphasis should be placed on context-dependent practices of "conceptualizing" that include retrieval cues, linguistic and embodied flexibility, and ad hoc instantiation) in Daniel Casasanto and Gary Lupyan, "All Concepts Are Ad Hoc Concepts," in *The Conceptual Mind: New Directions in the Study of Concepts*, edited by Eric Margolis and Stephen Laurence (Cambridge, MA: MIT Press, 2015), 543–66.

brought to the situation. Understanding religion as a practice necessitates considering it in the fullest sense of all that practices entail. That includes its habits that take place in specific settings and are constituted by temporalities, the improvisations with which people seek to engage the sacred, the feelings that characterize it, the narratives that give it meaning, its embodiment, its role in forging identities, and the communities that surround it. These regulated improvisations function as structuring practices that both condition and constitute experiences of the sacred and the meanings with which they are interpreted. Each of these topics is rich with generative insights from research in the social sciences and humanities and richer still with questions awaiting further investigation.

2

Situations

IN AN ESSAY about practicing religion, Courtney Bender describes an encounter on the train one day from Newark to Philadelphia between a man and woman seated near enough that she could overhear their conversation. The man remarked something about crazy terrorists, to which the woman responded that her husband was Muslim, which prompted the man to reply that of course not all Muslims are terrorists. The conversation continued as the woman told about her husband being put in jail for three weeks after 9/11 and how her Catholic family had felt about her marrying a Muslim. The pair, Bender says, was practicing religion.[1]

A rather different example is given in Andrew Johnson's study of a prison in Brazil. Pentecostalism is widely practiced in Brazil's prisons, Johnson argues, because it uniquely reflects the prison environment, solidifying tight-knit relationships among the inmates and helping them manage the harsh realities of incarceration. The situation in which the prisoners live shapes their faith, giving them a new identity and redeeming not only themselves but a shared space within the prison.[2]

These contrasting examples pose interesting questions about the role of situations in facilitating and influencing religious practices. Do situations provide cues of some kind that facilitate practicing religion? Is it the other people in the situation who have the greatest influence? What about the objects that are present in the situation? Are there power dynamics that matter? And how do people adapt to new situations based on what they have experienced in the past,

---

1. Courtney Bender, "Practicing Religions," in *The Cambridge Companion to Religious Studies*, edited by Robert A. Orsi (New York: Cambridge University Press, 2012), 273–95.

2. Andrew Johnson, *If I Give My Soul: Faith Behind Bars in Rio de Janeiro* (New York: Oxford University Press, 2017).

especially as the situations of which daily life is composed become increasingly diverse, fragmented, and non-local?

Although social scientists have long been interested in social situations, it has only been in recent years that the nature and functioning of situations has gained renewed interest. This interest reflects an awareness of the value of looking closely at the complexities of ordinary life instead of seeking broad generalizations about causal relations and it is connected closely to the growth of interest in practice theory. Bourdieu, for instance, stresses recurrent situations as the places in which we learn the "art of living," by which he means the norms of "appropriate conduct" through which we engage the ambiguities and uncertainties of daily life. Human behavior is in this perspective purposive, as arguments about goal orientations suggest, but purposive action necessarily takes account of the situations in which it occurs. Moreover, the point of investigating situations is not merely to identify how individuals adapt but to understand the practices that define and reproduce situations.[3]

Scholars come at the topic of situations from different perspectives and for this reason give situations differing definitions. Bourdieu mostly defines situations in terms of small-scale localized interactions that are structured by actors' dispositions and unequal resources. Situations are not instantaneous in his view but unfold over time and include both repetition and improvisation. Michael Burawoy argues for an "extended case method" in conducting interviews and ethnographic research that emphasizes the immediate contextual effects of co-presence among individuals, the resources and schemas that are invoked, and the interventions from the outside of regimes of power.[4] Randall

---

3. Pierre Bourdieu, *Outline of a Theory of Practice* (Cambridge, UK: Cambridge University Press, 1977), 8, 26, 40; Matthew Norton, "Mechanisms and Meaning Structures," *Sociological Theory* 32, 2 (2014), 162–87, reviews the literature and develops an argument about the situational construction of meaning; an approach that features Erving Goffman's "frame analysis" is developed in David Diehl and Daniel McFarland, "Toward a Historical Sociology of Social Situations," *American Journal of Sociology* 115, 6 (2010), 1713–52.

4. Michael Burawoy, "The Extended Case Method," *Sociological Theory* 16, 1 (1998), 4–33; Michael Burawoy, *The Extended Case Method: Four Countries, Four Decades, Four Great Transformations, and One Theoretical Tradition* (Berkeley and Los Angeles: University of California Press, 2009); and on the theoretical origins of the extended case method, Max Gluckman, *Analysis of a Social Situation in Modern Zululand* (Manchester: Manchester University Press, 1958); Max Gluckman, "The Utility of the Equilibrium Model in the Study of Social Change," *American Anthropologist* 70, 2 (1968), 219–37; and Bruce Kapferer, "Situations, Crisis, and the Anthropology of the Concrete: The Contribution of Max Gluckman," *Social Analysis* 49, 3 (2005), 85–122.

Collins defines situations more narrowly as "momentary encounters among human bodies charged up with emotions and consciousness because they have gone through chains of previous encounters."[5] Collins's definition, which serves his interest in rituals, can be usefully broadened, however, to include situations that are less "charged up with emotion" and, as many of his own examples suggest, are more than "momentary." The notion of "encounter" implies interaction between the person and the various physical, social, and dispositional aspects of the situation to which the person responds.[6] Practices may be solitary or include vicarious as well as in-person interaction. The study of situations is thus the investigation of how and the extent to which practices are shaped by and respond to these situational aspects.

Situations include the *spaces* in which the encounters occur. A space in these terms is a geographic place that has both a perceived identity and a material form.[7] In Michel de Certeau's apt phrasing, "space is a practiced place." It includes the artifacts—buildings, tables, chairs, paintings, icons—with which people interact and the significance of which is altered by the movement and positioning of bodies in interaction.[8] Henri Lefebvre writes that practices are necessarily spatial because they embrace the production and reproduction of "particular locations and spatial sets" and thus ensure "continuity" and "some degree of cohesion." Competence of performance, he says, is implied and required within given spatial practices.[9]

---

5. Randall Collins, *Interaction Ritual Chains* (Princeton, NJ: Princeton University Press, 2004), 3–4.

6. Social psychology literature on dispositional-situational interaction is reviewed in John F. Rauthmann et al., "The Situational Eight DIAMONDS: A Taxonomy of Major Dimensions of Situation Characteristics," *Journal of Personality and Social Psychology* 107, 4 (2014), 677–718, who list twenty-one different taxonomies of situations; see also John F. Rauthmann, Ryne A. Sherman, and David C. Funder, "Principles of Situation Research: Towards a Better Understanding of Psychological Situations," *European Journal of Personality* 29 (2015), 363–81, who plead for more "real-life" studies of situations.

7. Thomas F. Gieryn, "A Space for Place in Sociology," *Annual Review of Sociology* 26 (2000), 463–96.

8. Michel de Certeau, *The Practice of Everyday Life* (Berkeley and Los Angeles: University of California Press, 1984), 117; the emphasis on *practice* in this work notably contrasts with the focus on *perception* in Yi-Fu Tuan, *Space and Place: The Perspective of Experience* (Minneapolis: University of Minnesota Press, 1977), which has also been generative for scholarship concerned with place.

9. Henri Lefebvre, *The Production of Space*, trans. Donald Nicholson-Smith (Oxford: Basil Blackwell, 1991), 34.

A definition that captures the multiple aspects that constitute situations is given by Michael Hutter and David Stark, who write: "Situations are characterized by the particular social assemblage of persons and things that are in place and in motion during a span of time." This definition incorporates the fact that both interaction and place are essential, while also pointing to the importance of things that serve as situational affordances and the temporalities involved as situations unfold over time. The situations of greatest interest to Hutter and Stark are local—homes, laboratories, studios, art galleries, concert halls, and stores. But their view of situations is not limited to immediate face-to-face social interaction. The social assemblage that constitutes a situation can include people interacting at a distance as well, such as artists and scientists collaborating on projects through virtual media.[10]

A first take on what it means to say that religion is *practiced* necessitates emphasizing that practices take place in situations. Situations, such as worship services, occur repeatedly among the same assemblage of people and in the same space. But religious practices are highly portable, meaning that the fluid, often short-lived, interlaced situations in which they take place must be emphasized as well. An emphasis on situations advantageously shifts attention away from arguments suggesting that religion is essentially a means of achieving some long-term goal (such as assurance of one's eternal destiny) and for this reason can be investigated with respect to how rational or irrational it is. Human action is, as Hans Joas argues, contingent on and thus constituted by the situations in which it occurs. Situations, he says, befall us and confront us, but they also "are not mute," meaning that they "demand that we take action."[11]

In this chapter I discuss several lines of inquiry about situations that illuminate their role in religious practices: research on situational cues that reinforce habits, discussions of spaces and affordances that facilitate the formation of sacred space, and the power dynamics that occur in these spaces. Together, these cues, spaces, affordances, and power dynamics constitute a significant portion

---

10. Michael Hutter and David Stark, "Pragmatist Perspectives on Valuation: An Introduction," in *Moments of Valuation: Exploring Sites of Dissonance*, edited by Ariane Berthoin Antal, Michael Hutter, and David Stark (New York: Oxford University Press, 2015), 1–12; Hutter and Stark's definition of situations as performative "moments" of valuation is thus quite different from the face-to-face situationalism that is arguably too limited to take account of distances, virtual interaction, dispositions, and institutions; see Michèle Lamont and Ann Swidler, "Methodological Pluralism and the Possibilities and Limits of Interviewing," *Qualitative Sociology* 37, 2 (2014), 153–71.

11. Hans Joas, *The Creativity of Action* (Cambridge, UK: Polity Press, 1992), 160–61.

of the implicit rules that govern the meaning and composition of religious practices.

Situational Cues

An interest that has animated social psychological research for half a century or more is how human behavior responds to cues or stimuli in individuals' immediate context. Early studies cast in a behaviorist mold focused on responses to rewards and punishments and included attention to how habits are formed or broken by these stimuli. Recent studies have revived this interest in the role of situational cues by bringing cognitive science into the picture, first, to emphasize that cues function less as discrete stimuli and more as cognitive schemata that organize complex pieces of information, and second, to show the extent to which responses occur with or without deliberation.[12] Dual information processing studies that distinguish "fast" responses activated in an autonomous fashion without executive control from "slow" responses based on active conscious thought serve as the neurocognitive grounding for these discussions.[13] Situational cues, such as hearing a strange noise in a new house in the middle of the night, at first require deliberation (what's that noise?), but after repeated occurrences evoke hardly any thought (that's the furnace coming on). Recurrent cues that gradually generate unthinking responses are the basis of habits, which facilitate everyday behavior in terms of speed and efficiency. The responses become habitual if similar situations provide similar cues. Habits are then subsequently activated as a kind of default response when these situational cues occur. The fact that habits are "encoded in a conservative, slow-learning procedural memory system that reflects knowledge slowly accrued over repeated instances" renders them difficult to change.[14]

---

12. Wendy Wood and Dennis Rünger, "Psychology of Habit," *Annual Review of Psychology* 67 (2016), 289–314; and on cognitive schemata, Roy G. D'Andrade, *The Development of Cognitive Anthropology* (New York: Oxford University Press, 1995).

13. Daniel Kahneman, *Thinking, Fast and Slow* (New York: Farrar, Straus and Giroux, 2011); for a critical discussion of the dual processing literature, see Jonathan St. B. T. Evans and Keith E. Stanovich, "Dual-Process Theories of Higher Cognition: Advancing the Debate," *Perspectives on Psychological Science* 8, 3 (2013), 223–41.

14. Jeffrey M. Quinn et al., "Can't Control Yourself? Monitor Those Bad Habits," *Personality and Social Psychology Bulletin* 36, 4 (2010), 499–511, quote on page 499.

On this account, good habits are not maintained by willpower alone but by being in situations that cue the desired behavior.[15] This does not mean that a person's values and beliefs are unimportant, but that they often function outside of conscious awareness as the mental constructs, including the habits that people have acquired, through which people perceive and process information. The situational cues are triggers that prompt action guided by both the habits and the idiosyncrasies of the immediate context.[16] Bad habits function similarly, despite efforts to break them, when responses are automatically triggered by situational cues. Control of temptation accordingly requires finding ways to override the cues or avoid the situations. The takeaway for understanding religious practice is that situations provide cues that prompt and maintain certain kinds of religious activities.

Studies linking situational cues to habits must be qualified in two respects when applied to practices in ordinary life. The first is that the situation and the cue must always be the same or nearly the same for the result to occur. This may happen in the contrived space of a laboratory but is rarely true in actual situations. A person soon learns to commute to work without thinking much about it, even though the weather and traffic conditions vary from day to day. The second is the assumption that the situation largely determines how the individual behaves. This perspective, Candace Upton observes, "Claims that the situation a human being inhabits, or takes herself to inhabit, better predicts and explains her behavior than her putative traits of character."[17] Practice theory rejects this claim, arguing instead that individuals bring dispositions, narratives, and habits to their situations. Practice theory nevertheless recognizes that situations can and do activate, suppress, and redirect otherwise stable traits of character.

A constructive alternative to the situationist approach holds that practices are more firmly anchored in—cued by—certain situations than in others. For instance, people who routinely interact in certain situations may specify those

---

15. Evidence suggests that low willpower weakens people's ability to resist undesirable habits; David T. Neal, Wendy Wood, and Aimee Drolet, "How Do People Adhere to Goals When Willpower Is Low? The Profits (and Pitfalls) of Strong Habits," *Journal of Personality and Social Psychology* 104, 6 (2013), 959–75.

16. Rogers Brubaker, Mara Loveman, and Peter Stamatov, "Ethnicity as Cognition," *Theory and Society* 33, 1 (2004), 31–64.

17. Candace L. Upton, "Virtue Ethics and Moral Psychology: The Situationist Debate," *Journal of Ethics* 13, 2 (2009), 103–15.

situations as the "only" or "best-suited" places to engage in a practice—*and* establish practices of resistance toward competitors. Such instances are especially likely if "experts" are deemed necessary for the practice to be conducted successfully.[18] Moreover, these "institutionalized" situations provide the stable cues that produce habits, which in turn maintain recurrent actions that do not depend on conscious deliberation. For instance, research on voter turnout demonstrates that cognitive-based accounts that attribute turnout to beliefs, values, and candidate preferences provide significantly less explanatory power among voters who regularly vote (apparently as habit) than among infrequent voters.[19] A comparable pattern suggesting that deliberations about sermon quality, ambience, and programs play more of a role among new or sporadic attendees at religious services than among regular attendees is not hard to imagine. As interesting as it may be to observe religion being practiced on the train or in prison, therefore, the situations in which religion occurs are usually spaces in which relevant cues prompt habitual responses, including one of which individuals may be unaware. If, for instance, students who frequented events at a sport stadium raised their voices when incidentally shown an image of a stadium, as one study demonstrated, an image of a place of worship might be expected to trigger a lowering of voices among frequent attendees at religious services.[20]

Studies of motor learning demonstrate that not only the regularity and frequency of situational cues but also their salience affects the likelihood of habits being learned. Learning to play tennis, for example, is relatively unaffected by background lighting and ambient noise.[21] Similarly, learning to pray at mealtimes is unlikely to be affected by the day being cloudy or sunny. Why it is unaffected by the food served or the time of day, though, is a different matter. That depends on what people have learned to classify as salient. A person learns

---

18. Ann Swidler, "What Anchors Cultural Practices?" in *The Practice Turn in Contemporary Theory*, edited by Theodore R. Schatzki, Karin Knorr Cetina, and Eike von Savigny (New York: Routledge, 2001), 83–100.

19. John H. Aldrich, Jacob M. Montgomery, and Wendy Wood, "Turnout as Habit," *Political Behavior* 33, 4 (2011), 535–63.

20. David T. Neal et al., "How Do Habits Guide Behavior? Perceived and Actual Triggers of Habits in Daily Life," *Journal of Experimental Social Psychology* 48, 2 (2012), 492–98.

21. Daniel M. Wolpert and J. Randall Flanagan, "Motor Learning," *Current Biology* 20, 11 (2010), R467–R472; in contrast, physical locations are salient context cues for joggers—see Neal et al., "How Do Habits Guide Behavior?"

to pray, not when potatoes are served, but when a "meal" is served—and what counts as a "meal" depends on the situation.

Research indicates in fact that what defines eating situations as meals is a function of multiple cues. A study of American young adults, for example, found that eating events were significantly more likely to be considered as "meals" rather than "snacks" when eating occurred with family rather than alone, when the episode lasted longer, when people sat rather than stood, and when cloth napkins and ceramic plates were used rather than paper napkins and plates. Food cues also mattered, with expensive, high-quality, prepared food served in large portions cuing the situation as a meal, whereas inexpensive, lower quality, packaged food served in small portions defined the situation as a snack. In addition, the emotional valence of the situation mattered, with happiness being more associated with meals and boredom with snacks.[22]

When people have developed a habit of praying at meals, then, the situational cues that define food consumption as meals or snacks will likely influence the frequency with which they pray. A family gathering with people seated to enjoy exquisitely prepared food would be more likely to include a prayer than almost any other eating situation. A related possibility is that a decline in the frequency of people saying "table grace" might indicate less about religion than about people more often eating quickly prepared inexpensive packaged food alone.

Other situational cues that bear on activities being practiced as habits include the regularity and formality of their occurrence. Eating at scheduled times each morning, noon, and evening, for example, seems more likely to imply meals than consuming food at odd moments throughout the day, as would dressing for dinner and using special heirloom serving dishes. The counterpart in religion would be attending services regularly at the same hour on the same day of the week and wearing formal clothing or participating in a service spoken in Latin.

However, Durkheim's emphasis on the sacred being set apart adds a cautionary note. While regularity and formality may be the situational cues that perpetuate religious practice as habit, the same cues may not set the practice apart in any special way, at least not if the rest of daily life is scheduled and formal. It is therefore not surprising that reports of experiences people deem sacred often seem to imply an unscheduled event and that people periodically appear to revolt against religious formality. Meditating by a stream in the woods and

---

22. Brian Wansink, Collin R. Payne, and Mitsuru Shimizu, "'Is This a Meal or Snack?' Situational Cues that Drive Perceptions," *Appetite* 54, 1 (2010), 214–16.

gathering for a religious discussion at a bar become meaningful violations of habit-induced routines.

Situations in which cues encourage people to pray or worship are usually non-threatening. Whoever orchestrates the situation presumably assumes the outcome is desirable. But many situations are different. In Bender's example of the Muslim woman on the train, the man's remark about crazy terrorists could well have made the woman instantly more aware of being a member of a religious minority that many Americans disliked. She responded by asserting her identity. But what if she hadn't? Would she still have been practicing religion?

Research on "signaling threat" addresses such situations. Signaling threat is a situational cue that raises the salience of a person's identity in a way that makes the person feel vulnerable. Women in male-majority situations, as in science labs and corporate board meetings, frequently experience signaling threat. The salience of their identity as women is increased by the numerical predominance of men in the situation. It may also be increased by "mansplaining" and other patronizing remarks. Results in experimental studies show that typical responses to such signaling threats include a heightened sense of marginalization, a decrease in active participation or desire to participate, and increased vigilance both in physiological responses such as faster heart rates and cognitive responses such as paying greater attention to and retaining more in memory about the interaction taking place.[23]

Signaling threat has strong implications for understanding how people practice religion. Small sects that "retreat" from the world may do so because of doctrine but may also find that doctrine compelling because of exposure to signaling threat. Adherence to that doctrine may be further reinforced through the salient memories of such threats, as in the case of narratives about persecution.[24] Religious communities of greater size and social influence may generate cues that prompt signaling threat by magnifying the significance of an apparently hostile gesture on the part of another religious community or the "secular" society.[25] Yet another example of the significance of signaling threat is evident in research on religion and social class. This research suggests that

---

23. Mary C. Murphy, Claude M. Steele, and James J. Gross, "Signaling Threat: How Situational Cues Affect Women in Math, Science, and Engineering Settings," *Psychological Science* 18, 10 (2007), 879–85.

24. Bryan R. Wilson, *Religious Sects: A Sociological Study* (New York: McGraw Hill, 1970).

25. Christian Smith, *American Evangelicalism: Embattled and Thriving* (Chicago: University of Chicago Press, 1998).

people often gravitate to congregations of their own social class to avoid cues that make them feel vulnerable and out of place in other settings. These cues include the architecture and embellishments of the worship space and the style of language in which services are conducted.[26] Similarly, research suggesting that people gravitate to religiously homophilous networks suggests the need to investigate the cues that signal homophily or heterophily; e.g., surnames, phenotypical characteristics, dialect, grooming.[27]

The principal difficulty in drawing empirical inferences about situational cues is determining which of the many cues present in real-life contexts are most likely to be operative. One aspect of situations that increases the likelihood is if the cues converge to make the response over-determined. If prayer is more likely to accompany meals than snacks, its likelihood is increased by the number of meal-defining cues present (sitting with family, eating high-quality prepared food, etc.). A second aspect is the presence of an authority figure or authoritative group to define the situation. In the meal example, the head of the family may simply declare that a prayer is to be given, even if the situation is not defined as a meal. In the sect example, an individual who experiences a signaling threat may be disinclined to retreat from society, but a group that does is more likely to generate agreement about the need to retreat.

Besides aiming to maximize the likelihood of cues leading to desired responses, religious practices are also directed toward minimizing undesired behavior (e.g., discouraging drug use or sexual promiscuity). Understanding that these behaviors are products of habits *and* situations is useful. Behavior prompted by clear situational cues is likely to be affected by altering the situation, as in the case of students whose daily routines of newspaper reading and exercise were disrupted when transferred to a new university. When cues stem from multiple or unknown sources, though, as is frequently the case with smoking or over-eating, vigilant attention to the behavior itself is more likely to be effective, especially if monitoring cues (don't do it) can be attached to the behavior.[28]

---

26. Timothy J. Nelson, "At Ease with Our Own Kind: Worship Practices and Class Segregation in American Religion," in *Religion and Class in America: Culture, History, and Politics*, edited by Sean McCloud and William A. Mirola (Boston: Brill, 2009), 45–68.

27. Some evidence is included in Matt A. Barreto, *Ethnic Cues: The Role of Shared Ethnicity in Latino Political Participation* (Ann Arbor: University of Michigan Press, 2010).

28. Quinn et al., "Can't Control Yourself?"

While much of the interest in situational cues stems from concerns about invoking good habits and breaking bad habits, situational cues that disrupt ordinary life also play an important role. *Disruptive cues* shock us, redirect our attention, and prompt us to respond in ways we may not have expected. Disruptive cues are context-dependent, which means that the situation must be considered to understand why an act or event that is disruptive in one situation is not in another. Some happen naturally (the lights suddenly go out); others are staged (a speaker flips the lights on and off to signal that a meeting is about to begin). Any aspect of a situation that is "out of place"—speaking in the wrong register, wearing inappropriate clothes, muttering to oneself, laughing too loudly—can be a disruptive cue.

Research on disruptive cues suggests that they often evoke impulsive emotional responses, such as fear or anger, which can impede deliberative thought. Breaking news that leads with graphic images of violence, for example, typically prompts such responses and thus captures viewers' attention but worries critics that it sends misleading signals about the nature and causes of violence.[29] Religious practice is an interesting contrast because the violence in its traditions (war, murder, blood sacrifice) has been mentioned so often that it must be graphically amplified to be disturbing. Mel Gibson's *The Passion of the Christ*, as Stephen Prince shows, shocked its Christian viewers, but in a favorable way. "In any other context," Focus on the Family leader James Dobson said, "I could not in good conscience recommend a movie containing this degree of violent content. However, in this case, the violence is intended ... to emphasize the reality of the unspeakable suffering that our Savior endured."[30]

Gibson's movie illustrates a case in which people put themselves in a situation expecting to experience disruptive cues, much as a person visiting an amusement park or traveling to an underdeveloped country does. People *want* to be jarred. *Hazardous situational cues*, as Jennifer Keys calls them, can be sought to trigger a response that reinforces one's beliefs (people truly are suffering), but can also be avoided. Keys shows, for instance, how women seeking an abortion learn to "run the gauntlet" as best they can by dodging anti-abortion

---

29. Michael A. Milburn and Sheree D. Conrad, *Raised to Rage: The Politics of Anger and the Roots of Authoritarianism* (Cambridge, MA: MIT Press, 2016); Karen A. Cerulo, *Deciphering Violence: The Cognitive Structure of Right and Wrong* (New York: Routledge, 1998).

30. Stephen Prince, "Beholding Blood Sacrifice in *The Passion of the Christ*," *Film Quarterly* 59, 4 (2006), 11–22, quote on page 13.

rhetoric and pictures of brutalized fetuses.[31] The larger point is that cues are often known to be present in certain situations and people are frequently able to choose their situations accordingly.

If foundational beliefs and values, of which religion is a prominent example, must be triggered by situational cues to affect individuals' behavior, then it is essential for any conclusions about the nexus of beliefs to behavior to know what those triggers are. One example is an interesting study asking if religious values heightened concerns about the environment. The results from an analysis of survey data showed that general worries about the environment did not provide a trigger but that questions about genetically engineered organisms did—the latter apparently connoting a contravention of God's natural order more than the former.[32] In other studies, *priming*—the intentional manipulation of triggering words, such as preceding or not preceding a survey question about a presidential candidate with a question about religion—demonstrates the effects of subtle cues.[33]

Spaces

The spaces in which cues are evoked encompass intimate places such as living quarters and meeting rooms, formal places such as corporations and government buildings, and territorial places such as neighborhoods and entire cities. In all these instances, as Lefebvre argues, space is a social product, the reality of which is constituted in social interaction and in shared symbolism as spatial practice.[34] *Situational space* restricts the concept to the small-scale localized places in which face-to-face social interaction occurs. Bender's encounter on the train and Johnson's observations about a Brazilian prison fit this definition.

---

31. Jennifer Keys, "Running the Gauntlet: Women's Use of Emotional Management Techniques in the Abortion Experience," *Symbolic Interaction* 33, 1 (2010), 41–70.

32. Anders Biel and Andreas Nilsson, "Religious Values and Environmental Concern: Harmony and Detachment," *Social Science Quarterly* 86, 1 (2005), 178–91.

33. Paul A. Djupe and Brian R. Calfano, *God Talk: Experimenting with the Religious Causes of Public Opinion* (Philadelphia: Temple University Press, 2013); some examples are discussed in Robert Wuthnow, *Inventing American Religion: Polls, Surveys, and the Tenuous Quest for a Nation's Faith* (New York: Oxford University Press, 2015); for a thorough discussion of religion and priming, see Michael Tesler, "Priming Predispositions and Changing Policy Positions: An Account of When Mass Opinion Is Primed or Changed," *American Journal of Political Science* 59, 4 (2015), 806–24.

34. Lefebvre, *The Production of Space*.

Other examples of situational spaces in which religious practices occur include houses of worship, fellowship halls, soup kitchens, prayer closets, home altars, and art galleries. Situational spaces such as these that are public must further be distinguished from ones—backstage areas, as Goffman called them—that are truly private. In public situational spaces, individuals interact as representatives of publicly understood roles, such as physicians, customers, middle-class hosts, prisoners, and strangers on the train, whereas private situational spaces, such as family rooms and bedrooms, offer individuals greater freedom to behave informally and as representatives only of themselves or of intimately familiar others.[35]

Situational space refers not only to the physical place in which social interaction occurs but also to these representational ways that place envelops meaning and significance for the persons involved. The practices through which a place becomes space, in this sense, necessitate attention to the interpretations of events that have happened in the space before and are expected to happen again. De Certeau refers to a "feeling tone" that manifests itself in the events attached to specific places—a kind of emotional energy that seizes the participants because of what they know has gone on before or have experienced personally.[36] Walter E. A. Van Beek suggests in his study of Nigerian artisans that the place in which they work is a *dwelling*, which conveys an emotional attachment, "a dwelt-in space" with a "definite structure and a specific purpose, imbued with meaning and guiding action."[37]

The practices that define the meanings of situational space are typically relational, contrasting with practices that define different spaces and that sometimes supply contested meanings. Anthropologist Catherine Alexander, for example, suggests that English middle-class families' gardens are places of disorder—exuberance, excess, play—that contrast with and provide relief from the order that prevails within the house. The gardens, she suggests, also compete with religion, providing a *spatial Sunday* of innocence and repose in which

---

35. Erving Goffman, *The Presentation of Self in Everyday Life* (New York: Doubleday, 1959), 106–40.

36. Ian Buchanan, *Michel de Certeau: Cultural Theorist* (London: Sage, 2000), helpfully unpacks de Certeau's focus on narratives and feelings; the broader genealogy of the concept is discussed in Veronica Ng, "The Problem of *Place*: A Foucauldian and Discursive Analysis on *Place*," in *Space and Place, vol 3: Exploring Critical Issues*, edited by Didem Kilickiran, Christina Alegria, and Carl Haddrell (Oxford: Inter-Disciplinary Press, 2013), 185–204.

37. Walter E. A. Van Beek, *The Forge and the Funeral: The Smith in Kapsiki/Higi Culture* (East Lansing: Michigan State University Press, 2015), 16.

family bonds can be freely and playfully reinforced through casual conversation.[38]

As this example suggests, *discursive space* and situational space typically go together. Discursive space defines what can be talked about and how it can properly be discussed. Discursive space is often formally defined, as in the case of court hearings in which only certain arguments and kinds of evidence can be presented. In other instances, it is informally defined, as among friends who know from previous interaction not to talk about politics. Nina Eliasoph and Paul Lichterman call something similar a "group style" that tells people the appropriate way to talk in, say, a business meeting or a classroom.[39] What can be talked about is always subject to renegotiation as the persons present in the situation change and bring new experiences and concerns with them. In the same way that discussions of practice do, the concept of situational space therefore highlights both the stabilities and instabilities that arise from the multiple convergences of subjectivities, discourse, and action.

Sacred space is both situational and discursive. Its presence is evident in such examples as Notre Dame Cathedral, the Basilica of Guadalupe, the Dome of the Rock, and the Angkor Wat. These are spaces that have been consecrated publicly and over such a long period that it is difficult to think of them in any other way. Visitors feel that the buildings themselves are sacred. Consecration in these grand examples is established through the authority of powerful religious leaders, while on a smaller scale, sacred space consecrated through the loving work of local founders remembered for their carpentry and masonry skills is often equally powerful. In ordinary life, though, sacred space is usually harder to identify and often more difficult to say why it is sacred. Journalist Lisa Respers France, for example, wrote that the historic Fox Theater in Atlanta during a Prince concert—his last, as it happened—was transformed into a "sacred space" where "notes were prayers and performance was praise."[40] Perhaps she was the only person in the audience who felt this way and perhaps it was Prince's

---

38. Catherine Alexander, "The Garden as Occasional Domestic Space," *Signs* 27, 3 (2002), 857–71; Daniel Miller, *A Theory of Shopping* (Oxford: Berg, 1998), suggests that English garden centers where families shop on Sundays for plants and garden equipment also serve as substitutes for religious practices.

39. Nina Eliasoph and Paul Lichterman, "Culture in Interaction," *American Journal of Sociology* 108, 4 (2003), 735–94.

40. Lisa Respers France, "Prince's Last Concert Was a 'Sacred' Experience," *CNN*, April 22, 2016; cnn.com.

unique charisma that made the difference, but experiences like this require consideration.

Elaine A. Peña's ethnographic study of a community of Central American immigrants in suburban Chicago offers an instructive interpretation of how practices and space interact to create understandings of the sacred. Although their resources were limited, the immigrants had many possibilities at their disposal. For instance, they could have gathered in a public park and declared the space sacred, and they did in fact hold meetings in a high school gymnasium. However, they also created what they called Second Tepeyac, a replica of the hill in Mexico where the Virgin of Guadalupe appeared in 1531 and that later became the location of the Basilica of Guadalupe. Second Tepeyac, Peña observed, was sacred space because of the relationship between its symbolic connection to the virgin and the immigrants' practices. The sacred space was "infused with diverse cultural perspectives, distinct idioms, and different life experiences" drawn from the work over a ten-year period of the Guadalupan community in constructing it and from the consecrating services when it was finished, as well as the anti-immigrant sentiment the Guadalupans experienced. Sacredness no longer required the Virgin to have appeared but was preserved in the idea that "one grain of sand" was sufficient to consecrate a place. It was further manifested as shifting gatherings of devotees prayed, danced, made pilgrimages on bicycles, set up meetings with immigration lawyers, and learned of pending legislation.[41]

Second Tepeyac is an example of the broader adaptation of sacredness to the more transient lives people experience in the contemporary globalized world. People come and go as they please, pay their respects to the Virgin, and are on their way. Standing near the replica and knowing the story facilitates a meaningful inward experience that stays with the worshippers as they leave. But sacred space differs fundamentally from inward experience in one important respect. The difference is that sacred space exists in the physicality of its being and thus is subject to social control. The remarkable question about Second Tepeyac is how a community of immigrants could locate a space for it in

---

41. Elaine E. Peña, *Performing Piety: Making Space Sacred with the Virgin of Guadalupe* (Berkeley and Los Angeles: University of California Press, 2011), 18; and Elaine A. Peña, "Beyond Mexico: Guadalupan Sacred Space Production and Mobilization in a Chicago Suburb," *American Quarterly* 60, 3 (2008), 721–47.

suburban Chicago. The answer is that the Maryville Academy, which owned a ninety-seven-acre property, hosted it.

Unlike private spirituality that can easily be practiced in the sanctity of one's mind, sacred space—like any other space, only more so—implies the necessity of protecting a place that some group considers inviolable. Sacred space is rarely guarded by etiquette, superstition, or ritual alone. Its protection stems from power, whether in the hands of clergy, imposed by the state, or both. One of the more interesting historical examples is the murder of Thomas Becket, Archbishop of Canterbury, in Canterbury Cathedral in 1170. Besides the moral and political implications of the event so effectively dramatized in T. S. Eliot's *Murder in the Cathedral*, there was also the important matter of the murder happening in sacred space.[42] Canon law strictly regulated what constituted an offense of "Church Pollution," including the defacing of objects, brawling in the churchyard, and horseplay. Becket's death was abhorrent not only because he was murdered but also because blood, bones, and scrapings of his brain polluted the church floor.[43]

Modern examples of regulations governing sacred space include zoning laws and rules about building maintenance and fire exits. These regulations reflect the power of secular authorities, but religious groups improvise in responding to them.[44] When churches began moving to suburban locations in the 1950s, for example, municipal codes imposed new regulations governing site development and parking, but church planners decided in some cases to put parking spaces in front, with the idea that a full parking lot would cue newcomers to attend, while in other cases architects accommodated rear parking lots by shifting main entrances from front to back. Planners also adapted by purchasing larger spaces and designing buildings with future expansion in mind.[45]

Sacred spaces in homes—and homes *as* sacred space—contrast in interesting ways with public places of worship. Agnes Heller writes, "Integral to the average everyday life is awareness of a fixed point in space, a firm position from which we 'proceed' (whether every day or over larger periods of time) and to

---

42. T. S. Eliot, *Murder in the Cathedral* (New York: Harcourt Brace, 1935).

43. Laurence Etherington, "Canons of Environmental Law: Pollution of Churches and the Regulation of the Medieval 'Environment,'" *Legal Studies* 36, 4 (2016), 566–90.

44. The power of secular authorities is nicely illustrated in Anna Lea Berg, "From Religious to Secular Place-making: How Does the Secular Matter for Religious Place Construction in the Local?" *Social Compass* 66, 1 (March 2019), 35–48.

45. Gretchen Buggeln, *The Suburban Church: Modernism and Community in Postwar America* (Minneapolis: University of Minnesota Press, 2015).

which we return in due course. This firm position is what we call 'home.'"⁴⁶ As fixed space, homes are durable, familiar, and in most instances, secure bases of operation. They are, for most children, "our first universe," Gaston Bachelard observes, "the topography of our intimate being."⁴⁷ Stable cues in homes induce habits, and the regulated improvisation they require largely occurs within predictable limits. Homes are a kind of sanctuary, a place of retreat, against an external environment that, as David Harvey observes, is often "a place of mystery, the site of the unexpected, full of agitations and ferments."⁴⁸ But homes are also multifunctional, providing for bodily needs and leisure and social interaction, which locates sacred space within them amid ordinary activities and thus requires household rules to define it.⁴⁹

In many locations, home altars function as set-aside places that define sacred space within households. Improvisation adapts them to the household's specific interests and activities. Home altars among immigrant families illustrate these adaptations. A study of Vietnamese American home altars, for example, found that families arrange objects to include both Catholic and Buddhist traditions and that the altars are active, fluid spaces constituted by the placing and eating of fresh fruit, praying, cleaning, and rotating objects in commemoration of different ancestors and different religious holidays.⁵⁰ Hindu American home altars, which are often present in every room of the household, making it possible for each person to offer a private morning prayer, illustrate active participation as well.⁵¹

---

46. Agnes Heller, *Everyday Life* (London: Routledge and Kegan Paul, 1984), 239.

47. Gaston Bachelard, *The Poetics of Space* (Boston: Beacon Press, 1994), quoted in John Gatta, *Spirits of Place in American Literary Culture* (New York: Oxford University Press, 2018), 15.

48. David Harvey, *Consciousness and the Urban Experience* (Oxford: Basil Blackwell, 1985), 250.

49. Thomas A. Tweed, *Crossing and Dwelling: A Theory of Religion* (Cambridge, MA: Harvard University Press, 2006), 105, writes that "Home refers to an intimate controlled space, whether cleared or constructed, that provides for bodily needs—shelter, sleep, sex, healing, and food."

50. Linda Ho Peché, "'I Would Pay Homage, Not Go All Bling': Vietnamese American Youth Reflect on Family and Religious Life," in *Sustaining Faith Traditions: Race, Ethnicity, and Religion among the Latino and Asian American Second Generation*, edited by Carolyn Chen and Russell Jeung (New York: NYU Press, 2012), 222–40.

51. Shampa Mazumdar and Sanjoy Mazumdar, "Place Identity and Religion: A Study of Hindu Immigrants in America," in *The Role of Place Identity in the Perception, Understanding, and*

A study of Mexican American women's home altars showed similar improvisational responses and creative variation except that the objects venerated were national and ethnic as well as religious and included photos of children and grandchildren for whom the women prayed. The altars were also discursive spaces that occasioned stories of devotion, suffering, and loss.[52] This was true as well in Mexico among the women María Del Socorro Castañeda-Liles studied whose home practices reflected the fluidity of lived experience through the aromas of flowers, the taste of foods, and the images composing their home altars.[53] Similarly, research among Burmese American families in California found that most home altars included a bowl of fruit, two vases of flowers, and two candles—all traditionally Buddhist—with a few embellishments thrown in that may have represented a Catholic detour or the family's heritage. The discourse differed from the Mexican American study, though, because the immigrants' children mostly interacted with non-immigrant friends and thus had lost an understanding of the tradition and needed to have it explained.[54]

The hybridity evident in the mingling of objects from different religious and ethnic traditions in these examples illustrates the extent of control that families exercise over the space they designate as sacred in their homes. *Soka Gakkai* practices in Japan illustrate a different kind of control. A person who converts to *Soka Gakkai* is required by the group to destroy the traditional home altar and replace it with one approved by *Soka Gakkai*. The new member is also expected to convert the rest of the family as quickly as possible.[55] Power dynamics are evident, though, even in examples when external authority is absent. A home, Mary Douglas writes, is "space under control"—a space that in the extreme exercises "tyrannous control over mind and body"—regulating what its

---

Design of Built Environments, edited by Casakin Hernan and Bernardo Fatima (Danvers, MA: Bentham Books, 2012), 133–46.

52. Gabriella Ricciardi, "Telling Stories, Building Altars: Mexican American Women's Altars in Oregon," *Oregon Historical Quarterly* 107, 4 (2006), 536–52.

53. María Del Socorro Castañeda-Liles, *Our Lady of Everyday Life: La Virgen de Guadalupe and the Catholic Imagination of Mexican Women in America* (New York: Oxford University Press, 2018).

54. Joseph Cheah, "The Function of Ethnicity in the Adaptation of Burmese Religious Practices," in *Emerging Voices: Experiences of Underrepresented Asian Americans*, edited by Huping Ling (New Brunswick, NJ: Rutgers University Press, 2008), 199–217.

55. Felix Moos, "Religion and Politics in Japan: The Case of Soka Gakkai," *Asian Survey* 13, 3 (1963), 136–42.

inhabitants are expected to do and refrain from doing.[56] Home altars are no exception. In each of the immigrant American examples, it was the matriarch of the family who decided what should be placed on the altar—as one young woman explained, "it always had to go through a last check with Mom"—and whose authority was demonstrated by making these decisions.[57]

The *prayer closet* in early modern Europe became a space in which individuals could truly seek the sacred in seclusion; and yet, these places were also subject to local authority and custom. Samuel Richardson's Clarissa, for example, withdrew to a closeted space that she could lock from the inside, as was the custom among seventeenth-century women, to read, write, and reflect, but such practice was widely considered an "absurd affectation" unless it included prayer, which enjoyed the blessing of the clergy. Closeted prayer and reflection occurred in dedicated space that was used for no other purpose. And as bourgeois homes increased in size, it became typical both in Europe and in the American colonies for them to include prayer closets.

Amanda Vickery's rich account of household life in late-seventeenth-century England shows that without prayer closets, daily religious practice typically enjoyed only a modicum of separation from ordinary routines. Devout Protestants nevertheless took the King James Version of Matthew 6.6 literally: "When thou prayest, enter into thy closet, and when thou hast shut thy door, pray to thy Father which is in secret, and thy Father which seeth in secret shall reward thee openly." Oxfordshire gentlewoman Anne Dormer, for example, wrote in her diary and letters that she retreated daily to the safety of her closet to pray. The closet was an escape from the clutter and disturbances elsewhere in the house. Vickery's story of Anne Dormer is also a reminder that the situations in which religious practices occur are never fully set apart from daily life. The reason Dormer considered her prayer closet a "safe shelter" was that her husband was abusive. He patrolled the house "like a gaoler," sometimes kicking in doors looking for her. The household clutter from which she hid was his. The prayer closet was her only place to indulge her feelings unobserved.[58]

Prayer closets may have offered seclusion, but they illustrate how the meanings of sacred space reflect the social practices through which they were

---

56. Mary Douglas, "The Idea of a Home: A Kind of Space," *Social Research* 58, 1 (1991), 287–307; quotes on pages 289 and 303.

57. Pech, "I Would Pay Homage," 229.

58. Amanda Vickery, *Behind Closed Doors: At Home in Gregorian England* (New Haven, CT: Yale University Press, 2009), 196.

constituted. Closets used for other purposes were special places in which valuables could be protected. Their presence marked both the status of the homeowner and the homeowner's capacity to control a significant space. They connoted "room for improvement" in the case of closets used for solitary intellectual work, "intimacy" when used for assignations, and "privacy" when sought as a retreat from public responsibilities. When Protestants heeded admonitions to enter their *closet* (not simply a room or chamber, as earlier Bible translations said), all these connotations inflected the practice. The prayer closet circumvented priestly intervention between the individual and God, empowered the individual to enjoy an intimate relationship with God, and ultimately played a role in devotion becoming a private matter of the heart.[59]

Besides illustrating how power is present, these examples also show that space does not become sacred by being set apart in the manner that Durkheim suggested. Space is not enduringly set apart as sacred by being sharply divided from the profane through purification rituals. It is sacred because people act upon the space and the objects within it in ways that they have already decided are religious or of potential spiritual significance, whether as a place legally designated for worship or a room in which to pray.[60] There is of course an order of expectations about what is appropriate in the space, but it is more akin to Mary Douglas's understanding of purity than to Durkheim's. Her well-known assertion that "dirt is matter out of place" is meant to emphasize these culturally specific expectations. A "dirty" spoon is not dirty in all contexts but in specific situations in which the participants define it as such. Similarly, a child's toy on a home altar may be "matter out of place" in one context and have a quite

---

59. Informative surveys of the extensive historical literature on closets and closeted prayer are included in Danielle Bobker, "The Literature and Culture of the Closet in the Eighteenth Century," *Digital Defoe* 6, 1 (2014), 1948–1802; Danielle Bobker, "Coming Out: Closet Rhetoric and Media Publics," *History of the Present* 5, 1 (2015), 31–64; Lena Cowen Orlin, *Locating Privacy in Tudor London* (New York: Oxford University Press, 2007); Susan Comilang, "Through the Closet: Private Devotion and the Shaping of Female Subjectivity in the Religious Recess," *Renaissance and Reformation* 27, 3 (2003), 79–96; and Charles E. Hambrick-Stowe, *The Practice of Piety: Puritan Devotional Disciplines in Seventeenth-Century New England* (Chapel Hill: University of North Carolina Press, 1982).

60. Although reports of sacred experience in everyday life frequently emphasize that the experience was "spontaneous," interview studies also suggest that people anticipate these events by demarcating a physical space; see, for example, Will Adams, "Discovering the Sacred in Everyday Life: An Empirical Phenomenological Study," *Humanistic Psychologist* 24, 1 (1996), 28–54.

different meaning in another.⁶¹ Moreover, the boundaries that set apart even such familiar spaces as homes are provisional and processual, rendering them subject to varying interpretations, as Bridget Purcell discovered in studying Muslim women in Turkey who drew and redrew the boundaries of their homes depending on shifting family relations and domestic activities.⁶²

The fluidity of everyday life that practice theory seeks to emphasize suggests a further reason to embrace Douglas's interpretation: the fact that spaces are frequently designated for multiple purposes rather than only one. A soup kitchen may double as a space to fix meals and discuss theological understandings of suffering and death. A church basement is likely to house a nursery school during the week and perhaps a yoga class on Friday evening. A cathedral may be a work of art as much as a place for worship. Thomas Bremer's ethnographic study of the San Antonio Missions National Historical Park, for example, shows how "touristic practices" in which sightseeing, picture taking, and souvenir shopping developed and had to be negotiated with the historic definitions of sacred space that current worshippers at the mission churches wanted to preserve.⁶³

Power to control the uses of sacred space must be part of the negotiations when space is shared in these ways. In the missions case, the Catholic Church gave up its exclusive authority and joined with the National Park Service and the state of Texas to attain sufficient funds to preserve the historic San Antonio missions. Although the practices of worshippers and tourists differed significantly, preserving the missions' historic architecture was in the interest of both. In other cases, the architecture itself defines the space in a way that empowers some of the practices that happen in the space more than others. Frederick Borsch's account of multi-faith worship services being held in Princeton

---

61. Mary Douglas, *Purity and Danger: An Analysis of the Concepts of Pollution and Taboo* (London: Routledge, 1966), 48; Robbie Duschinsky, "Recognizing Secular Defilement: Douglas, Durkheim and Housework," *History and Anthropology* 25, 5 (2014), 553–70.

62. Bridget Purcell, "The House Unbound: Refiguring Gender and Domestic Boundaries in Urbanizing Southeast Turkey," *City and Society* 29, 1 (2017), 14–34.

63. Thomas Bremer, *Blessed with Tourists: The Borderlands of Religion and Tourism in San Antonio* (Chapel Hill: University of North Carolina Press, 2004), 27; other examples of mixed-use spaces are discussed in Courtney Bender, *Heaven's Kitchen: Living Religion at God's Love We Deliver* (Chicago: University of Chicago Press, 2003); Courtney Bender, *The New Metaphysicals: Spirituality and the American Religious Imagination* (Chicago: University of Chicago Press, 2010); and Wendy Cadge, *Heartwood: The First Generation of Theravada Buddhism in America* (Chicago: University of Chicago Press, 2005).

University's cruciform Gothic-style chapel building, for example, demonstrates the constraints arising from well-established physical cues.[64] At the same time, architectural constraints themselves may be fungible to the point of being managed for effect, as, for instance, in the redesign of ancient shrines to have greater symbolic meaning for present-day pilgrims.[65]

Affordances

The concept of affordances complements the study of situational cues and space. Affordances are the relationships of people and "things" that facilitate practices, where facilitation may occur directly by putting them to use or indirectly by supplying information about what is or is not feasible. James Gibson, whose work in ecological psychology originated the concept, insisted that affordances cut across the dichotomy of subjective and objective, reframing the latter toward perceptions of what they offered or furnished, for good or ill. Cognitive scientist David Kirsch defines an affordance as "a dispositional property of a situation defined by a set of objects organized in a set arrangement, relativized to the action repertoire of a given agent."[66] A mailbox, for example, is an affordance the purpose of which is generally understood based on its cultural meanings and the specific relevance of which is determined by the person's desire to mail a letter. The ordering and arrangement of affordances refers to their temporal and spatial relevance, as in the case of various kitchen utensils used at different times and places in preparing a meal. An affordance's elasticity refers to the range of purposes to which it can be put; e.g., water's elasticity is greater than a mailbox's. Affordances also vary in terms of how reliable the relationship between object and perception is; e.g., a chair's affordance for sitting is highly

---

64. Frederick Borsch, *Keeping Faith at Princeton: A Brief History of Religious Pluralism at Princeton and Other Universities* (Princeton, NJ: Princeton University Press, 2012).

65. Judit Kis-Halas, "Pilgrims on the Rosary Route," *Material Religion* 14, 1 (March 2018), 148–52.

66. David Kirsh, "The Intelligent Use of Space," *Artificial Intelligence* 73 (1995), 31–68; see also Carl Knappett, *Thinking Through Material Culture: An Interdisciplinary Perspective* (Philadelphia: University of Pennsylvania Press, 2005), 35–63; James J. Gibson, *The Senses Considered as Perceptual Systems* (New York: Houghton Mifflin, 1966); James J. Gibson, *The Ecological Approach to Visual Perception* (New York: Taylor and Francis, 1986); and James J. Gibson, "The Theory of Affordances," in *Perceiving, Acting, and Knowing: Toward an Ecological Psychology*, edited by Robert Shaw and John Bransford (Hillsdale, NJ: Lawrence Erlbaum, 1977), 67–82.

probable, whereas a rock's affordance for sitting is not.[67] When affordances function reliably and as expected, they rarely require conscious attention even though they constitute the "things" of the immediate situation. "We begin to confront the thingness of objects," Bill Brown writes, "when they stop working for us: when the drill breaks, when the car stalls, when the windows get filthy."[68]

While affordances such as kitchen utensils, hammers, and chairs are utilitarian in the sense of assisting us in getting things done, our interaction with material objects is also constraining, just as our relationships with people are. Bruno Latour, whose "actor network theory," as he calls it, includes such relationships with things, observes that the usefulness of these relationships is often present in how they *limit* what we do: fences that keep us from trespassing, road signs that remind us of speed limits, classroom walls that discourage our minds from wandering. In these respects, they exercise power in our lives.[69]

Affordances are not to be associated only with utilitarian purposes. Sociologist Tia DeNora emphasizes the role of affordances in aesthetic practices. A song, painting, or dramatic performance is a resource—an affordance—for an experience, idea, or creative endeavor. An affordance, she suggests, is an event-situated object around which action can be organized that in turn assists the participants in constructing an interpretation of it and themselves, thereby enhancing clarity about who they are.[70] Similarly, psychologist Marketta Kyttä, suggests that affordances for experiences of sociality, such as playgrounds for children, can usefully be conceptualized and compared.[71]

If homes are "space under control," as Mary Douglas suggests, affordances are how that control is accomplished. The home's roof, walls, floor, and furnishings are the minimum affordances of everyday life. Things of this nature manage our relationship with the physical world. Additional affordances assist in relating with people (phones, coffee shops) and define us in terms of taste and

---

67. This and further distinctions are discussed in Andrea Scarantino, "Affordances Explained," *Philosophy of Science* 70, 5 (2003), 949–61.

68. Bill Brown, "Thing Theory," *Critical Inquiry* 28, 1 (2001), 4.

69. Bruno Latour, "Where Are the Missing Masses? The Sociology of a Few Mundane Artifacts," in *Shaping Technology/Building Society: Studies in Sociotechnical Change*, ed. Wiebe E. Bijker and John Law (Cambridge, MA: MIT Press, 1992), 151–80; Bruno Latour, *Reassembling the Social: An Introduction to Actor-Network Theory* (New York: Oxford University Press, 2005).

70. Tia DeNora, *Music in Everyday Life* (Cambridge: Cambridge University Press, 2000).

71. Marketta Kyttä, "Affordances of Children's Environments in the Context of Cities, Small Towns, Suburbs and Rural Villages in Finland and Belarus," *Journal of Environmental Psychology* 22 (2002), 109–23.

status (arts, sports equipment). Their meaning, as Arjun Appadurai suggests, is inscribed in their use and is conditioned by the spaces in which they are located and the practices that occur in these spaces. The affordances that appear and reappear as objects in familiar spaces develop a biography that connects with the person's past and projected future. Accordingly, they convey an implicit feeling tone that seems right, as the grip of a familiar hammer does. But affordances also constrain. A slaughterhouse conveyor belt dictates the pace of work, a book is read from front to back, and web surfing provides opportunities for scattered viewing and yet constrains the positioning of hands and eyes. Moreover, the biographies of affordances reveal expenditures of time and energy devoted to their care, maintenance, and preservation.[72]

DeNora's example of Lucy who listens to Schubert's *Impromptu* in G flat major and finds herself soothed by the music illustrates the active relational aspect of affordances that distinguishes them from material artifacts. The music soothes Lucy as she retreats from the rest of the world that she can no longer bear. The music is an affordance because Lucy situates herself in a quiet room at home in a comfortable chair and recalls how she was soothed to sleep as a child by her father playing the piano. She actively pulls together "a range of things (furniture, speakers, memories, current emotional state, musical recordings, a temporal interval)." In these respects, Lucy is truly an accomplice in the music's work as an affordance. Her relationship to the music and the music's relationship to her constitute an event, DeNora says, that carries a sense of power and communicates a special message or mood within the circumstances of its use.[73]

Affordances for religious practices vary along a continuum of facilitation and constraint, typically with elements of both. Their facilitating and constraining power arises from the situation in which they occur—a cross in a Christian

---

72. Arjun Appadurai, "Introduction: Commodities and the Politics of Value," in *The Social Life of Things: Commodities in Cultural Perspective*, edited by Arjun Appadurai (New York: Cambridge University Press, 1986), 3–63; Charles Spinosa, "Derridian Dispersion and Heideggerian Articulation: General Tendencies in the Practices that Govern Intelligibility," in *The Practice Turn in Contemporary Theory*, edited by Theodore R. Schatzki, Karin Knorr Cetina, and Eike von Savigny (New York: Routledge, 2001), 209–22, emphasizes the subjective mood or sense of purpose that makes one "feel at home in dealing with the thing" (p. 217); preservation is discussed in Julka Almquist and Julia Lupton, "Affording Meaning: Design-Oriented Research from the Humanities and Social Sciences," *Design Issues* 26, 1 (2010), 3–14.

73. Tia DeNora, *Music in Everyday Life* (New York: Cambridge University Press, 2000), 41–43.

home or a mezuzah on the doorpost of a Jewish home—and the extent to which they have been consecrated. Consecration depends on prior acts performed by authorities, such as priests or shamans. In a culture of mass consumption, consecration of sorts occurs indirectly through the way artifacts are marketed; for example, as being branded by a religious community, having been blessed, originating from a holy place, or having bestowed special powers on previous purchasers. If the mere fact of marketing is deemed an act of profanation, as some argue, then practices of segmentation may be sufficient as means of quasi-consecration: purchasing an artifact at a holy site or while on a pilgrimage, making a home-stitched wall hanging, passing along a family Bible as a gift, or ordering an item through a religious organization. In *Set in Stone: America's Embrace of the Ten Commandments*, for example, Jenna Weissman Joselit describes how Christian and Jewish organizations marketed "power-ranger" action figures of Moses to families, apparently believing that children's spiritual lives would be enriched.[74]

Affordances are a way of thinking about the role of material culture in religious practice that avoids suggesting that material culture determines human action, on the one hand, or is merely the result of human action, on the other hand. The prevalence of material culture in religious practice is well established. In a nationally representative survey of US adults, 56 percent of those who prayed at least several times a year included sacred objects, such as a cross or painting, candles, music, or poetry. Those who included them, moreover, were more likely than those who did not to say they felt close to God.[75]

Research by historians Sally M. Promey and David Morgan illustrates the role of material culture as affordances in religion. Hard benches and straight-backed pews in colonial American churches facilitated austerity and respect among the faithful. Warner Sallman's widely distributed 1946 "Christ at the Door" painting beckoned believers to invite a friendly white Jesus into their hearts. Carvings, wall hangings, and illustrated children's books assisted

---

74. Jenna Weissman Joselit, *Set in Stone: America's Embrace of the Ten Commandments* (New York: Oxford University Press, 2017); Mormon action figures are described in Jana K. Riess, "Stripling Warriors Choose the Right: The Cultural Engagements of Contemporary Mormon Kitsch," *Sunstone* (June 1999), 36–47; family Bibles, Catholic kitsch, and other objects of veneration are discussed in Colleen McDannell, *Material Christianity* (New Haven, CT: Yale University Press, 1995).

75. Robert Wuthnow, *All in Sync: How Music and Art Are Revitalizing American Religion* (Berkeley and Los Angeles: University of California Press, 2003), 88–92; no causality is implied, given the cross-sectional nature of the survey.

worshippers' interaction with saints and angels. Yiddish New Year's postcards reinforced shared identity among Jewish American immigrants. In each instance, the material content of the object interacted with a person's intentions as a vehicle for the furtherance of those intentions—furtherance as *possibility* for the concretization and communication of conviction in practice.[76] In recent work, Morgan also suggests that affordances frequently become anthropomorphized and function as a source of enchantment even though they may not be associated with religion. When we name our automobiles and yell at our computers, they become objects of worship and derision.[77]

Technology is perhaps the source of greatest interest in affordances, posing questions for religious practice (as in other areas) about the influences of television, computers, the Internet, mobile phones, and other devices. Technological affordances that render distant communication possible reduce the need for in-person gatherings, on the one hand, and, on the other hand, enable such gatherings through efficient means of communication, forming "synthetic situations" in which people who are not physically co-present nevertheless coordinate their activities and feel connected.[78] While virtual communication may undermine the location of religious practices in physical places, virtual activities nevertheless occur in physical places and thus are more likely to alter practices in these places than replace them. A study of an online forum for young Hindu American women provides a suggestive example. The women typically participated in the forum from a specific place in their home that acquired meaning almost as a home altar in the extent to which it reinforced Hindu identity, provided information about Hindu websites and area temples, and included references to sacred texts, while also giving the women freedom to interpret Hindu practices in novel ways.[79]

---

76. David Morgan, "Imaging Protestant Piety: The Icons of Warner Sallman," *Religion and Culture* 3, 1 (1993), 29–47; David Morgan and Sally M. Promey, eds., *The Visual Culture of American Religions* (Berkeley and Los Angeles: University of California Press, 2001); David Morgan, ed., *Religion and Material Culture: The Matter of Belief* (New York: Routledge, 2009); David Morgan, *Sacred Gaze: Religious Visual Culture in Theory and Practice* (Berkeley and Los Angeles: University of California Press, 2005).

77. David Morgan, *Images at Work: The Material Culture of Enchantment* (New York: Oxford University Press, 2018).

78. Karin Knorr Cetina, "The Synthetic Situation: Interactionism for a Global World," *Symbolic Interaction* 32, 1 (2009), 61–87.

79. Madhavi Mallapragada, *Virtual Homelands: Indian Immigrants and Online Cultures in the United States* (Champaign: University of Illinois Press, 2014).

The delicacy with which religious affordances function in relation to local practices is evident in Birgit Meyer's discussion of Jesus pictures among Pentecostals in southern Ghana. As material objects, Jesus pictures can be understood as the result of mass production and distribution in international markets. As affordances, however, they are both powerful and dangerous—powerful because of how they are looked upon as a resource for the strengthening of visual piety; dangerous because of being fetishized in the way of animistic religion. For Ghanaian Pentecostals, Meyer asserts, Jesus pictures are an instance of material religion, but require that "material" be understood in interaction with the local practice in which it is interpreted.[80]

Meyer's example suggests that religious affordances can be *spiritual* as well as material. Saints, angels, and other spiritual beings, Robert Orsi argues, should be included among the interlocutors with which religious practitioners interact.[81] These interlocutors function as affordances: imbued, as sociologist Timothy Nelson writes, with a "capacity and the inclination to intervene in the on-going affairs of the social and physical world."[82] They assist people in securing good fortune and avoiding temptation. They also forge a bond among believers who benefit from similar affordances and, as among Ghanaian Pentecostals, understand the powers and dangers involved. Historian Leigh Schmidt's study of eighteenth-century American examples of people hearing divine voices demonstrates further how situational cultures affected the interpretations of these experiences. Believers sought and welcomed them as sources of blessing, comfort, and guidance. Skeptics schooled in Enlightenment philosophy interpreted them as superstition or, in some instances, suggested novel scientific explanations.[83]

---

80. Birgit Meyer, "'There Is a Spirit in That Image': Mass-Produced Jesus Pictures and Protestant-Pentecostal Animation in Ghana," in *Things: Religion and the Question of Materiality*, edited by Dick Houtman and Birgit Meyer (New York: Fordham University Press, 2012), 296–320.

81. Robert A. Orsi, *Between Heaven and Earth: The Religious Worlds People Make and the Scholars Who Study Them* (Princeton, NJ: Princeton University Press, 2005).

82. Timothy J. Nelson, *Every Time I Feel the Spirit: Religious Experience and Ritual in an African American Church* (New York: NYU Press, 2005), 50.

83. Leigh Eric Schmidt, *Hearing Things: Religion, Illusion, and the American Enlightenment* (Cambridge, MA: Harvard University Press, 2000); see also Jeffrey C. Alexander, "Iconic Experience in Art and Life: Surface/Depth Beginning with Giacometti's Standing Woman," *Theory, Culture, and Society* 25, 5 (2008), 1–19, and Jeffrey C. Alexander, "Iconic Consciousness: The Material Feeling of Meaning," *Theory, Culture, and Society* 103, 1 (2010), 10–15, who notes

A hammer that feels right or an encounter with a spirit that seems comforting suggests a further aspect of affordances: persons who feel right about the hammer are also likely to feel right about *themselves* using the hammer. Feeling right about themselves means doing the right thing; it implies confidence in one's judgment, skill, and experience. Webb Keane calls this evaluative stance an *ethical affordance*. An ethical affordance is an interaction between an individual and a material object or spiritual force that bears on the person's sense of being good or bad, where the criteria for good or bad are traits such as fair and honest or relative positions such as privileged and worthy.[84] While many affordances (such as skill at using a hammer) communicate values implicitly and reflexively, affordances may also convey ethical messages directly. David Morgan, for example, argues that images in nineteenth-century Protestant American children's literature communicated that literacy was not only a practical skill but also a moral virtue by associating it with Christian benevolence.[85]

Affordances for practicing religion nearly always bear ethical as well as practical implications. A person who understands and makes use of a religious affordance knows—and perhaps discloses to significant others—that she is a believer who takes her faith seriously. She feels that she is doing the right thing in inserting the affordance into her interaction. Frank Schaeffer's story of the "gospel walnut," which he recounts as an amusing anecdote from his childhood, is a striking example. Schaeffer was the son of Edith and Francis Schaeffer, the internationally known evangelical Protestant writers and founders of the L'Abri Christian training center in Switzerland. The gospel walnut was a hollowed walnut shell from which a ribbon printed with a Bible verse could be unwound. As a child traveling by train with his mother, Schaeffer's task was to deploy the gospel walnut as a tool in witnessing to strangers, often with a make-do affect impossible to sustain without a bit of playfulness.[86] As a more serious example, Sally K. Gallagher argues in *Getting to Church: Narratives of Gender and Joining*

---

the iconic blending of the material and spiritual, writing "we must try to understand how meaning, soul, and spirit manifest themselves through materiality" (p. 12).

84. Webb Keane, *Ethical Life: Its Natural and Social Histories* (Princeton, NJ: Princeton University Press, 2016), 27–32.

85. David Morgan, "For Christ and the Republic: Protestant Illustration and the History of Literacy in Nineteenth-Century America," in *The Visual Culture of American Religions*, edited by David Morgan and Sally M. Promey (Berkeley and Los Angeles: University of California Press, 2001), 49–67.

86. Frank Schaeffer, *Portofino: A Novel* (New York: Carroll & Graf, 1992).

that the affordances of materiality—architecture, size and layout of the building, its location, seating arrangements and style, bulletins and newsletters, and what appears on its website—is the stuff of congregational culture that encourages people to come in the first place, to return, to feel at home, and to worship.[87]

The skill in utilizing ethically charged affordances adds an interesting perspective on the much-discussed topic of religious belief. Belief is traditionally regarded as a set of ideas or convictions, often expressed in propositional form, that believers hold to be true (for instance, that Jesus died, was buried, and rose on the third day). And in survey research assessing religious commitment, questions asking for assent to such doctrinal beliefs are a standard means of determining whether commitment is holding steady or declining. But when, as is often the case, decline is identified, the response from religious leaders sometimes focuses revealingly more on restoring lost skills than on shoring up faltering convictions. For instance, an essay responding to one of the many recent polls about rising levels of non-religiosity among American young people suggests not that firmer theological grounding is needed but that Christians should do a better job at communicating their faith, especially in answering questions that the unchurched apparently are asking. In short, *skill* in talking about beliefs is key.[88]

Skill as the situational capacity to deploy affordances is thus a learned and adapted practice that combines action and the practical cognitive knowledge required to enact belief. "In practice theory," Omar Lizardo and Michael Strand write, "the main sort of socialization 'content' that is transmitted to persons as a result of being exposed to and encompassed by a given social environment does not consist of consciously held, propositionally stated 'beliefs.' . . . Instead socialization implies the acquisition of irreducibly embodied schemes of action, stored in procedural memory and manifested as a form of 'skill.'"[89] Jeanne Kormina and Sonja Luehrmann in their study of contemporary Russian

---

87. Sally K. Gallagher, *Getting to Church: Narratives of Gender and Joining* (New York: Oxford University Press, 2017), especially chapter 2.

88. J. Warner Wallace, "Young Christians Are Leaving the Church—Here's Why," *Fox News*, September 9, 2018.

89. Omar Lizardo and Michael Strand, "Skills, Toolkits, Contexts and Institutions: Clarifying the Relationship between Different Approaches to Cognition in Cultural Sociology," *Poetics* 38 (2010), 204–27; quote on pages 211–12.

Orthodox prayer call this kind of skill "practical competence." It is demonstrated, they suggest, in how competently people pray (or testify or witness) both in terms of the sincerity of belief expressed and the cultivation of social relationships.[90]

Ethical affordances typically reveal and sharpen status differences among those who make use of them. Ghanaian Pentecostals who understood the proper meaning of Jesus pictures considered themselves to be of higher status than persons who interpreted the pictures differently. The high status of early-eighteenth-century Americans who heard divine voices diminished as Enlightenment worldviews gained popularity. Status differences within a single situation also affect and reinforce how affordances are interpreted. For example, nineteenth-century Russian commissars interpreted popular practices surrounding relics and icons as irrational vestiges of folk culture and Orthodox priests said they were symbolic prototypes, while peasants considered them to have divine power that could "crop up anywhere" and bestow special power on believers. In short, the same tradition in the same villages was understood differently and in ways that corresponded with the status of its different populations.[91]

As this example suggests, affordances symbolize status differences not only in such expected ways as high-status people displaying more expensive accoutrements (e.g., fancier clothing or membership at high-priced spiritual retreat centers) but also in less expected ways such as interpreting the meaning of religious symbols differently. A study of Hindu women's adornments in Nepal identified an interesting difference between younger, better educated women in the city and their less educated mothers in rural areas. The rural women wore *pote*—a thick, long multi-strand of small green, red, and yellow glass beads with a large gold ornament strung in the middle—from the day they received it from the groom at their wedding until they died without ever removing it from their neck. Wearing the *pote* was deeply symbolic of their beliefs as Hindu women regarding their domestic and spiritual responsibilities. Its power as an affordance lay in the fact that its meaning was communicated from mother to daughter.

---

90. Jeanne Kormina and Sonja Luehrmann, "The Social Nature of Prayer in a Church of the Unchurched: Russian Orthodox Christianity from Its Edges," *Journal of the American Academy of Religion* 86, 2 (June 2018), 394–424.

91. Webb Keane, "Rotting Bodies: The Clash of Stances toward Materiality and Its Ethical Affordances," *Current Anthropology* 55, S10 (2014), S312–21; quote on page S319.

Moreover, it went with the women from room to room and from home to market, rather than being worn only on special ritual occasions. The younger urban women, in contrast, improvised because the traditional *pote* was heavy and sometimes cumbersome. They wore lighter beads, substituted safety pins with a few of the traditional beads for the multi-strand ornaments, adapted colors to match their clothing, and took off the *pote* when showering, exercising, or sleeping. In short, they displayed their urban status by exhibiting greater individual variation in how they wore *pote*.[92]

The *pote* example illustrates one of the important ways in which practice theory's focus on situations differs from earlier approaches. The difference between rural and urban women's practice would likely have been viewed in earlier approaches as an instance of secularization; specifically, as a gradual abandonment of tradition and an increase in individualistic adaptations that would gradually lead to *pote* itself being a relic of the past. The study's authors, though, suggest a different interpretation. They claim that the urban women they interviewed still associated *pote* with its traditional meanings. Indeed, the deliberations in which they engaged by finding ways to improvise gave the practice additional meaning. *Pote* was an affordance they could carry with them, even in new work and family settings, and was a material way in which to connect their identities as Hindus and modern women.[93]

Power Dynamics

Power is a ubiquitous feature of situations, and the situations in which religion is practiced are no exception. The reason some situational cues are more salient than others is typically the result of real and implied power dynamics: the Vietnamese American mother who arranges the home altar and sets the rules for its use or the pastor of a storefront church who selects music that makes its congregants feel at home. The space for practicing religion is usually controlled by someone: the park commission that makes space available for Mexican

---

92. Megan Adamson Sijapati and Tina Harris, "From Heavy Beads to Safety Pins: Adornment and Religiosity in Hindu Women's Pote Practices," *Material Religion* 12, 1 (2016), 1–25.

93. Hillary Kaell, "Seeing the Invisible: Ambient Catholicism on the Side of the Road," *Journal of the American Academy of Religion* 85, 1 (2017), 136–67, offers a similarly suggestive way of thinking about affordances (wayside crosses) as objects that engage with secularism rather than serving merely as instances of secularization.

American immigrants or the bourgeois householder who escapes to her prayer closet and locks the door from the inside. Similarly, the possibilities affordances offer depend on who can use them: the family background that trains a person to appreciate Schubert or that gives a nineteenth-century child the opportunity to read books.

I emphasize power because contemporary religious practice is mostly regarded as *voluntaristic*, and rightly so, in that individuals *choose* which religion to practice or to practice no religion. The lesson social science teaches, though, is that choices are never entirely free—not in the marketplace and not in religion. Choices are structured; not determined, but constrained. Practice theory emphasizes the processes through which choices are constrained *and* how the decisions people make alter those constraints and produce new ones. Cues, spaces, and affordances are among the specific aspects of situations that shape and are shaped by the practices that occur within them.

For religion to be as voluntaristic as it is, the power to control the situations in which it is practiced is a fundamental requirement. A person who chooses to drive to a place of worship twenty miles away instead of attending the one down the block has the means to make the commute. A person who dislikes organized religion and instead pays a hefty price to visit an ashram in India has the capacity to consider the trip a spiritual affordance as does (less expensively) the person who takes an afternoon from work for spiritual renewal at the park that the community has provided. An hourly wage worker on the cutting line at the slaughterhouse does not have that freedom.

In these examples, power is exogenous to the immediate situation. Power, in the sense of being enacted in the situation, is endogenous as well. The Russian peasant who claims to be in intimate audible communication with God is empowered in a way that her neighbor to whom God has not spoken isn't. The same is true of an adept compared to a novice in a yoga class. In these comparisons, power inheres in the fact that immediate temporally bound situations are rarely free of the experiences and dispositions practitioners import from previous situations. The adept is not only more skilled but also is better acquainted with the available affordances and can speak knowledgeably about them.

Although power accrues from practice in similar situations, it is often transferrable to dissimilar situations. Mary Pattillo-McCoy's study of African American churches in Chicago demonstrates how the style of speaking and interacting at church transferred to other situations in the community. The church "styles," she says, are useful [i.e., are affordances] in providing the "hows" of social action, specifically in the way meetings are convened, testimonies are given, and handshakes are performed.[94]

An opposing observation is that religious practices can be appropriated for use by external wielders of power. Liston Pope's 1942 *Millhands and Preachers*, conducted in Gastonia, North Carolina, is a classic investigation of powerful corporate owners using preachers to deter union organizing.[95] Similarly, among wage workers at twenty-first-century slaughterhouses, the company-paid chaplain may be an affordance for counseling but may also be a lackey that management employs to get around labor disputes and accusations of human rights violations.[96]

Religion in the service of dominant power structures, finally, is the reason studies of religion also emphasize situations in which its practice provides a mode of resistance. An interesting example occurred at the cave of La Sainte-Baume in southern France in the closing years of the twentieth century. By tradition the cave was the place where Mary Magdalene spent the latter part of her life. It became a destination for pilgrimages in the Middle Ages, and eventually a church and a Dominican convent were constructed at the site. By the end of the twentieth century, alternatives accompanied these traditional practices. Inspired by New Age and Neopagan ideas, these alternatives consisted of pilgrimages that venerated the site as a tribute to Mary as the female equivalent of Jesus and to Mother Earth. Pilgrims came in search of healing from gender discrimination and sexual abuse. They abhorred the patriarchal symbolism of the Catholic images and felt violated by their presence. The Catholic images nevertheless provided a focus with which to deconstruct their traditional meanings. An ethnographer described how women sat on the ground feeling the energy of Mother Earth as they prayed. They reimagined Mary as a wounded healer instead of a fallen woman. The cave became a symbol of the womb and of birth. Some left menstrual blood near the altar. Some went away feeling renewed; others felt conflicted, unsure of how they felt about what they had

---

94. Mary Pattillo-McCoy, "Church Culture as a Strategy of Action in the Black Community," *American Sociological Review* 63, 6 (1998), 767–84.

95. Liston Pope, *Millhands and Preachers: A Study of Gastonia* (New Haven, CT: Yale University Press, 1942).

96. Robert Wuthnow, *Small-Town America: Finding Community, Shaping the Future* (Princeton, NJ: Princeton University Press, 2013), 248–49.

experienced. Had it been right? Was it empowering? Those were the questions.[97]

Situations then are rich with implications worthy of further exploration in the study of religious practice and, indeed, the study of other practices as varied as consumption, participation in the arts, and the use of electronic devices that connect persons meaningfully with material affordances and the spaces in which they are used. A focus on situations contrasts epistemologically with decontextualized approaches that seek to establish theoretical generalizations by identifying a single explanatory factor that may give only small purchase on what happens in real life. The focus is rather on the multiple interactions that occur between individuals and other individuals and with the cues and affordances that facilitate and constrain these interactions. Situations have histories that guide the unfolding interactions that take place within them. And situations are the places in which the control of space and the availability of relevant affordances become important aspects of the power dynamics and possibilities for resistance that shape practices.

A focus on situations contributes to better understanding the ethical implications posed in studies of habit and improvisation. Habits that guide behavior in desirable directions, such as toward generosity and compassion, are learned in stable situations that provide reinforcing cues and yet also become dispositions that transcend situations. An altruistic person, for instance, should behave generously despite changing circumstances. Research is needed, though, to determine if that is indeed the case or if, as other arguments suggest, people respond strategically to whatever the situation demands. One scenario implies ethical training that instills enduring dispositions; the other points more toward shaping situations and people's choices of situations.[98]

---

97. Anna Fedele, "Gender, Sexuality and Religious Critique among Mary Magdalene Pilgrims in Southern France," in *Gender, Nation and Religion in European Pilgrimage*, edited by Catrien Notermans and Willy Jansen (New York: Routledge, 2012), 55–70.

98. Gilbert Harman, "Skepticism about Character Traits," *Journal of Ethics* 13, 2/3 (2009), 235–42, draws on Sartre and Goffman to suggest a recasting of virtue ethics that takes greater account of situations. Empirical studies suggesting that altruistic dispositions are relatively strong in predicting charitable behavior across diverse situations include Tamas Bereczkei, Bela Birkas, and Zsuzsanna Kerekes, "The Presence of Others, Prosocial Traits, Machiavellianism: A Personality Situation Approach," *Social Psychology* 41, 4 (2010), 238–45; and Brent Simpson and Robb Willer, "Altruism and Indirect Reciprocity: The Interaction of Person and Situation in Prosocial Behavior," *Social Psychology Quarterly* 71, 1 (2008), 37–52. At-risk sexual behavior is shown to be relatively more affected by situational factors; see M. Lynne Cooper, "Toward a

The numerous examples in which studies of religious practice illuminate the role of situations demonstrate the necessity for further research of paying close attention to the fluidity and variability of religious practice in ordinary life. Prayers, veneration of saints, feeling close to God, and talking about one's beliefs and doubts, among other things, whether on a train, in a prison, at home, or in a cathedral, are practices that can be better understood by taking account of the habits that are cued by the situation, the disruptions that may necessitate improvisation, and whether the space is sufficiently private to be under personal control or public enough to have come under ecclesial or governmental control. As much as they may be shaped by material affordances, such as home altars and prayer rugs, situations are above all spaces in which social relationships are present or implied. Those relationships are clearly present when the practices are communal and they are implied when the solitary practices of individuals bear the imprint of power, opportunity, and control.

Person × Situation Model of Sexual Risk-Taking Behaviors: Illuminating the Conditional Effects of Traits Across Sexual Situations and Relationship Contexts," *Journal of Personality and Social Psychology* 98, 2 (2010), 319–41.

3

Intentions

INTENTIONS ARE A NOTABLE emphasis in the practices of most religious traditions. Muslim scholars argue that the Qur'an identifies intention (*niyya*) as the criterion by which the religious value of an act is to be judged. The *Bhagavad Gita* teaches that the intention of a charitable act is what produces its merit. In Vietnam, followers of the syncretic religion known as *Tam Giáo* call to spirits of the dead in rituals that explicitly enact the intentions of human and divine agents. Roman Catholics in many parts of the world recite the rosary for the benefit and intention of living and deceased family members. Evangelical church-growth consultants argue that congregations falter unless they are "intentional." Episcopalians express their intention to seek and serve Christ with the vow, "I will, with God's help." The "absolute intentionality" of Black Pentecostal preaching, Ashon Crawley observes, includes an intensity that provides "the accretional peaks and points of departure for spontaneous, improvisatory praise." To speak of religious practice necessarily is to speak of intentions. Christian Smith writes, "Religious practices are spiritually significant habits *intentionally* engaged in for the purpose of being shaped by them toward the good as known by a religious faith."[1]

---

1. Paul R. Powers, "Interiors, Intentions, and the 'Spirituality' of Islamic Ritual Practice," *Journal of the American Academy of Religion* 72, 2 (2004), 425–59; Torkel Brekke, "Contradiction and the Merit of Giving in Indian Religions," *Numen* 45, 3 (1998), 287–320; Kirsten W. Endres, "Engaging the Spirits of the Dead: Soul-Calling Rituals and the Performative Construction of Efficacy," *Journal of the Royal Anthropological Institute* 14, 4 (2008), 755–73; Nathan D. Mitchell, *The Mystery of the Rosary: Marian Devotion and the Reinvention of Catholicism* (New York: NYU Press, 2009); Diana Pasulka, "Purgatory in the Carolinas: Catholic Devotionalism in Nineteenth-Century South Carolina," in *Southern Crossroads: Perspectives on Religion and Culture*, edited by Walter H. Cosner Jr. and Rodger M. Payne (Nashville: University Press of Kentucky, 2008), 275–302; Randy Pope, *The Intentional Church: Moving from Church Success to*

While the nature and meaning of intention has been debated extensively in philosophy, relatively few studies of religious practice in ordinary life have examined it. Indeed, the emphasis in practice approaches on what people do and say instead of what they think and believe represents a significant bias toward neglecting intention and minimizing its importance. Yet to do so fails to address how action can be considered as problem-solving behavior without taking intention into account or how dispositions, as Bourdieu argues, can be considered. To set intention aside, moreover, is to ignore such important arguments about religion as Weber's suggestion that religion functions as a "switchman" in guiding ethical orientations and Geertz's inclusion of "long-lasting moods and motivations" among the definitional elements of religion.

Researchers who study religion with ethnographic methods and qualitative interviews frequently confront questions that would benefit from closer consideration of intentions. When a person describes a religious experience as having happened unexpectedly and another person discusses effort expended over an extended period to become more spiritual, for example, how are these accounts to be interpreted? What evidence is needed to assess their credibility? Should it matter that one person's experience seemed unintentional and the other's apparently was intentional? Or, when an author concludes that a congregation intentionally practiced segregation, how do we evaluate this claim? Questions like these come up in quantitative research as well. In studying the possible effects of religion on recovery from addiction, for example, how important might it be to know the strength of subjects' intentions to recover and whether it mattered that those intentions were verbalized publicly?

This chapter's argument develops in four parts. The first section discusses the treatment of intention in mainstream social theory and traces the reasons it has been sidelined. The second section introduces a distinction between prior intention and intention in action and discusses several emendations of this distinction in the philosophical literature. The third section argues that a clearer understanding of intention's relevance to religious practice can be attained by specifying the questions it poses as problems of sustaining, aligning, and assessing intention. The final section suggests how religion understood as

---

Community Transformation (Chicago: Moody, 2006); Episcopal Church, *The Book of Common Prayer* (New York: Church Hymnal Corporation, 1979), 305; Ashon T. Crawley, *Blackpentecostal Breath: The Aesthetics of Possibility* (New York: Fordham University Press, 2017), 84; Christian Smith, *Soul Searching: The Religious and Spiritual Lives of American Teenagers* (New York: Oxford University Press, 2005), 45, italics added.

practice addresses these problems through rewards, habits, social interaction, and rhetoric.

Intention in Social Theory

Discussions of intentions in social theory appear traditionally under the rubrics of motives and goals. Motives are the subjective states that propel actors toward certain lines of action and away from others. Goals are the desired end-states that guide actors to engage in certain actions and not others. Motives and goals are in these formulations nearly indistinguishable as mental influences on action in the case of individuals and as cultural constraints in the case of collectivities, both preceding actions taken and differing mainly insofar as motives prompt or initiate acting while goals are the teleological ends toward which it is directed. A murderer's motive, it might be said, is wanting money, while the murderer's goal is to obtain money, which in turn is driven by a culture in which wealth is a valued goal.[2] The concepts' meanings are even more closely associated in treatments suggesting that values "motivate" people to pursue "goals."[3] Motives and goals nevertheless receive differing emphases in different theoretical traditions and as such are the focus of differing objections.

Intentions as motives receive greatest attention in theoretical discussions grounded in phenomenology. Particularly in the lineage of Edmund Husserl, these discussions foreground the immersion of all consciousness in intentionality and emphasize that subjectivity influences action and can be distinguished but also inferred from observing action.[4] Alfred Schutz, for instance, conceptualizes intention as an act of will that envisions action and then differentiates action from movement based on its presence. Intention functions pragmatically in everyday life to distinguish among its spheres of relevance.[5]

---

2. This example is mentioned in Guillermina Jasso, "Principles of Theoretical Analysis," *Sociological Theory* 6, 1 (1988), 1–20; for a recent example of the motives-and-goals approach to religion, see Ann Taves, *Revelatory Events: Three Case Studies of the Emergence of New Spiritual Paths* (Princeton, NJ: Princeton University Press, 2016), especially chapter 12.

3. See, for example, essays in Michael Hechter, Lynn Nadel, and Richard E. Michod, *The Origin of Values* (New York: Aldine de Gruyter, 1993).

4. Edmund Husserl, *Ideas Pertaining to a Pure Phenomenology and to a Phenomenological Philosophy, First Book* (The Hague: Matinus Nijhoff, 1982).

5. Alfred Schutz, *Collected Papers VI. Literary Reality and Relationships*, edited by Michael Barber (New York: Springer, 2013), 93–100; Alfred Schutz, *Life Forms and Meaning Structure* (London: Routledge, 1982), 34.

Berger and Luckmann argue that a person waking up at night following an altercation and seeing a knife embedded in the wall can reasonably infer that the knife "expresses a subjective intention of violence, whether motivated by anger or by utilitarian considerations, such as killing for food." Subjective intentions, they suggest, become objectified in like manner, as actions and objects "proclaim" the actor's motives, although they qualify the argument by conceding that specific motives may be knowable only with additional information about the situation (an important concession, as I discuss later). Motives nevertheless tend to be "internalized in primary socialization," which Berger and Luckmann argue is the basis for considering intentions to be stable and enduring as well as identifiably different from one society, social class, religion, or subculture to the next. The behavior of a person raised in a devout religious family, therefore, should be expected to be guided by religious motives, whereas utilitarian motives might dominate the behavior of a person socialized in a different context.[6]

Intentions as goals are the focus of Talcott Parsons's formulation of action theory. Parsons calls "a future state of the actor-situation system . . . which [the actor] attempts actively to bring about (including the prevention of events he does not want to happen)" a "goal." Goals are intentional, unlike responses to stimuli, in that they involve the actor taking meaningful action with the aim of influencing events per the actor's wishes or interests. Wishes or interests, in turn, occur as motivations, which are organized within an actor's personality via the socialization process, and as goals must be symbolized as envisioned end-states. Moreover, while goals can be private and idiosyncratic, the goals individuals pursue tend to reflect larger cultural orientations. Parsons's essential claim is thus that human action can be understood as the individual and collective pursuit of anticipated future states of affairs, which when attained result in gratification.[7]

Insofar as action is goal-oriented, the line of inquiry this observation suggests is whether the actor's intentions (i.e., anticipated future states) are consistent with the action that ensues. Goal-oriented intentions are assumed to remain constant, guiding decisions about actions bent toward achieving those intentions in the most effective and efficient manner possible. How consistency is ascertained includes the actor's adaptation to the various physical,

---

6. Peter L. Berger and Thomas Luckmann, *The Social Construction of Reality: A Treatise in the Sociology of Knowledge* (New York: Penguin, 1966), 49–50, 155.

7. Talcott Parsons, *The Social System* (New York: Free Press, 1951), 4.

cultural, and social constraints and opportunities on which the successful pursuit of goals depends. One means of achieving such adaptation is through habit, as in pursuing career success by habitually showing up at work on time. Given changing circumstances, the more likely mode of adaptation is through conscious, reasoned deliberation. Planning of this sort differs from habit in the extent to which active thought is present and from "stream of consciousness" in the extent of coherence, logic, temporal orientation, and references to intentionality. The anticipated goal is thus manifestly in the foreground, pulling the actor forward and shaping which courses of action are taken.[8]

Differences in emphasis notwithstanding, discussions of intention necessarily bring motives and goals together, insofar as intentions occur prior to action and yet look forward to the goal anticipated to be accomplished from that action. This in fact is Weber's reason for insisting that social action be understood as meaningful action: action's meaning is constituted not only by the coordination of means and ends, as commonly suggested, but also by the relationship of motives and goals. A person chopping wood to earn wages, Weber argues, is assumed to be operating from a "rational" motive because the action can be understood in "an intelligible and more inclusive context of meaning"; in contrast, a person chopping wood in a fit of rage is "an irrational case" because the motivation is "affectually determined." The distinction between rational and irrational of course runs through Weber's corpus. However, the example's relevance to Weber's understanding of intention is its primary concern. A motive is the "intended" or subjective meaning, he writes, "which seems to the actor or the observer an adequate ground for the conduct in question"; hence, an interpretive grasp of that meaning requires investigating the intended meanings of individuals' concrete actions, the intended meanings of collective actions, and the kinds of meanings associated with ideal types of common phenomena. Intentions will in some instances align with observable outcomes. However, numerous reasons exist, he says, for this not to be the case: actors may have repressed or concealed their motives, similar actions may occur from multiple motives or be interpreted differently, and conflicting motives may be present.

---

8. John A. Bargh, "The Four Horsemen of Automaticity: Awareness, Intention, Efficiency, and Control in Social Cognition," in *Handbook of Social Cognition*, edited by Robert S. Wyer and Thomas K. Srull (Hove, UK: Erlbaum, 1994), 1–40; and as developed more fully in Julie Y. Huang and John A. Bargh, "The Selfish Goal: Autonomously Operating Motivational Structures as the Proximate Cause of Human Judgment and Behavior," *Behavioral and Brain Sciences* 37 (2014), 121–75.

While a causal interpretation requires consideration of both intentions and action, therefore, Weber posits that inconsistency may be as important as consistency.[9]

Reasonable as these arguments may be, discussions of intentions have prompted considerable resistance. Sociological accounts grounded in Marxian and structural emphases on inequitable distributions of power and economic resources suggest that intentions, values, beliefs, and tastes should always be considered derivative of those distributions rather than of importance as causal explanations.[10] Ryle's critique of the "myth of volitions" identifies another central issue. "To say that a person pulled the trigger intentionally," he writes, "is to express ... the occurrence of one act on the physical stage and another on the mental stage [and] that the bodily act of pulling the trigger was the effect of a mental act of willing to pull the trigger." The empirical difficulty is that mental acts "remain a mystery." "One person can never witness the volitions of another. Nor could it be maintained that the agent himself can know that any overt action of his own is the effect of a given volition."[11]

Cultural theorists' response has been to agree that mental acts are unobservable but to argue that traces are evident in expressive acts that differ from the physical acts through which intentions are pursued. For Geertz, the "moods and motivations" of which religion is composed are at least minimally observable in winks, nods, and gestures. C. Wright Mills's influential 1940 essay argued that motives should not be understood as private inward states of individuals but as *vocabularies* by which individuals communicate. A student who says, "I intend to spend this evening in the library," on this account, is not disclosing a hidden mental imperative, but is justifying a future act in terms that will be acceptable to the student's interlocutors. A justification of this kind, Mills suggests, is not without consequences. Were the interlocutors to say, "that's silly, you've already studied enough," their refusal of the justification might persuade the student to spend the evening differently.[12]

---

9. Max Weber, *Economy and Society*, edited by Guenther Roth and Claus Wittich (Berkeley and Los Angeles: University of California Press, 1978), 8–11.

10. For instance, see the discussion of "culture" in Douglas S. Massey, *Categorically Unequal: The American Stratification System* (New York: Russell Sage Foundation, 2007), 204–6.

11. Gilbert Ryle, *The Concept of Mind* (London: Mayflower Press, 1949), 62–66.

12. C. Wright Mills, "Situated Action and Vocabularies of Motive," *American Sociological Review* 5, 6 (1940), 904–13.

The idea that motives are "strategies of action," as Mills calls them, leaves unanswered many of the questions about intentions' relation to action, even as it opens interesting considerations about language. Consistency between the student's verbalization of plans to spend the evening in the library and then spending the evening there appears to depend entirely on the verbalization being acceptable to the student's interlocutors. Indeed, Mills ventures that motives must not only be agreeable but unquestionable, citing as an example skepticism about John D. Rockefeller's avowed religious motives as evidence that secularization is making such avowals less credible. Mills concedes that in pluralistic settings, individuals may be conflicted about which account serves best to justify their actions, but offers no remedy for the conflicts.

Ann Swidler's widely read essay on culture in action, which adopted Mills's idea of motives as strategies of action, developed the claim that actors were not driven by the kind of deeply socialized values that Parsons and Weber identified as goal orientations, but did what they needed to do to accomplish short-term ends—and adopted language from a repertoire of available scripts to justify their actions. Like Mills, Swidler argues that certain actions are more likely if agreeable interpretations could be articulated to render them meaningful to the actor and to significant others.[13] However, the fit between action and expressed intentions remains complicated. After-the-fact justifications arguably may have little relation to what a person has done or plans to do next. Articulated intentions may fail to communicate because words and gestures are polysemic. Intentions may not be articulated at all when interlocutors implicitly "know" why certain actions are taken.[14] Moreover, as Bourdieu points out, private motives that a person discusses, say, among family may be quite different from those expressed publicly; indeed, the more the two differ, the more ostentatiously the public ones may be expressed.[15]

In view of these difficulties, efforts to revive interest in unconscious, deeply ingrained values and dispositions that give rise as intentions or motives to various decisions and actions occur periodically. Dispositions that underlie and

---

13. Ann Swidler, "Culture in Action: Symbols and Strategies," *American Sociological Review* 51, 2 (1986), 273–86.

14. Theodore R. Schatzki, "Practice Minded Orders," in *The Practice Turn in Contemporary Theory*, edited by Theodore R. Schatzki, Karin Knorr Cetina, and Eike von Savigny (New York: Routledge, 2001), 50–63, example of pupils' intentions being inscribed in the classroom's spatial arrangement, page 51.

15. Pierre Bourdieu, *Outline of a Theory of Practice* (New York: Cambridge University Press, 1977), 38–42.

guide conscious behavior offer one such point of entry within practice theory, as do arguments about the unconscious, values, and dual processing modes of cognition. However, an alternative approach that has enduring appeal in the social sciences is to focus on concrete action and the concrete resources on which it depends instead of attempting to understand the role of unobservable and perhaps trivial mental inclinations. What counts is action, structure, power arrangements, economic resources, oppression, markets, demography, not intentions. Marxian emphasis on infrastructural determinants is one example, while American pragmatism is another. As Dewey once observed, "Without smoothed roads, signals and junction points, traffic authorities and means of easy and rapid transportation . . . civilization could relapse into barbarism in spite of the best of subjective intention and internal good disposition."[16] Religion may be the exception, insofar as beliefs and values remain of interest; and yet, in some discussions the materiality of religion serves as a way of circumventing thorny questions about intentions. These questions nevertheless are difficult to avoid when religion is viewed, not through a Cartesian lens in which thoughts and actions occupy separate spheres, but as practices that combine the two.

Conceiving of religion as practice raises the stakes for including intentions and lowers one of the difficulties in investigating them. Practices are purposive and agentic, which means they cannot be adequately examined without asking what the person intended to do, whether what they did was intentional, and how their actions in the moment signal something about their intentions. In interviews and surveys that ask only for self-reports of the person's intentions and actions (usually at one time), it is difficult to establish much except the often trivial conclusion that a person who intended to do x did or did not actually do x. To find out more, it is necessary to gather more information of the kind that practice theory implies, either through direct observation or further questioning.

For example, suppose you observe someone sitting quietly in a coffee shop with their eyes closed. You assume the person is doing something intentional, but how do you ascertain what those intentions are? Besides observing the person, you probably take note of what you can about the situation. If the person's eyes open after a few moments and look expectantly around, you may conclude that the person intends to meet someone and is waiting patiently for that person

---

16. John Dewey, *Human Nature and Conduct: An Introduction to Social Psychology* (New York: Henry Holt, 1922), 75.

to arrive. If, however, you see a copy of the Upanishads in the person's lap, you may conclude that the person's eyes were closed with the intention of meditating. Were you to return the next day and make the same observation, you might decide that your initial interpretation of the person's intentions was correct. You might also verify your guess by asking the person.

In collecting these bits of information, you would have been assisted by recognizing that practices, whether short or long, are better understood by considering a person's intentions than by observing only their actions and that intentions require bringing in information about the situation. Had you assumed that an intention is only a mental state that you cannot probe—and about which even the person may not have been aware—you would have been significantly hindered in understanding what you observed. Bringing the context into the picture, perhaps making repeated observations, and perhaps speaking with the person provided substantially more information. Recognizing that in ordinary life we in fact routinely make guesses about people's intentions—often guessing correctly—has been the basis for an epistemological shift from assuming that intentions are locked away in individuals' private consciousness toward considering how they are expressed in actions and discourse and through the situations in which they occur.

Two Kinds of Intentionality

The distinction between first- and second-degree murder is that the former is premeditated while the latter is not. Both are intentional (unlike voluntary manslaughter), but first-degree murder is planned ahead of time while second-degree murder occurs in the heat of the moment, still with the intent to kill or with the use of force with a high likelihood of killing even though the event was not planned in advance. John Searle's account of intentionality captures the difference by distinguishing *prior intention* from *intention in action*. Prior intentions are the desires, goals, plans, and decisions that a person formulates in advance of acting; for example, intending to vote in the next election or intending to get married. Whether they anticipate a specific act or one that is less clearly defined, prior intentions require a complex set of interrelated beliefs and desires and a set of assumptions about one's abilities, which Searle terms respectively the "network" and the "background" of mental presuppositions. Intention in action is distinguished from prior intention by occurring during the performance of the action itself. Intention in action is an event—voting, rather than planning to vote—or more precisely the psychological event that accompanies the bodily event. It is what the person is trying to do, as in purposefully and consciously voting for one candidate rather than another, or doing something spontaneously yet purposefully such as raising one's arm to fend off a blow. Intention in action is the self-monitoring feedback mechanism that tells us we are acting toward a goal and how we are doing toward achieving the goal.[17]

Neither prior intention nor intention in action is necessarily observable to an interested bystander, but both are *potentially* observable and at different times and in different ways. The prior intention of the person at the coffee shop perhaps happens the day before and is known because the person discusses it with a friend, makes a phone call, or places a backpack near the door. A prior intention of this kind, Searle argues, is in turn guided by certain background dispositions; perhaps in this case by a conviction that time socializing or meditating is well spent. But there is no reason to insist that the prior intention has become so unconscious that the person could not begin to verbalize it. It is different from observable action only because it happens earlier, not because it is submerged in a subterranean level of unawareness.[18] Intention in action valuably specifies that what follows a prior intention is not simply a completed goal-oriented action, but a series of in-the-moment intentions that occur as a person executes an action and that are interpretable in the context of that action. The coffee shop patron's intentions in action, for instance, are noticeable in the person's movements and affordances.

The distinction between prior intention and intention in action, Searle argues, demonstrates that an understanding of intentionality's role in human behavior necessitates consideration of both. Prior intention follows from Husserl's observation that consciousness is intentional, by which he meant that perception is both grounded in the broader phenomenology of a person's beliefs and experience and directional toward certain content, as in looking at a door or making plans to open the door. Prior intention further implies a

---

17. John R. Searle, *Making the Social World: The Structure of Human Civilization* (New York: Oxford University Press, 2015), 31–35; see also G.E.M. Anscombe, *Intention* (Oxford: Basil Blackwell, 1957), whose classic discussion includes the distinction between "intention for the future" and "intention in action."

18. Stephen Vaisey, "Motivation and Justification: A Dual-Process Model of Culture in Action," *American Journal of Sociology* 114, 6 (2009), 1675–1715, in my view, unnecessarily locates motivation in the unconscious.

belief or judgment that an anticipated act is desirable. Intention in action is in part shown in a person's bodily positioning and movement. Merleau Ponty gives the example of an organist who "sits on the seat, works the pedals, pulls out the stops, gets the measure of the instrument with his body, incorporates within himself the relevant directions and dimensions, settles into the organ as one settles into a house."[19] We who may be observing infer that the organist is acting intentionally. The same is true, Rowland Stout argues, when an unexpected act can nevertheless be interpreted as occurring on purpose. "As I swerve the car to avoid a pedestrian I intend to swerve the car," he writes, "but I did not intend to swerve it before I did it. The moment I started intending to swerve the car was the moment I started swerving the car."[20]

Whether they are prior dispositions or occur as habits devoid of deliberative thought or as improvisations in which intentions and action happen in the same moment, intentions are an integral aspect of practice. As complex sequences of action that unfold over time, practices include successive prior intentions and intentions in action, which necessarily are situated. An intention is "embedded in its situation," Wittgenstein writes, "in human customs and institutions."[21] Intentionality in playing chess, for instance, includes the fact that the game exists, participants' plans and overall strategy for the game, and their aims in each individual move. There is an "accordion effect," Searle suggests, that relates separate intentions in action to previous and future ones and to prior intention as well as reflexively to the person's self-understanding.[22] Thus, the satisfaction that a person derives from a sequence of complex actions is not merely that the actions have been completed but also that one's intentions have been fulfilled.

In this perspective, the question to which social science discussions are usually addressed should be understood as the ways in which a person's intentions are communicated to other people and interpreted by those people, not as matters of intentions *causing* action. Considered in this view, for instance, Berger

---

19. Maurice Merleau-Ponty, *Phenomenology of Perception* (London: Routledge, 2012, originally published 1945), 145.

20. Rowland Stout, *The Inner Life of a Rational Agent: In Defence of Philosophical Behaviourism* (Edinburgh: Edinburgh University Press, 2006), 150.

21. Ludwig Wittgenstein, *Philosophical Investigations* (London: Blackwell, 1953), 58.

22. Searle, *Making the Social World*, 37; referencing Joel Feinberg, *Doing and Deserving: Essays in the Theory of Responsibility* (Princeton, NJ: Princeton University Press, 1970), 34.

and Luckmann's discussion of motives is largely consistent with the idea of intentions in action. They argue that an actor's subjective intentions are better known to other people in familiar face-to-face situations than in the abstract or among strangers. Intentions are knowable because they tend to be pragmatic, at least in everyday life, serving as a kind of shared "recipe knowledge" that reflects "competence in routine performances." Moreover, in actions that unfold over time, motives operative at one step in the process may be influenced by social interaction and thus be different in the next step. Finally, a person attempting to guess another person's motives usually relies to some extent on "typifications," meaning ideas about what people in similar situations usually do and intend to do.[23]

Sustaining, Aligning, Assessing

Conceiving of intentionality as sequences of prior intention and intention in action places them in the context of regulated improvisation that Bourdieu's version of practice theory emphasizes. Intentions, accordingly, are subject to the revisions that ordinarily take place as people are confronted with changing constraints and opportunities and as the situations in which these confrontations occur are guided by subjective dispositions, behavioral habits, and situational affordances. The situational fungibility of intentions in practice poses three fundamental questions: (1) how are intentions sustained, (2) how are actors' intentions aligned with those of other actors, and (3) how do actors assess their own and others' intentions?

An example given by Donald Davidson of a person named James going to church nicely illustrates the question of how intentions are *sustained*. Davidson's interest is distinguishing among the possibilities of considering the status of James's intentions as causes or reasons for his behavior, including the role of beliefs and judgments. But Davidson's positing that James went to church with the intent of impressing his neighbors suggests an issue of equal importance. Is James fulfilling a spiritual intention he may have formed early in life, or has that intention not been sustained if he now goes to church only to impress the neighbors? What if James thinks he goes to church to gain spiritual knowledge but in fact goes to church to impress his neighbors? Does it matter that his neighbors think he goes to church to impress them even though that is not his

---

23. Berger and Luckmann, *Social Construction*, 36, 56, 59, 74.

reason? And does it matter whether his childhood intentions have been sustained if he continues to go?[24]

There is reason to argue that James's intentions—both his prior intention and his intention in action—*should* matter. Religion's defining characteristics, Geertz argues, include *long-lasting* moods and motivations. These are "tendencies, capacities, propensities, skills, habits, liabilities [that] lend a chronic character to the flow of [a person's] activity." They have a "directional cast," "a chronic inclination" grounded in "mental traits" and "psychological forces" that raise the probability of certain actions being performed repeatedly over an extended period. But Geertz is student enough of Ryle to argue that this is not all that moods and motivations are. They are also observable in activity, which "gets them out of any dim and inaccessible realm of private sensation into that same well-lit world of observables in which reside the brittleness of glass [and] the dampness of England."[25]

On this account, James's regular attendance at church over the years would satisfy Geertz that long-lasting moods and motivations were present. However, it would not satisfy Davidson's concern that James may be attending church to impress the neighbors. Something about James's moods and motivations as plans, decisions, and purposes must be long-lasting, just as in other practices. Does he still intend to demonstrate love to his wife after many years of marriage with sincerity or merely to avoid conflict? Does he intend to be an enthusiastic sales representative or does he merely show up at work every day? It is not enough that he keeps on doing what he has done in the past. If his reason for going to church is to practice religion and not merely to impress the neighbors, his *intentions* for doing what he does must be sustained. He needs somehow to be reminded of his prior intentions and his intentions in action. And for that to happen, social interaction, rituals, and discourse that periodically bring these intentions to conscious thought are likely to play an important role. In fact, the church services he attends probably reinforce not only his actions but also his intentions.

Intentions are *aligned* when people consider it important to be "playing on the same team," "pulling together," "working toward a common goal," "reading from the same page." Alignment assures participants that their actions have a common purpose and are oriented toward the same goal even though there may

---

24. Donald Davidson, *Essays on Actions and Events* (New York: Oxford University Press, 1980), 8.
25. Geertz, *Interpretation of Cultures*, 90, 95, 96.

be a division of labor among their actions. Aligned intentions can be signaled through embodied positioning and motion, as paired figure skaters do from extensive practice, or as a crowd does that runs for shelter from a sudden cloudburst. In other situations, such as a cocktail party, nonverbal cues such as the nod of a head or the direction of a gaze may suggest common intentions, their effectiveness at communication depending on prior interaction. When circumstances change, verbal alignment of common intentions becomes more imperative, especially when questions arise about interlocutors' commitment to a shared agenda.

Alignment of intentions among individuals interacting in the same situation resembles the intersubjectivity emphasized in phenomenological accounts of everyday life, but with an important difference. Intersubjectivity is the shared understanding of reality broadly conceived that derives from shared memories and experiences and enables persons to interact with others as fellow human beings. It tells us that the here and now world of everyday reality, Berger and Luckmann write, "is as real to others as it is to myself."[26] In Searle's terms, it constitutes the background beliefs and assumptions that make prior intentions possible. Aligned intentions are more specific, referring to shared aims, plans, and intentions in action.

While the alignment of intentions is most obvious in social situations, it is also present when isolated individuals act in solitary situations. Barry Barnes illustrates the point with the example of an acupuncturist whose practice occurs in the absence of other acupuncturists. The solo acupuncturist nevertheless must act as a member of the acupuncturist community, following its rules and performing per accepted standards of practice. The acupuncturist's intentions unless articulated to the client are unobservable in the situation, but are explicitly aligned in professional meetings and through certification processes.[27]

It is reasonable to assume that the acupuncturist's intentions bend toward the profession's aims and rules because of its authority to certify or withhold certification. Power of one sort or another is typically a feature of the alignment process. Instructors assert their authority by declaring the lesson's objective for the day. Students affirm that authority as they write down the objective and

---

26. Berger and Luckmann, *Social Construction of Reality*, 37.

27. Barry Barnes, "Practice as Collective Action," in *The Practice Turn in Contemporary Theory*, edited by Theodore R. Schatzki, Karin Knorr Cetina, and Eike von Savigny (New York: Routledge, 2001), 25–36.

make it their own. A child affirms a parent's authority by agreeing, yes, I want to obey better from now on. Verbal alignment of this kind further reinforces power through what Charles Tilley calls emulation: "the transfer of chunks of social structure that happen to include unequal categories." Examples would include military units, schools, prisons, segregated restaurants, and patriarchal households, which structure expectations about the proper alignment of intentions.[28]

Assessing intentions refers to a person's evaluative moral imputation of another person's intentions or of one's own. In the case of James going to church, his intentions do not have to align with those of his neighbors if none of them go to the same church, but his neighbor may wonder what to think of James as a neighbor: is James sincere in his apparent religious motives or is James superficial and simply doing things for show? The neighbor's interest may be idle curiosity or may matter because James needs a character witness. James's own assessment may be that he wants to attend church for spiritual reasons but knows he attends for show and thus assesses his action negatively in view of his prior intention.[29]

Assessments of intentions vary along several vectors of generality. In many situations an initial consideration is whether a person has acted intentionally at all, and thus should be held accountable, or can be excused. A second consideration is whether a person's intentions are sincere and have been expressed truthfully, which we assess in terms of the language used, the relationship of intentions and behavior, and the situation's conventions and norms. In most situations, a third consideration is whether the expressed intention seems "reasonable" in terms of what we ourselves would do or would expect others to do in similar circumstances. A fourth consideration is an evaluative assessment of whether our estimation of the person is elevated or reduced in terms of the relationship between our values and the person's intentions.[30]

---

28. Charles Tilley, *Durable Inequality* (Berkeley and Los Angeles: University of California Press, 1998), 95.

29. Alfred R. Mele, *Springs of Action: Understanding Intentional Behavior* (New York: Oxford University Press, 1992), 156–58, on aversive evaluative assessments versus desires.

30. The various literatures that address the assessment of intentions include speech act theory, attribution theory, and framing theory; e.g., John R. Searle, *Speech Acts* (Cambridge, UK: Cambridge University Press, 1969); Catherine Sanderson, *Social Psychology* (New York: John Wiley & Sons, 2010); Erving Goffman, *Frame Analysis* (Cambridge, MA: Harvard University Press, 1974).

Evaluative assessments are made on grounds of conformity or deviation from moral principles, such as attributing a person's intentions to courage and self-sacrifice, on the one hand, or to cowardice and selfishness, on the other hand. Insofar as religious traditions uphold such principles, they provide the narratives through which assessments are made; for example, comparing a person's intentions to those of a saint. However, an alternative mode of assessment is to emphasize certain aspects of the situation to demonstrate that the intention in action should be judged more seriously because it also reflected a prior intention and had been implemented before. For instance, in bringing a sexual harassment suit against a distinguished college professor whose legendary status in the field endangered the charge from being investigated, the seriousness of the offender's action is significantly increased if the complainant demonstrates that the offender has engaged in harassment in other situations, has a penchant for viewing pornography, and has explicitly verbalized harassing intentions.

The capacity to manage how one's intentions are assessed reflects the situation's power differentials. The merely curious neighbor's power increases to the extent that James needs a character witness or the neighbor presides over a community organization to which James wishes to be appointed. James can reinforce his devout prior intentions by participating in a church group in which he publicly affirms them and receives positive feedback for his affirmations. At issue is the question of James's sincerity. If he wishes to be regarded as sincere in his intentions, he can improve the chances of his significant others making that assessment by how he discloses his intentions. It will help his case if he attends a church that provides regular occasions for James to give a testimony about his faith, to pray and lead meetings, and to engage in service activities. James demonstrates that his intentions are sincere by their consistency and duration.

James's situation is an occasion for affirming the sincerity of his intentions in two respects. One is through the illocutionary force of the speech acts the situation provides. As James and the other religious practitioners recite their creeds and pledge to abide by divine rules, they declare their intentions. The more James participates verbally as well as bodily, the more his actions carry illocutionary force. The second is through the situation's typifications, as Berger and Luckmann suggest. James may be a silent participant, but his presence is an implicit public declaration that encourages other participants to assess his intentions as being like their own.

Were the situation different, the concealment of intentions would be an important strategy. On an evening in which James and his neighbor are playing poker, for example, each knows that the other's prior intention is to win and this intention is aligned by the rules of the game, but it is in neither's interest to disclose intentions in action from one hand to the next. Concealment is to their advantage. Or suppose the neighbor has intentionally spread false rumors about James's business dealings and now is worried that James is planning revenge. Keeping one's opponent "in the dark about one's intentions," Bourdieu suggests, may be an appealing strategy in a situation like this. The longer James manages to keep the neighbor in the dark, the longer the neighbor must worry about what will happen and when it will occur. Time is working for James, Bourdieu would say.[31]

Intention in Religious Practice

The James example suggests several of the ways in which intentions may be affirmed in religious contexts. These relationships can be described by considering the role of *rewards, habits, social interaction,* and *rhetorics of intention*. These mechanisms operate in the context of practices that unfold over time to sustain, align, and regulate the assessment of intentions.

The *rewards* of practicing religion are often extrinsic, such as companionship and opportunities to impress the neighbors, but are also intrinsic, such as assurance in anticipation of death and meaning in the face of suffering. The latter pertain to a practitioner's intentions. The intrinsic rewards from a person's religious practices can reinforce the person's intentions as well as the person's activities, just as becoming proficient at playing the piano can stiffen one's resolve to keep practicing. In short, a person's prior intention is gratified by attaining one's goal. Moreover, being one of the faithful means trying to be faithful, whether one succeeds at it or not. In *America's Pastor*, for example, Grant Wacker suggests that Billy Graham revivals functioned this way. Despite upwards of 70 percent of those who participated being regular churchgoers, participation rewarded participants with feelings of divine acceptance while at the same time reinforcing both a desire to be saved and an act of declaring that desire. "It's better to be a backslider time and time again," a journalist noted, "than never to make an effort to move forward at all."[32]

---

31. Pierre Bourdieu, *The Logic of Practice*, trans. Richard Nice (Stanford, CA: Stanford University Press, 1990), 106.

32. Ronald C. Wimberley et al., "Conversion in a Billy Graham Crusade: Spontaneous Event or Ritual Performance?" *Sociological Quarterly* 16, 2 (1975), 162–70; Grant Wacker, *America's*

Erin Johnston's study of yoga and centering prayer practitioners demonstrates something similar. Practitioners developed a "highly desirable but ever-elusive aspirational identity," which prompted Johnston to wonder why in the absence of rewards they continued practicing. By all indications, they were acting irrationally, pursuing an objective in the absence of rewards. What she found was that the participants who stuck with it used the experience of failing to reinterpret their intentions. The goal of practicing, for instance, was not to achieve transcendence or enlightenment but to demonstrate perseverance or to gain greater self-awareness. Trained leaders in both groups assisted participants in formulating these reinterpretations. Just as in the Billy Graham example, the recurring nature of the practice as it unfolded gave participants the occasion to reflect on their intentions.[33]

To suggest that *habit* may be a way that intention is inscribed in religious practice runs counter to the notion that habit occurs in the absence of conscious thought. In fact, a substantial literature suggests that intentions and habits function in opposing ways: intentions influence actions when habits are weak and matter less when habits are strong.[34] However, it is a well-established characteristic of habits that they are not simply weak or strong but situationally cued and of necessity subject to improvisation because of situational variation. "Implementation intentions," as Peter Gollwitzer calls them, take into account this variation by specifying in advance one's inclination to respond to a given situation in a specific manner; for instance, "When I receive a solicitation, I will write a check" or "I will hold my tongue if my boss yells at me."[35] While habits to a considerable degree facilitate the execution of such intentions, the fact that situations vary necessitates cognitively prompted adaptations. Living as we do in less than perfectly predictable worlds, Michael Tomasello writes,

---

Pastor: Billy Graham and the Shaping of a Nation (Cambridge, MA: Harvard University Press, 2014), 265.

33. Erin Johnston, "The Enlightened Self: Identity and Aspiration in Two Communities of Practice," *Religions* 7 (2016), 1–15; Erin Johnston, "Failing to Learn, or Learning to Fail? Accounting for Persistence in the Acquisition of Spiritual Disciplines," *Qualitative Sociology* 40, 3 (September 2017), 221–35.

34. Judith A. Ouellette and Wendy Wood, "Habit and Intention in Everyday Life: The Multiple Processes by Which Past Behavior Predicts Future Behavior," *Psychological Bulletin* 124, 1 (1998), 54–74.

35. Peter M. Gollwitzer, "Implementation Intentions: Strong Effects of Simple Plans," *American Psychologist* 54, 7 (1999), 493–503.

intentionality empowers us "to recognize novel situations and to deal flexibly [with] unpredictable exigencies."[36]

The literature on habit asks what predicts action but generally does not consider the role that intentions may play in the formation of habits or the possibility that habits may reinforce mindfulness of intentions, as would be the case if the act at issue was not brushing one's teeth but reciting a short prayer about one's desire to serve God. If habits are learned, as of course they are, then intention must be understood as integral to the learning process. The prior intention is not to achieve a long-term goal but to learn the habit, even if the habit is brushing one's teeth; and intention in action is the purposeful "trying" that occurs as the habit is being learned, such as reminding oneself that brushing must be done correctly. Ryle explains it this way: "Learning to apply instructions by deliberate and perhaps difficult and alarming practice is . . . peculiar to creatures with minds. It exhibits qualities of character . . . since the novice is making himself do something difficult and alarming with the intention to develop his capacities. To say that he can swim if he tries is, therefore, to say both that he can understand instructions and that he can intentionally drill himself in applying them."[37]

The applicability of this perspective on habit can be illustrated with reference to the standard argument in rational-choice theories of religion that people participate in religious activities because religion offers a promise of eternal life—and that the stronger the promise, the more likely people are to participate.[38] But if people are sure they are going to heaven, why do they need to participate in religion at all? Indeed, one version of rational-choice theory suggests that the best kind of religion would assure people of a blessed afterlife and *discourage* them from attending services because attending is an inefficient use of their time.[39] To understand why they attend, intentions' role in habits is key. Prior intentions do not have to refer to an ultimate goal such as eternal life but to the habit of attending, which means that attending is not a means to a goal but is the goal, as in teaching a child that it is good (pleasing to God) to

---

36. Michael Tomasello, *A Natural History of Human Thinking* (Cambridge, MA: Harvard University Press, 2014), 8.

37. Ryle, *The Concept of Mind*, 129.

38. Malcolm Hamilton, "Rational Choice Theory: A Critique," in *The Oxford Handbook of the Sociology of Religion*, edited by Peter B. Clark (New York: Oxford University Press, 2009), 116–33.

39. Robert J. Barro and Rachel M. McCleary, "Religion and Economic Growth Across Countries," *American Sociological Review* 68, 5 (2003), 760–81.

attend Sunday school regularly. And intention in action is present as the person learns the habit; for instance, when attendance includes reading a story about God being pleased when children attend Sunday school. In both ways, intentions are sustained in practice. In this example, they are also aligned in the context of other children attending, and how they are assessed is reinforced by the lesson suggesting that the children's attendance pleases God.

An interesting example of intention in action consciously modulating behavior that otherwise ran mostly on habit occurred in Thomas J. Csordas's research on charismatic healing practices. Some of the healers used massage as a form of therapeutic touch for the purpose of "calling forth God's positive energy." The healers were trained to the point that they could use their hands without having to think much about the motions. However, they knew that clients responded differently depending on differences in bodily sensitivity and fears of intimacy. "What's really important is the intention," one of the healers told Csordas. "You need to be very careful [with massage] in the way of intention," she explained. Keeping her intention in action in mind as she performed massage helped her to improvise in each situation to avoid bringing up too much affect and releasing too much negative energy.[40]

Social interaction in religious practice can be oriented strictly toward the accomplishment of certain activities, such as worship or service, but it can also be directed toward sustaining, aligning, and assessing intentions. Unsurprisingly, experimental-design studies demonstrate that individuals are more likely to affirm certain intentions if they perceive group support for those intentions.[41] Practice theory stresses that social interaction also extends through time and thus can be considered behaviorally in conjunction with both prior intention and intention in action. Andrew Johnson's study of Pentecostal religion in a Brazilian prison, for example, illustrates both. By convening at regular times in a prison space that became known as sacred space, the participants not only worshipped but signaled in advance their intention to worship. The space and the

---

40. Thomas J. Csordas, *The Sacred Self: A Cultural Phenomenology of Charismatic Healing* (Berkeley and Los Angeles: University of California Press, 1997), 53.

41. For example, self-reported intentions toward atheists are examined in conjunction with variations in perceptions of the frequency of atheism in Garrett L. Strosser et al., "When Private Reporting Is More Positive Than Public Reporting," *Social Psychology* 47, 3 (2016), 150–62; bystander studies demonstrate the variable effects (positive and negative) of bystanders on intentions to assist someone needing help; e.g., Tobias Greitemeyer and Dirk Oliver Mügge, "When Bystanders Increase Rather Than Decrease Intentions to Help," *Social Psychology* 46, 2 (2015), 116–19.

social arrangement of the participants cued their intentions, and the meetings regularly affirmed participants' intention to reform through verbalizations of their intentions.[42]

One of the conclusions from studies of pilgrimages is that intentions become clearer as the journey proceeds. Paula Elizabeth Holmes-Rodman's account, for example, describes her participation among a group of devout Catholic women on a pilgrimage to Chimayo in New Mexico during which verbalized intentions shifted from furthering the church, being devout, and praying for others to disclosing personal intentions concerning the healing of physical illnesses, quieting worries and doubts, and overcoming loneliness. As the women talked about these concerns, they realized that intentions they imagined deviated from the group were closely aligned with others', and thus came away with more positive assessments of their motives. Holmes-Rodman says they also became enmeshed in one another's stories.[43]

Although social interaction frequently has unintended consequences, it stands to reason that social interaction engaged in with intentionality is likely to have different outcomes than social interaction lacking intentionality. Grace Yukich and Ruth Braunstein's research on interfaith advocacy provides an example. They identified two kinds of interfaith practices: "aggregative practices" that combined symbols and activities from different religious traditions but left each tradition identifiable; and "integrative practices" that involved the "intentional and creative mixing of religious symbols, language, and practices." The two appeared similar in public settings, but the latter derived from intentional private backstage interaction dedicated to building trust and solidarity. These backstage events included rituals and discourse in which integrative intentions were explicitly discussed.[44]

A contrasting example is illustrated in Andrew L. Whitehead's study of small groups in congregations. Whereas Yukich and Braunstein observed social interaction in which intentions were discussed, Whitehead argued that a

---

42. Andrew Johnson, *If I Give My Soul: Faith Behind Bars in Rio de Janeiro* (New York: Oxford University Press, 2017).

43. Paula Elizabeth Holmes-Rodman, "'They Told What Happened on the Road': Narrative and the Construction of Experiential Knowledge on the Pilgrimage to Chimayo, New Mexico," in *Intersecting Journeys: The Anthropology of Pilgrimage and Tourism*, edited by Ellen Badone and Sharon R. Roseman (Champaign: University of Illinois Press, 2004), 24–51.

44. Grace Yukich and Ruth Braunstein, "Encounters at the Religious Edge: Variation in Religious Expression Across Interfaith Advocacy and Social Movement Settings," *Journal for the Scientific Study of Religion* 53, 4 (2014), 791–807.

congregation could institutionalize "collective intentionality" through the way it structured social relationships. Congregations, he found, achieved greater accountability among their members, involvement in congregational activities, and financial contributions by structuring their social relationships through formalized participation in small groups. These effects, he argued, were not the result simply of dense social networks among individuals but of congregations' deliberate planning to achieve more structured relationships.[45]

Intention in these instances consisted of prior intention being included in planning meetings and then enacted by shaping subsequent social interaction to accomplish the desired goal. In other studies, intention is present more clearly as intention in action. A study of high school community service volunteers, for example, found that journaling and debriefing sessions helped the volunteers to reflect on their intentions at each stage of preparing for and implementing service activities, with the effect of clarifying the steps involved and of forging stronger intentions to continue volunteering in the future.[46] The journaling and debriefing sessions also provided opportunities for the volunteers' leaders to establish "criterion of intention," as Frank Cioffi has called them, particularly that the volunteers should attach greater significance to the altruistic intentions they became aware of after the fact than the prior intentions that usually consisted of only fulfilling a course requirement.[47]

In much of everyday life, intentionality is not this explicit. Intentions are communicated implicitly through mental and bodily attention. Reflecting on what he had learned as a child from his elders, Augustine wrote, "Their intention was shewn by their bodily movements, as it were the natural language of all peoples: the expression of the face, the play of the eyes, the movement of other parts of the body, and the tone of voice which expresses our state of mind in seeking, having, rejecting, or avoiding something."[48] Wittgenstein gives a similar example in describing how a person is guided by a partner in a dance: "you make

---

45. Andrew L. Whitehead, "Financial Commitment Within Federations of Small Groups: The Effect of Cell-Based Congregational Structure on Individual Giving," *Journal for the Scientific Study of Religion* 49, 4 (2010), 640–56.

46. Robert Wuthnow, *Learning to Care: Elementary Kindness in an Age of Indifference* (New York: Oxford University Press, 1995).

47. Frank Cioffi, "Intention and Interpretation in Criticism," in *On Literary Intention*, edited by David Newton-DeMolina (Edinburgh: Edinburgh University Press, 1976), 55–73; and discussed further in Julia Tanney, "The Color Flows Back: Intention and Interpretation in Literature and in Everyday Life," *Journal of European Studies* 38, 3 (2008), 229–52.

48. Augustine, *Confessions*, I, 8; quoted in Wittgenstein, *Philosophical Investigations*, 2.

yourself as receptive as possible, in order to guess his intention and obey the slightest pressure." Wittgenstein's point is that the intention is communicated as an "ethereal, intangible influence" without you having to be conscious of it in the moment. Thought and deliberation about what happened occurs after the fact.[49]

Ritual attention theory argues that the spatial arrangement, pacing of interaction, and interdependence of the people involved play a significant role in sustaining and aligning their intentions. A worship service conducted in a space in which pews face an elevated pulpit from which a speaker gives an engaging sermon after which the congregation sings collectively, for example, is geared toward maximum sharing of attention and intention.[50] As a different example, Laura Clawson's study of Sacred Harp singing in the rural American South shows that the singers' squared spatial arrangement and coordination of voices during practices produced a common intention in action that bridged demographic and economic differences among the participants.[51]

Whether the intentions in such ritualized settings are fleeting or are sustained in ordinary life is a harder question. Stephen Jaeger's study of Depression era motion pictures offers a suggestive counterpoint to the idea that practices constitute actionable intentions. Fred Astaire and Ginger Rogers's "Cheek to Cheek" dance sequence, beautifully choreographed and brilliantly executed against a lavishly romantic setting, inspired downtrodden audiences who wanted to believe that they too could achieve their dreams. Perhaps they did return home with a renewed commitment to work harder and live happier. Or more likely, as Jaeger suggests, audiences went home knowing what they saw on screen was a grand illusion. Astaire's and Rogers's movements were "more graceful and charming" than anything observable in real life. Viewers could imagine that happy citizens enjoyed lives of "perfect rhythm and grace" but knew themselves to be "trapped in a reality where the human body and limbs move by cruder

---

49. Wittgenstein, *Philosophical Investigations*, 70.

50. J. David Knottnerus, "Religion, Ritual, and Collective Emotion," in *Collective Emotions*, edited by Christian von Scheve and Mikko Salmela (New York: Oxford University Press, 2014), 312–25.

51. Laura Clawson, "'Blessed Be the Tie that Binds': Community and Spirituality among Sacred Harp Singers," *Poetics* 32, 3–4 (2004), 311–24; Laura Clawson, *I Belong to This Band, Hallelujah! Community, Spirituality, and Tradition Among Sacred Harp Singers* (Chicago: University of Chicago Press, 2011).

laws."⁵² Religion, too, is no stranger to illusion and disappointment. Insofar as routine practices are concerned, attention to one's intentions is as much a reminder of falling short as it is of making progress. Echoes of Saint Paul's lament—the things that I want to do, I do not do—undoubtedly feature in practitioners' frustrations in realizing their intentions.

Rhetorics of intention refer to the discourse that explicitly sustains, aligns, and assesses intentions. Examples would include plans, proposals, and declarations that stipulate individuals' or groups' prior intention to engage in some future action; and progress reports, statements about tactics, and feedback telling practitioners how actions in the moment relate to intentions in action. Zohreh Kermani's ethnography among pagan families affiliated with the Spiral Winds Coven, for example, found that pagan children were given a rich repertoire of magical stories, songs, and rituals with which to improvise, and yet had to be guided in how to orient their intentions toward these repertoires. In one instance, children made full use of a labyrinth, not quite understanding what to make of it, but were guided by signs asking them to "declare your intention to travel to the heart" and conversations encouraging them to express their intentions by lighting incense, meditating, and becoming aware of the energy they might be experiencing.⁵³

Intentions expressed in discourse provide ways of guiding, interpreting, and communicating the meanings of action. They assist the actor in establishing control over other people's assessments of an act that otherwise may have multiple interpretations. And control of this sort, which may happen as an after-the-fact interpretation, serves as a meaningful link between an act that occurs in the moment and a person's durable dispositions and identity, which are expected to be present in the future. Wittgenstein asks, "Why do I want to tell [someone] about an intention, as well as telling what I did? Not because the intention was also something which was going on at that time. But because I want to tell him something about *myself*, which goes beyond what happened at that time."

The need to correct mistaken assumptions about who you are and what your actions may convey about your intentions is a frequent occurrence in ordinary life. As Alessandro Duranti observes, "interpretation relies on conventionality

---

52. C. Stephen Jaeger, *Enchantment: On Charisma and the Sublime in the Arts of the West* (Philadelphia: University of Pennsylvania Press, 2012), 300.

53. Zohreh Kermani, "Playing with Fire (and Water, Earth, and Air): Ritual Fluency and Improvisation among Contemporary Pagan Children," in *The Study of Children in Religions: A Methods Handbook*, edited by Susan B. Ridgely (New York: NYU Press, 2011), 108–20.

as much as on intentionality," which means that "an audience may respond to what they judge to be contextually relevant conventions" rather than a speaker's intentions.[54] Rhetorics of intention may be used to reinforce the speaker's intentions or the speaker may attempt to alter the contextually relevant conventions. An interesting illustration emerged in Samuel Perry's study of evangelical women engaged in religious fund-raising. Single women attempted to communicate clearly and directly that they were engaged in professional fund-raising. However, as a statement of their prior intention, the message frequently was ignored by single men who took their cues from the situation and interpreted it as an occasion to request reciprocation in the form of a romantic relationship. To counter this misinterpretation, the women restated their prior intention during the fund-raising event and managed the situation to include different cues about their intentions in action, such as meeting in a public place, bringing a male colleague, and going out of their way to speak in a professional register.[55]

Rhetorics of intention in broader contexts are one of the means by which Searle's emphasis on background beliefs connects to the idea that intention is directional. Background beliefs are evident in the example of James if the fallacy of singular intention is removed and James can attend church to worship *and* to impress the neighbors. Holding both intentions equally requires James to draw on background beliefs that enable the two to be reconciled. Perhaps he intentionally makes a show of going to church so that he can explain to his neighbor why he attends. Perhaps his church has taught him that he should encourage his neighbor to attend. Alternatively, James may factor in his desire to impress his neighbor by identifying as a secondary intention attending at a specific church, such as a downscale church that will also demonstrate his intention of being a servant leader. These are the kinds of background beliefs that

---

54. Alessandro Duranti, "Intentionality," *Journal of Linguistic Anthropology* 9, 1/2 (1999), 134–36, quote on page 135; cultural variations in the conventions through which intentions are said to be unknowable or inexpressible are discussed in Rupert Stasch, "Knowing Minds Is a Matter of Authority: Political Dimensions of Opacity Statements in Korowai Moral Psychology," *Anthropological Quarterly* 81, 2 (Spring 2008), 443–53, and related essays in the same issue.

55. Samuel L. Perry, "She Works Hard(er) for the Money: Gender, Fundraising, and Employment in Evangelical Parachurch Organizations," *Sociology of Religion* 74, 3 (2013), 392–415. Rachel Kraus, "They Danced in the Bible: Identity Integration among Christian Women Who Belly Dance," *Sociology of Religion* 71, 4 (2010), 457–82, illustrates another context in which gendered intentions are commonly misunderstood, arguing that her subjects at least satisfied themselves that their intentions were spiritual.

James could probably articulate if he were pressed to do so. Moreover, the process of articulation, as discourse that has been learned, tried, experimented with, and improvised, is an aspect of practice that has a modulating effect. As Bourdieu observes, discourse "outruns the conscious intentions of its apparent author and constantly offers new pertinent stimuli to the *modus operandi* of which it is the product and which functions as a kind of 'spiritual automaton.'"[56]

Rhetorics of intention are the vocabularies by which singular motives that conform to group legitimacy can be expressed, as Mills suggests, but their discursive flexibility also enables them to articulate the common situation in which motives are over-determined "like wringing the neck of a chicken."[57] For example, one of the specific intentions emphasized in religious practice is helping the needy, and studies generally demonstrate that actively religious people are more likely than average to say they would help if someone was in need. And yet, when asked to explain their intentions, discursive flexibility comes into play to articulate complex motives and beliefs, which are not at all unusual in modern, culturally pluralistic contexts influenced not only by religion but also by self-help groups, advertising, corporations, and education. A corporate executive who spends his lunch breaks volunteering for Meals on Wheels, for instance, explained his intentions during an interview this way: "I'm convinced that true, true happiness in life comes from helping people," but then he changed intonation and quickly added, "I have people say to me, 'Oh Martin, you're doing so many things.' Or they try to make me seem like such a great guy. But I say, 'Look, wait, I'm not, I'm doing it for a very selfish reason: it makes me happy.'"[58]

In this example of multivocality—*heteroglossia*, in Bakhtin's terms—Martin speaks both for himself and for "other people."[59] On the surface, the statement merely underscores Martin's insistence that his intention in doing volunteer work is to find happiness. However, it also allows Martin to introduce by inference the idea that his intention is altruistic and for that reason admirable.

---

56. Bourdieu, *Logic*, 57.

57. Carlo Emilio Gadda quoted in Italo Calvino, *Six Memos for the Next Millennium* (Cambridge, MA: Harvard University Press, 1988), 104.

58. Robert Wuthnow, *Acts of Compassion: Caring for Others and Helping Ourselves* (Princeton, NJ: Princeton University Press, 1991), 65.

59. Mikhail M. Bakhtin, *The Dialogic Imagination: Four Essays* (Austin: University of Texas Press, 1981), 293–97.

Heteroglossia like this assists Martin in sustaining the ambiguity of his intentions without having to select one that does not ring true to him. It aligns his volunteering with people he knows who also volunteer without setting himself apart from them. And his statement manages to include an apparent assessment of his intentions from others while also pushing against that assessment.

While multivocality of this sort illustrates discursive flexibility, rhetorics of intention are constrained by social norms. A person cannot willy-nilly offer any account that happens to come to mind. Martin apparently knows it is socially acceptable in his circle of acquaintances to do volunteer work to be happy *and* to be helpful, but not acceptable to appear as too much of a "goody-goody." Were Martin a member of a religious community, which he is, his rhetorics of intention would also be constrained by its teachings. If, for instance, he announced to his congregation that he intended to help at its homeless shelter but did not carry through, he would likely feel shame or guilt at not having lived up to his commitments.

However, suppose Martin is a frail octogenarian. Martin then might engage in what Robert A. Wicklund and Jostein Rise call *symbolic contributions* through the mere expression of intentions. Symbolic contributions, they argue, are valuable when a person is known to be ill-equipped or has neither the time nor the opportunity to carry out a given performance. A person limited in these ways can then show support for the performance that cannot be materially advanced through words as well as small deeds that express supportive intentions.[60] Examples include a person sending a birthday card ("wish I could be there") to a geographically remote loved one, a poorly prepared student demonstrating good intentions by trying to answer the questions on an exam, a person without means to purchase a piano telling friends about desiring to have one, and a spectator cheering for the home team at an athletic event. In each of these examples, the goal to be enacted is socially desirable, but conventions have also been established for persons who cannot achieve the goal to express their intentions.

Religion is among other things a practice established for people to make symbolic contributions by expressing their intentions. Prayer is one of the practices that serves this purpose. Martin may be too frail or too busy to help the homeless, but he can demonstrate his desire to help them by praying that God will give them comfort and assistance. Creedal affirmations function similarly.

---

60. Robert A. Wicklund and Jostein Rise, "Intentions and Other Symbolic Contributions to Society," *Social Psychology* 39, 4 (2008), 205–12.

The congregants who promise "we will" when asked during a baptismal rite if they will assist an infant to live a Christian life must understand that the chances of doing anything of tangible benefit are extremely low, but they willingly express their intention anyway. In addition, religion is perhaps unique in the normative constraint it exercises over such rhetorics of intention through positing that they must align with God's intentions and not merely the congregation's. Although theological arguments vary, one strand of Christian theology, for instance, argues that God's intention is for humans to be saved ("salvific intent") and that humans should align their intentions with God's by conforming their wills to Jesus through coming close to Jesus and living similarly to Jesus.[61]

These examples do not exhaust the ways that intentions are expressed and enacted in religious practice. They nevertheless underscore the importance of keeping intentions in the picture when considering religion rather than opting for a perspective that focuses only on the behavioral aspects of attendance, service activities, or for that matter demographic trends and membership statistics. The further point is that intentions are ill-conceived if they pertain only to questions about the possible impact of mental states on subsequent action or are considered only as after-the-fact justifications. An emphasis on the practice of religion heightens sensitivity to the fact that it occurs in ordinary life, thus including the plans that people formulate as prior intentions and the intentions in action that guide the implementation of plans. To the extent that religion is practiced, it is a matter not simply of action but of expressing and interpreting intentions. Practice provides the opportunities in rituals, conversation, and social interaction for people to articulate and enact their intentions and to have their intentions reinforced, aligned, and favorably assessed.

---

61. For example, see John Read, *Catherine Booth: Laying the Foundations of a Radical Movement* (Cambridge, UK: Lutterworth Press, 2013), 47–49.

4

Feelings

TO IMAGINE religion without imagining it with feelings would be to deny almost everything we know about it, whether from ethnographic, textual, or even statistical sources. It would be to ignore the terrifying wrath of the gods, the compassionate concern of the saints, the reverential awe and the depths of despair reported in the accounts of mystics, the desperate pleas of sinners at the mourners' bench, and the tears of parents at the graves of young children. To dwell on exceptional moments of reverie and awe, as some accounts of sacred experience do, would also be to miss the role of feelings in ordinary life, where there is evidence that feelings as intuitive promptings guide decisions about moral action. Moreover, religion in ordinary life is impossible to grasp without considering the feelings a person may carry from childhood warnings about sin or from living in a culture of instant gratification. By some accounts, feelings are the last outposts of cultural colonization, the inner preserve of our personal identity that we are willing to expend precious resources on seeking to manage.[1]

Wayne Proudfoot identifies two reasons for an increase of interest among scholars of religion in the investigation and analysis of feelings. One is the view

---

1. For example, see Kelly Oliver, *The Colonization of Psychic Space: A Psychoanalytic Social Theory of Oppression* (Minneapolis: University of Minnesota Press, 2004), and earlier treatments in Philip Rieff, *The Triumph of the Therapeutic: Uses of Faith After Freud* (New York: Harper & Row, 1966); Daniel Bell, "Beyond Modernism, Beyond Self," in *Art, Politics, and Will: Essays in Honor of Lionel Trilling*, edited by Quentin Anderson, Stephen Donadio, and Steven Marcus (New York: Basic, 1977), 213–53; and Christopher Lasch, *The Culture of Narcissism: American Life in an Age of Diminishing Expectations* (New York: Norton, 1979). For a retrospective examination of this line of cultural criticism, see Antonius A. W. Zondervan, *Sociology and the Sacred: An Introduction to Philip Rieff's Theory of Culture* (Toronto: University of Toronto Press, 2005).

that feelings, unlike deliberate acts and statements that are subject to voluntary control, cannot be manipulated. They arise unbidden from somewhere deep in our inner selves, or so we assume, and are thus an authentic expression of who we are. A second is that feelings, unlike language and customs, "appear to be invariant across cultures" and thus, in spanning religious traditions, suggest underlying commonalities in religious experience. To these might be added a third: feelings are popularly regarded as the arbiters of moral claims. As Bellah and his colleagues argue critically in *Habits of the Heart*, "In the absence of any objectifiable criteria of right and wrong, good or evil, the self and its feelings become our only moral guide." And, whether as moral guides or as claims about the sacred, feelings are uniquely powerful because the person is the final authority in making assertions about them: mistaken or not, no one else can show the person to be in error.[2]

Heightened popular interest in feelings appears to be driven in part by the pluralistic culture in which we live. In the homogeneous settings we imagine people in the past to have lived, it is possible to believe in whatever common wisdom prevails, which may include austere theological tenets. It is harder today to be sure that transubstantiation or consubstantiation is correct, or, for that matter to care. It may be equally difficult to decide if it is okay to be a Catholic who practices transcendental meditation or a Jew who marries a Buddhist. Uncertainties of these kinds push propositional knowledge to the background in many situations compared to what we know from personal experience, especially from situations in which we "feel" deeply moved or "feel" that something is right or wrong. In *Spiritual Marketplace*, Wade Clark Roof captures this rising emphasis, writing that "religion has not been abandoned but is expressed in a mood, style and discourse" based on feeling rather than doctrine. We look increasingly to feelings, Roof says, but have trouble knowing how to express them and how to find a way to feel happy about ourselves.[3]

---

2. Wayne Proudfoot, *Religious Experience* (Berkeley and Los Angeles: University of California Press, 1985), 76; Robert N. Bellah et al., *Habits of the Heart: Individualism and Commitment in American Life* (Berkeley and Los Angeles: University of California Press, 1984), 76; and on persons as the final authority about feelings, William P. Alston, "Feelings," *Philosophical Review* 78, 1 (1969), 3–34. Ruth Leys, "The Turn to Affect: A Critique," *Critical Inquiry* 37, 3 (2011), 434–72, surveys the broader interest in feelings and emotions in the social sciences and humanities, suggesting that an underlying motif is a desire to contest an over-emphasis on reason and rationality.

3. Wade Clark Roof, *Spiritual Marketplace: Baby Boomers and the Remaking of American Religion* (Princeton, NJ: Princeton University Press, 1999), 115; Grace Davie, *The Sociology of*

The literature on feelings makes several distinctions that serve usefully to delimit what is at stake in religious practice. Feeling statements that take the form "I feel like going shopping" can mostly be set aside on grounds that "feel like" is readily substitutable with "plan to" or "think I will." Most to the point are what Ryle calls "general condition" feelings or, as Alston renames, "adjectival feelings," examples of which include "I feel anxious," "I feel afraid," and "I feel angry." Adjectival feelings differ in terms of the pleasantness or unpleasantness of the affect (e.g., depressed or elated, fearful or confident), the intensity with which they are experienced, their temporality (acute or chronic), and whether they are focused (worried about a test) or diffuse (pervasively anxious). Feelings have visceral manifestations, although these vary in intensity and bodily location: feeling angry, for instance, is of a different order than saying something "felt right." The cognitive aspect of feelings also varies, from relatively non-deliberative moods (such as feeling "down") to complexly interpreted self-reflexive feelings (such as feeling ashamed or guilty about having done something that violates ethical norms). As Proudfoot observes, a person doesn't feel proud of the sky or ashamed of the rain; pride and shame require deliberation about one's self.[4]

Religion (London: Sage, 2007), 144, expresses a similar view, writing that the most dynamic popular forms of religion emphasize sensation, feeling, emotion; for an interesting account of emotions experienced by a non-religious person experimenting with contemporary religious services, see Corinna Nicolaou, *A None's Story: Searching for Meaning Inside Christianity, Judaism, Buddhism, and Islam* (New York: Columbia University Press, 2016).

4. Gilbert Ryle, "Feelings," *Philosophical Quarterly* 1, 3 (1951), 193–205; Alston, "Feelings"; Proudfoot, *Religious Experience*, 88; or, as Ricoeur says in emphasizing the self-reflexivity of feeling, "its function is to abolish the distance between knower and known," Paul Ricoeur, "The Metaphorical Process as Cognition, Imagination, and Feeling," *Critical Inquiry* 5, 1 (1978), 143–59, quote on page 156; see also Norbert Elias, "On Human Beings and Their Emotions: A Process-Sociological Essay," in *The Body: Social Process and Cultural Theory*, edited by Mike Featherstone, Mike Hepworth, and Bryan S. Turner (London: Sage, 1991), 103–25, who suggests that emotions can be conceptualized as including behavior, bodily responses, and feelings, but that in practice emotions and feelings are typically used interchangeably; and Jonathan H. Turner and Jan E. Stets, "Sociological Theories of Human Emotions," *Annual Review of Sociology* 32 (2006), 25–52, whose survey of the role of emotions in five standard theoretical approaches notes the infrequency with which anything less generic than "positive emotional energy," "negative emotional energy," "arousal," and "emotion expectation" is discussed; further distinctions are drawn in "affect theory" between affect and emotions, which, place affect closer to the present discussion of feelings; see Devika Sharma and Frederik Tygstrup, eds., *Structures of Feeling: Affectivity and the Study of Culture* (Berlin: De Gruyter, 2015).

Feelings are of interest in a wide variety of studies about religion. Surveys and experimental-design studies, for instance, ask people if they have ever "felt close to God," had a "deeply moving religious experience," or felt "forgiven," "cleansed," or "saved." Quantitative studies also examine relationships between religious participation and such adjectival feelings as happiness, anxiety, and depression. Qualitative research includes information about instances in which individuals feel distraught or ecstatic and in which groups express emotional fervor. Inspiration from Durkheim, Friedrich Schleiermacher, Rudolf Otto, William James, Clifford Geertz, and others has prompted discussions especially of what constitutes the intense affective experiences people attribute to the sacred. Indeed, the emotional power of the sacred, as Durkheim suggests, and the long-lasting moods that Geertz emphasizes are taken in some accounts as constitutive of the meaning of religion itself. Transcendence, fulfillment, wholeness, well-being are *feelings* in these accounts.[5] And in less philosophical accounts, feelings are the focus of empirical investigation concerned with religion's role in promoting positive outlooks on life—and with the "therapeutic culture's" impact on religion.[6] At the same time, students of religion express caution about following too closely the Durkheimian argument about sacred and profane being distinguished principally on the basis of emotional intensity. Ann Taves, for instance, suggests that "religious experience" be considered in terms of multiple "building blocks" rather than singling out intense feelings as the defining feature.[7]

Recent scholarship on feelings in settings other than religion suggests important, and yet relatively unexplored, implications for critical inquiries about religion. Criticisms of religion have charged that it privileges feelings rather than

---

5. For example, Robert N. Bellah, *Beyond Belief: Essays on Religion in a Post-Traditional World* (Berkeley and Los Angeles: University of California Press, 1970), 196–207.

6. Rieff, *Triumph of the Therapeutic*; James Davison Hunter, *American Evangelicalism: Conservative Religion and the Quandary of Modernity* (New Brunswick, NJ: Rutgers University Press, 1983), 73–100; Andrew J. Polsky, *The Rise of the Therapeutic State* (Princeton, NJ: Princeton University Press, 1991); James L. Nolan Jr., *The Therapeutic State: Justifying Government at Century's End* (New York: NYU Press, 1998); Eva Illouz, *Saving the Modern Soul: Therapy, Emotions, and the Culture of Self-Help* (Berkeley and Los Angeles: University of California Press, 2008); for an overview, see Katja Rakow, "Therapeutic Culture and Religion in America," *Religion Compass* 7, 11 (2013), 485–97.

7. Ann Taves, *Religious Experience Reconsidered: A Building Block Approach to the Study of Religion and Other Special Things* (Princeton, NJ: Princeton University Press, 2009).

thought and thus promotes behavior based on intuition and impulse instead of rationality and reflection. Religion is thus the antithesis of science, a repository of superstition and irrationality that will inevitably fade into the recesses of the past as rational thought proceeds.[8] But studies examining the presence of emotions in rational decision-making about moral issues and in scientific discoveries have muddied these binaries. Similarly in observations of ordinary life, "the wonder of minor experiences," as Jane Bennett terms it, is a reminder that even in modernity enchantment remains in the pleasurable feelings of being charmed by the unexpected and in the childlike excitement of impulsive decisions.[9] Paying greater attention to feelings as information, as forms of intelligence, in social interaction, and as things people do has necessitated attending more closely to the complexities of feelings in religious practice.[10] Critical discussions of what Bellah called "enlightenment fundamentalism," in which the affective power of icons and symbols are neglected, has contributed crucially as well.[11]

The direction this research leads is toward the need to shift from decontextualized assumptions about interior moods and instead contextualize the feelings people experience and report. In this perspective, feelings remain an important aspect of the subjectivity that phenomenology has always insisted on acknowledging, but feelings occur as a feature of social practices, whether in the comforting mood that "feeling at home" in a familiar space and among valued people and material objects provides or the sudden outburst of anger that a traffic accident evokes. Feelings are cued by the events and affordances present, which is not to say that they derive only from specific situations, but how they are expressed and interpreted is influenced by situational norms.

---

8. Among other sources, religion as non-rational emotion-based superstition is emphasized in Richard Dawkins, *The God Delusion* (Boston: Houghton Mifflin, 2006), and Daniel C. Dennett, *Breaking the Spell: Religion as a Natural Phenomenon* (New York: Penguin, 2006); Wayne Glausser, "The Rhetoric of New Atheism," *Style* 50, 1 (2016), 1–18, provides an interesting discussion of the extent to which these writers also induce emotional responses.

9. Jane Bennett, *The Enchantment of Modern Life: Attachments, Crossings, and Ethics* (Princeton, NJ: Princeton University Press, 2001), 5.

10. On criticisms of religion based on a cognitive versus emotions split, see Bellah, *Beyond Belief*, 237–57; and Catherine Bell, *Ritual Theory and Ritual Practice* (New York: Oxford University Press, 1992), 14–15.

11. Robert N. Bellah, "Confessions of a Former Establishment Fundamentalist," *Bulletin of the Council on the Study of Religion* 1, 3 (1970), 3–6.

Moreover, we engage with feelings purposively in attempting to manage them, doing so in relation to what we somatically experience but also in terms of the rules and meanings available to us.[12]

In this chapter I discuss how run-of-the-mill emotions as well as intense feelings, which are often described as a feature of religious experiences, are structured by situational rules governing their expression. Situations supply cues that elicit or suppress emotions much like habits are elicited or suppressed. Habits learned from religious socialization cue implicit messages about feeling loved and suppressing anger. Habits also produce long-lasting dispositions that shape the feelings individuals experience. Habits fail, though, amid the uncertainties of daily life, prompting feelings that guide improvisation. Religious practice contributes rules that are subject to competing dynamics for the experience and display of emotions. On the one hand, religious practices include ritualized events that include a controlled display of feelings in a way that would not be appropriate in everyday life. On the other hand, religious practices include stylized beliefs and activities geared toward explaining and guiding feelings that arise within everyday life. In both instances, the fact that feelings are often attributed to impulses that arise unbidden complicates how religious practices are observed. Among other things, religious practices inform people's thinking about why feelings occur and what an appropriate response to them should be. Moreover, these situational influences take shape amid wider discursive formations in which feelings serve as cultural representations. I begin with the relationship of habits and feelings, discuss contributions focusing on feeling rules, examine the role of authorities and rituals, and briefly consider feelings as culture.

---

12. Lila Abu-Lughod and Catherine A. Lutz, "Introduction: Emotion, Discourse, and the Politics of Everyday Life," in *Language and the Politics of Emotion*, edited by Catherine A. Lutz and Lila Abu-Lughod (New York: Cambridge University Press, 1990), 1–23; Monique Scheer, "Are Emotions a Kind of Practice (And Is That What Makes Them Have a History)? A Bourdieuian Approach to Understanding Emotion," *History and Theory* 51, 2 (2012), 193–220; and Ole Riis and Linda Woodhead, *A Sociology of Religious Emotion* (New York: Oxford University Press, 2010), who emphasize the social and material *relationality* of emotions; Jenna Supp-Montgomerie, "Affect and the Study of Religion," *Religion Compass* 9/10 (2015), 335–45, who draws on Gilles Deleuze and Sara Ahmed, emphasizes the energy that works through social interaction in its dynamism of coming together and falling apart.

Habit and Feelings

In many discussions of feelings' role in religion, habit is the starting point. Habit and the skills and propensities associated with them instill the dispositions and moods in which religious commitment is affirmed, and religion in turn is expected to inculcate habits that produce certain desirable emotions and restrain others.[13] A devout person, for example, learns to be steadfast in confidence that divine mercy will triumph in the face of despair, to give a soft answer rather than responding angrily, and to exercise patience instead of succumbing to anxiety. Habits are expected to work most of the time to keep a person's unwanted emotions under control, and when trouble occurs, to provide fallback solutions that have worked in the past. It was these impulse-regulating mechanisms that encouraged many religion writers and developmental psychologists to focus attention on the cultivation of good habits in children. Besides facilitating or restraining emotions, habit contributes to the tasks of daily life in terms of familiar routines instead of being guided by one's feelings. Moreover, habits such as prayer and meditation can become sources of divine assurance and joy—sources of the habitual surrender, Schleiermacher wrote, "in which [pious] emotions take their rise."[14]

The literature on habit that describes it as non-deliberative behavior registers general agreement that habit is behavior devoid of heightened self-conscious emotion. Experimental research suggests that people engaged in routine non-deliberative habitual activities experience fewer stressful emotions than those engaged in non-habitual behavior, apparently because repeated activities have fewer arousal-inducing interruptions, evoke fewer emotion-inducing discrepancies between activities and goals, and provide participants with a greater sense of self-control.[15] In everyday life, habitual behavior is routine, mundane,

---

13. Veena Das, "Wittgenstein and Anthropology," *Annual Review of Anthropology* 27 (1998), 171–95, offers a valuable discussion of the role of habit in the work of Wittgenstein and Stanley Cavell.

14. Friedrich Schleiermacher, *On Religion: Speeches to its Cultured Despisers* (Cambridge: Cambridge University Press, 1996 [1799]), 25; John Dewey, *Human Nature and Conduct: An Introduction to Social Psychology* (New York: Henry Holt, 1922), deals extensively with the contrast between habit and emotion-driven impulses.

15. Wendy Wood, Jeffrey M. Quinn, and Deborah A. Kashy, "Habits in Everyday Life: Thought, Emotion, and Action," *Journal of Personality and Social Psychology* 83, 6 (2002), 1281–97.

dull (there is little to be excited about when brushing one's teeth). Habit smooths the functioning of daily life by reducing the frequency of anxiety-producing decision-making situations. Indeed, it is the disruption of habit rather than its ordinary functioning that prompts emotional outbursts: *Damn, where did I put my keys?* Moreover, the normative impetus to learn good habits and to put them into practice is to be in control, as in learning to hold one's tongue instead of displaying anger. Habit in these instances is a practice that keeps emotions in check. Its relation to emotion lies in the fact that emotion, too, is often understood to be non-deliberative, experienced as a mood that overtakes us, as somatic and unwilled, arising spontaneously, viscerally. This is as true of pleasurable feelings—joy, happiness, elation—as it is of anxiety, fear, and anger.[16]

The notion that habit serves to suppress emotion is only partially accurate, though. Habit also facilitates emotional states, which are appropriately termed *states* because they are sustained non-deliberatively through the routines and situational cues habits provide. A study of participation in political events among young adults offers an interesting case in point. As political participation became habitual, the participants' anger about politics became their customary response. They also expressed less fear about threatening events, which, combined with anger, appeared to facilitate their sense of political efficacy.[17] Research on the emotional aspects of political rhetoric suggests a similar pattern: viewers who habitually watch certain campaign advertisements or who regularly listen to partisan talk radio programs become habituated to feelings of anger, alarm, or excitement to the point that the feelings become both expected and desired.[18]

Although habit and feelings may be non-deliberative, they are situational, facilitated by routines and repetitive cues, and, as I have argued in the case of habit, to a degree intentional. The habit of putting one's keys in the same spot

---

16. On emotion as non-deliberative, see Joseph LeDoux, *The Emotional Brain: The Mysterious Underpinnings of Emotional Life* (New York: Simon & Schuster, 1996); and see Leys, "The Turn to Affect," for criticism of this perspective, a close reading of which suggests the need to differentiate arguments emphasizing complete automaticity and arguments focusing on the inclusion of cognitive schema and semiotic effects; see also William E. Connolly, "The Complexity of Intention," *Critical Inquiry* 37, 4 (2011), 792–99, and Ruth Leys, "Affect and Intention: A Reply to William E. Connolly," *Critical Inquiry* 37, 4 (2011), 799–805.

17. Nicholas A. Valentino, Krysha Gregorowicz, and Eric W. Groenendyk, "Efficacy, Emotions, and the Habit of Participation," *Political Behavior* 31, 3 (2009), 307–30.

18. Ted Brader, *Campaigning for Hearts and Minds: How Emotional Appeals in Political Ads Work* (Chicago: University of Chicago Press, 2006).

every day is possible because of having planned at some point to do so and being able to control the space of one's home, whereas the impossibility of always parking in the same location at the shopping mall requires deliberation to fix the location in mind each time. Emotion is similarly situational, in that some situations (a dentist appointment) are typically more anxiety-producing than others (a leisurely walk). Prior intention is an anticipation of what to expect and how to act in different situations. Intention in action is the online monitoring that occurs in the situation. A visit to the dentist is intentional in the sense of wanting to care for one's teeth and in planning to be calm by doing what helps lower one's anxiety moment to moment.

These are the background features of daily life into which religious practices fit. The role of habit is implied or explicitly acknowledged. The literature stemming from Weber and running through Geertz, and Berger and Luckmann, argues that religion mitigates the emotional pain of suffering and trauma by providing explanations—theodicies—that account for these events while affirming the divine goodness of the sacred. Theodicies are thus cognitive answers to the "why" and "why me" questions that arise from the depths of human suffering. But the beliefs in which these answers are cast must be maintained if they are to be available when suffering occurs. They can be affirmed periodically in rituals, as Durkheim understood, such as an annual event in which stories are told and enacted. Or in everyday life they can be affirmed, as Berger and Luckmann emphasized, in the routines and conversations that constitute the reality of taken-for-granted experience. Indeed, much about religion is concerned with managing one's emotions in ordinary affairs. Habits guide practitioners to avoid situations in which guilt or anger might result, to cultivate certain feelings of joy and praise, and to learn prayers and devotional recitations conducive to comforting emotions. Explicit cues, such as a Lenten blessing asserting "As believers, we look to God for comfort," offer guidance. Habits and social relationships are behind the subjective well-being, happiness, relief from anxiety, and peace of mind to which polls and surveys often attest. Just as other aspects of practice do, the relationship of religion to feelings therefore requires examining the situations, rules, authorities, rituals, and symbols that constitute this relationship.[19]

---

19. Yang Yang, "Social Inequalities in the United States, 1972–2004: An Age-Period-Cohort Analysis," *American Sociological Review* 73, 2 (2008), 2004–26; Christopher G. Ellison, "Religious Involvement and Subjective Well-Being," *Journal of Health and Social Behavior* 32, 1 (1991), 80–99, which suggests that "existential certainty" is the mediating factor between attendance

Habits regulate emotions most reliably when the habits are cued by stable and enduring situations. The clearest examples are full-time religious professionals (Buddhist monks, for instance) whose daily lives are regimented around meditation and prayer. In ordinary life, the daily routines of eating and sleeping, personal cleanliness, and accomplishing regular household tasks may sustain habits of mindfulness or spontaneously uttering a brief prayer. A person who attends worship services several times a week may be inspired by the idea of living a "joy-filled spiritual life." The Lenten blessing appears as an email or tweet as a brief reminder of divine comfort amid a busy work day. Yet, the realities of daily life are rarely stable and enduring enough to ensure that habits alone will govern emotions. Only in the imagined worlds of pre-set long-term goals pursued through unimpeded rational activities is it possible to assume that life is that orderly.

Habits' relationship to emotions lies as much in the fact that habits are breached by the unanticipated contingencies of daily life, as in the expectation that they will be maintained. Nina Bandelj writes that even in economic transactions, where rationally planned activities are expected, the routines are rarely stable and enduring. The reasons, she suggests, are (a) that goals are hard to define in advance and typically evolve during the process of decision making, (b) the effectiveness of activities directed toward goals is likely to be uncertain and to require modification as situations change, (c) the personnel involved may change, (d) timing and time constraints may change, and (e) it is impossible to anticipate or control all the possibly relevant events and circumstances. Bandelj says these are the reasons decision-makers must be adept not only in planning but also at improvisation. And, while there are many ways to improvise, her research finds numerous instances in which decision-makers base their improvisations on emotions: trust their gut feelings, listen to their heart, follow their intuition, get a feel for the situation, and simply do what feels right.[20]

Religious practices are ways of justifying the improvisations that *feel right* when uncertainty is present. D. Michael Lindsay's interviews with evangelical executives, for instance, found numerous examples of feelings being invoked to explain business decisions. As one CEO remarked, "When you're doing the

---

and "life satisfaction"; sociologists' interests in research on happiness more than doubled in the 1990s and on emotions more than tripled, judging from articles published in *American Sociological Review*, *American Journal of Sociology*, and *Social Forces*.

20. Nina Bandelj, "Emotions in Economic Action and Interaction," *Theory and Society* 38, 4 (2009), 347–66.

right thing, your heart feels light and good." Another said it "wouldn't feel right" to drive a $50,000 car. But Lindsay's observations led him to conclude that executives often used religious language to "feel better" about spending money on themselves.[21] Other studies suggest that feelings play a role when breaches occur in people's religious habits. Susan Crawford Sullivan's research among low-income single mothers, for instance, found that feelings were often the basis for leaving a church or joining another one. As one mother explained, she felt angry and uncomfortable at her former church; and as another remarked about wanting to join a church, "I think it would help me feel better about a lot of things."[22]

The notion that feelings intensify when habits are broken is complicated by another pattern that surfaces frequently in research on religious practices. These are the practices people learn that become habitual as preparation for and indeed in anticipation that *intense extraordinary feelings may result*. Courtney Bender's story of Cathy Morton, a woman who experienced an emotional "whooshing" out-of-body experience, is an example. Morton's experience came during a Reiki master training course in which she hoped to learn the practice of energetic healing. As she said more about her experience, she also associated it with previous courses and conferences as well as childhood Sunday school attendance. Morton was still surprised by the "whooshing" but understood that it was a legitimate outgrowth of her practices.[23] Other studies demonstrate instances in which the relation between habit and intense feeling is more direct. Thomas Csordas's research among Catholic Charismatics, for example, found that regular participants felt unworthy and distressed as they faithfully practiced until they eventually achieved a breakthrough of spiritual cleansing.[24]

Bender suggests that experiences like Cathy Morton's necessitate scholarship that more closely aligns habitual and seemingly nonhabitual religious experiences. The nonhabitual "happenings" that seem to be so unexpected and so unusual that they constitute the "feelings, acts, and experiences of individual

---

21. D. Michael Lindsay, *Faith in the Halls of Power: How Evangelicals Joined the American Elite* (New York: Oxford University Press, 2007), 172, 192, 204.

22. Susan Crawford Sullivan, *Living Faith: Everyday Religion and Mothers in Poverty* (Chicago: University of Chicago Press, 2011), 113–14.

23. Courtney J. Bender, "Touching the Transcendent: Rethinking Religious Experience in the Sociological Study of Religion," in *Everyday Religion: Observing Modern Religious Lives* (New York: Oxford University Press, 2007), 202–27.

24. Thomas J. Csordas, *The Sacred Self: A Cultural Phenomenology of Charismatic Healing* (Berkeley and Los Angeles: University of California Press, 1997), 49–50.

men in their solitude," as William James wrote, who then "stand in relation to whatever they may consider the divine" are experienced that way because of the conditions, habits, and practices that allow such experiences to happen. The feelings that validate a person's unique individual relationship to the divine must themselves be validated by practices that assert the authority of individuals and the value of feelings. Even in the examples James considered, solitude was contingent on the spaces in which individuals conducted their lives and on their capacity to imagine that they were unique solitary individuals despite the expectations about feelings to which they were accustomed. The deeply emotional moments they experienced occurred in situations sought for solitude, whether in walks along the seashore or in monastic retreats where quieting the mind and disciplining the body were practiced and were described in after-the-fact accounts that selectively set the writer apart for having had such wondrous moments.[25]

Well-being

To argue that feelings are situational is not to suggest that they are shaped entirely by moment-to-moment events. Studies that seek to measure transitory feelings retrospectively or in real time find that feelings are situationally variable and nonspecific. Variability depends on the activities in which people are participating; for instance, Daniel Kahneman and colleagues found that positive feelings such as feeling happy and enjoying oneself were most common when people were socializing, relaxing, and eating, and, at least among a small minority, engaging in prayer or meditation, while negative feelings such as frustration, annoyance, and anxiety were highest during commuting, working, and housework. Not surprisingly, the social interaction in which positive feelings occurred most often was among friends and relatives, while negative feelings occurred when alone or interacting with a boss or co-workers. The research nevertheless showed that people aggregated their feelings in ways that

---

25. William James, *The Varieties of Religious Experience* (New York: Penguin, 1982 [1903]), 4, 306, 382; Josiah Royce's criticisms of James along these lines and how James might have responded are imaginatively discussed in Hans Joas, "Religious Experience and Its Interpretation: Reflections on James and Royce," in *The Varieties of Transcendence: Pragmatism and the Theory of Religion*, edited by Hermann Deuser et al. (New York: Fordham University Press, 2016), 219–35.

corresponded with overall descriptions of feeling states, such as happiness and well-being.[26]

The standard method of assessing the relationship between religious practice and well-being has been through self-reports of overall feeling states. Positive relationships between religious involvement and feelings of happiness and well-being are found often enough that several interpretations have been adduced.[27] One is that religion may be a way of attaining assurance about an important lifetime goal, such as glorifying God, doing good works, or gaining entry to heaven, that well-being essentially results from feeling that one is doing the right thing in terms of achieving an important goal. This interpretation suggests that marriage and career involvement may function similarly as sources of well-being because of their relationship to lifetime goals.[28] A second interpretation posits that supportive social relationships, such as the kind people may experience in a religious congregation, are key. In this view, religious goals and beliefs may also be a factor, but, as an emphasis on practice suggests, it is the affirming cues from the spaces, affordances, and social interaction that matter most.[29] A third perspective suggests, as Bourdieu emphasizes, that people bring dispositions with them that influence how they respond in situations. Thus, a person who has had a happy upbringing, for instance, would be expected to feel

---

26. Daniel Kahneman et al., "A Survey Method for Characterizing Daily Life Experience: The Day Reconstruction Method," *Science* 306, 5702 (2004), 1776–80; Daniel Kahneman and Alan B. Krueger, "Developments in the Measurement of Subjective Well-Being," *Journal of Economic Perspectives* 20, 1 (2006), 3–24; the real-time alternative to the Day Reconstruction Method is described in Saul Shiffman, Arthur A. Stone, and Michael R. Hufford, "Ecological Momentary Assessment," *Annual Review of Clinical Psychology* 4 (2008), 1–32.

27. Michael Hout and Andrew Greeley, "Religion and Happiness," in *Social Trends in American Life: Findings from the General Social Survey since 1972*, edited by Peter V. Marsden (Princeton, NJ: Princeton University Press, 2012), 288–314, is a statistically rigorous analysis of data in the United States and other countries, with appropriate controls, suggesting that regular attendance and feeling close to God are consistently and positively related to happiness; Sara Ahmed, *The Promise of Happiness* (Durham, NC: Duke University Press, 2010), is essential reading for a critical perspective on the culture of happiness.

28. C. Daniel Batson and W. Larry Ventis, *The Religious Experience* (New York: Oxford University Press, 1982).

29. For a review of these studies, see Michael Argyle, "Causes and Correlates of Happiness," in *Well-Being: Foundations of Hedonic Psychology*, edited by Daniel Kahneman, Ed Diener, and Norbert Schwarz (New York: Russell Sage Foundation, 1999), 353–73; Argyle also mentions studies suggesting that religion's relationship with happiness is due to better health habits.

happier whatever the circumstances might be than someone from an unhappy background.[30]

Although the general picture from large cross-sectional studies is of positive relationships between religion and happiness, studies also document exceptions. In an analysis of data from the National Comorbidity Survey of Adolescents, for example, Heather Kugelmass and Alfredo Garcia found that teens with no religion or who were atheists or agnostics were significantly more likely than teens who were religiously affiliated to have experienced mood and anxiety disorders; however, underscoring the possible effects of family conflicts, nonreligious teens with two religious parents were most likely to have experienced these disorders.[31] Other studies suggest that religiously legitimated parental abuse of children may be among the *sources* of low or non-religiosity among teens or adults.[32] The effects of harsh punishment of children on children's emotional well-being, though, appear to depend on the contexts in which punishment is given. Although harsh punishment is shown to result in lower indications of emotional well-being, conservative Protestantism appears to mitigate these effects, possibly because strict punishment is accompanied by other parenting activities that are more affirming.[33] Yet another line of research, prompted by interest in people disaffiliating from religion, has examined

---

30. While the prevailing interest in religion's relationship with feelings of well-being is understandable, some attention has also been given to feelings of gratitude, humility, and sympathy; for example, Neal Krause and R. David Hayward, "Humility, Compassion, and Gratitude to God: Assessing the Relationships Among Key Religious Virtues," *Psychology of Religion and Spirituality* 7, 3 (2015), 192–204.

31. Heather Kugelmass and Alfredo Garcia, "Mental Disorder Among Nonreligious Adolescents," *Mental Health, Religion and Culture* 18, 5 (2015), 368–79.

32. Alex Bierman, "The Effects of Childhood Maltreatment on Adult Religiosity and Spirituality: Rejecting God the Father Because of Abusive Fathers?" *Journal for the Scientific Study of Religion* 44, 3 (2005), 349–59; for an overview of the literature on religion and childrearing patterns, see John P. Bartkowski and Christopher G. Ellison, eds., *Children and Childhood in American Religions* (New Brunswick, NJ: Rutgers University Press, 2009).

33. Christopher Ellison, Mark A. Musick, and George W. Holden, "Conservative Protestants and Corporal Punishment," *Journal of Marriage and Family* 73, 5 (2011), 946–61; W. Bradford Wilcox, "Conservative Protestant Child Rearing: Authoritarian or Authoritative?" *American Sociological Review* 63 (1998), 796–809; and on gendered emotion work in conservative Protestant families, W. Bradford Wilcox, *Soft Patriarchs, New Men: How Christianity Shapes Fathers and Husbands* (Chicago: University of Chicago Press, 2004).

"spiritual struggles," finding them to be associated with depressive symptoms, generalized anxiety, and unhappiness.[34]

Situational variability in well-being has attracted greater interest in recent years due to the difficulties of learning much from correlational studies of well-being beyond the influence of such general factors as religion, age, gender, and socioeconomic status. The study of situational feelings has required shifting from large-scale population sample surveys to smaller-scale methods of sampling situations. The Ecological Momentary Assessment method prompts people periodically through a typical day to record what they are doing and who they are with and to answer a series of questions about what they are feeling. Though labor-intensive, this method avoids recall bias, such as people remembering positive feelings more clearly than negative feelings. The Day Reconstruction Method, which is more easily administered, asks people first to construct a diary of their previous day's sequence of events and then to answer questions about the feelings they associated with each event.

Besides the relatively unsurprising findings about situations associated with positive or negative feelings, situational studies examining variation in the gender, homophily, time horizons, and familiarity of interacting partners have opened opportunities for thinking about feelings in ways that emphasize the constitutive features of practices.[35] One such contribution is the study of temporality in the sequencing of events and practices. For instance, evidence can be brought to bear on such notions that an emotionally jarring experience can ruin a person's outlook on life for the rest of the day or that a few minutes spent in centering prayer can have an enduring uplifting effect. A related contribution is clearer evidence about the effects of clinical interventions, such as talk therapy, and clinical-like experiences, such as listening to relaxing music. Closer to questions about social interaction, the differential effects on feelings of different relationships can be examined; for instance, showing, as one study did,

---

34. Hisham Abu-Raiya et al., "Robust Links Between Religious/Spiritual Struggles, Psychological Distress, and Well-Being in a National Sample of American Adults," *American Journal of Orthopsychiatry* 85, 6 (2015), 565–75.

35. For example, Nina Vogel et al., "How the Social Ecology and Social Situation Shape Individuals' Affect Valence and Arousal," *Emotion* 17, 3 (2017), 509–27, report findings suggesting that positive affect is associated with interaction among family and friends whereas emotional intensity (arousal) is higher in nonfamily interaction. Time horizons are examined in Da Jiang et al., "Limited Time Perspective Increases the Value of Calm," *Emotion* 16, 1 (2016), 52–62.

that husbands' feelings significantly influence wives' feelings when the husbands come home from work, but not vice versa.[36]

Situational research, whether conducted through systematic experiential sampling or qualitatively, brings the study of feelings that may be associated with religion, divinity, or the sacred significantly closer to the dynamics of everyday life than has been the case in traditional studies of religious experience. Polls and surveys that document percentages of populations having been born again or having had a religious awakening remain useful for the purposes for which they were intended but leave much to be desired. As Saul Shiffman writes in another context, "Research methods that examine this landscape from 10,000 feet cannot shed light on how this landscape is shaped at ground level."[37] Everyday life is influenced, to be sure, by relatively stable dispositions and personality traits. But we know from our experiences of ordinary life that how we feel can vary dramatically depending on what may just have happened as well as on the rules that inform us about how we are supposed to register those feelings.

Feeling Rules

Feeling rules are the implicit—and sometimes explicit—norms that guide people about the kinds of emotions they should expect in various situations and how appropriate or inappropriate it is to express these emotions. Feeling rules locate emotions in situational space, suggesting that feelings are not only directed toward or evoked by other people but also experienced and displayed in patterned ways. Arlie Hochschild's study of flight attendants, for example, provides a vivid illustration of feeling rules. The attendants experienced apprehension, stress, anger, and even fear on long, crowded flights, openly expressing them in private spaces after the flights in Hochschild's presence. But they were trained to stifle these emotions during flights, smiling graciously and behaving as if they were completely calm and in control. They knew that if they did not, they would likely be fired. Moreover, the training largely succeeded,

---

36. Reed Larson and Maryse H. Richards, *Divergent Realities: The Emotional Lives of Mothers, Fathers, and Adolescents* (New York: Basic Books, 1994).

37. Saul Shiffman, "Dynamic Influences on Smoking Relapse Process," *Journal of Personality* 73 (2005), 1715–48.

Hochschild argued, in persuading the trainees that they were indeed feeling calm and in control.[38]

In this example, the feeling rules were explicitly taught and nearly always followed in the situations to which they applied. In everyday life, feeling rules are more likely to be learned implicitly as people participate in situations and observe what other people do and say. At a neighborhood meet-and-greet for newcomers, for instance, the newcomers may observe that everyone smiles, laughs, and speaks quietly or, in a different neighborhood, that people tensely and angrily confront one another, especially after a few drinks. Erving Goffman concluded from observing social interaction in such situations that a second kind of feeling rules was also operative. These rules came into play when breaches occurred in implicit norms, functioning to resolve disagreements, save face, and restore what had been broken. Breaches in feeling rules are among the instances in which such restorative mechanisms become important. The reason is that emotions cannot always be controlled, arising spontaneously without deliberation as they are assumed to do, or if a breach is planned, the restorative mechanisms include defining them as something deep, authentic, and spontaneous.[39] These restorative mechanisms are themselves subject to the feeling rules prevalent in the situation, which can be the source of conflict between the desire to express one's feelings and fear about the consequences of expressing them.[40]

Melissa Gregg suggests that contemporary workplace cultures add to the difficulties of expressing feelings honestly and directly. Work is often de-skilled and alienating, especially when it is repetitive and technology-based, yet workers are expected to feel engaged with their work and refrain from venting negative feelings toward co-workers. The outlet, she says, is passive-aggressive snark expressed in emails, on online platforms, and through edgy humor, all occurring indirectly and in stylized ways rather than in person. The emoticon, she

---

38. Arlie Hochschild, "Emotion Work, Feeling Rules, and Social Structure," *American Journal of Sociology* 85, 3 (1979), 551–75; Arlie Hochschild, *The Managed Heart: Commercialization of Human Feeling* (Berkeley and Los Angeles: University of California Press, 2012 [1979]).

39. Erving Goffman, *Interaction Ritual: Essays on Face-to-Face Behavior* (Garden City, NY: Anchor Books, 1967).

40. Jennifer L. Bryan et al., "God, Can I Tell You Something? The Effect of Religious Coping on the Relationship Between Anxiety Over Emotional Expression, Anxiety, and Depressive Symptoms," *Psychology of Religion and Spirituality* 8, 1 (2016), 46–53, in three experimental studies, found that turning to God as an outlet for inexpressible feelings was less effective than hypothesized.

writes, has become the acceptable means of communicating affect through the screen.[41]

Feeling rules that construct feelings to appear authentic resemble the mechanisms through which intentions are authenticated, but with an important difference. Deliberation facilitates the authenticity of intention by communicating that one's plans are thoughtful, but undercuts the authenticity of feelings by suggesting that they are calculated. When televangelist Jimmy Swaggart shed tears in 1988 while confessing to having visited prostitutes, for example, critics wondered if the emotion was genuine or staged. The few times Hillary Clinton became teary-eyed during the 2008 and 2016 presidential campaigns, in contrast, received fewer critical comments because they appeared spontaneous. The gendering of feeling rules was arguably relevant as well, giving Clinton wider latitude to express feelings because of being a woman, although critics claimed she was "playing the woman card."

A second dynamic was present in both instances. Feeling rules are different in public than in private, which means that public figures like Swaggart and Clinton may be suspected of expressing feelings appropriate to their public roles that are not congruent with their private lives. This possibility is furthered in some instances by signals being given indicating that one's public feelings are indeed staged. Among flight attendants, for example, the practiced smiles, stylistic speech, and uniforms communicate, *this is not who I am and this is not what I may truly be feeling*. Similarly, a common device in police procedural fiction is to observe that the suspect smiles but the smile does reach the suspect's eyes. Incongruities like these between the situational rules governing the public expression of feelings and the private feelings a person experiences inside become part of the self-presentational tensions that interested Goffman. The options are situational, varying with the intensity of the mismatch and the power dynamics in place: resolve the tension by exiting the situation, changing it, or accepting it. Research also suggests that situations construct participants' willingness to act *as if* the feelings displayed are authentic even though they are recognizably staged. For instance, a study revealed that Disney World visitors understood staff's cheerful smiles to be fake but proceeded to talk as if they were real.[42]

---

41. Melissa Gregg, "On Friday Night Drinks: Workplace Affects in the Age of the Cubicle," in *The Affect Theory Reader*, edited by Melissa Gregg and Gregory J. Seigworth (Durham, NC: Duke University Press, 2010), 250–68.

42. Karen Klugman et al., *Inside the Mouse* (Durham, NC: Duke University Press, 1995), 110–11.

Studies in which people talk about praying find that "praying about it" surfaces not only in relation to making important decisions such as choosing a career but also in dealing in the moment with feelings that are incongruent with situational feeling rules. Todd Starnes's book about conservative Christians who felt the government was attacking their traditional values describes a manager of a food bank who was angry and worried about losing government support but whose situation ruled out publicly expressing those feelings. "I'm not called to worry about it," she said. "I pray about it."[43] Similarly, Michael Lindsay's interviews with corner-office evangelical executives found that they often prayed privately rather than publicly revealing their anxiety about risky business ventures.[44] Experimental-design studies examine similar possibilities about praying as a substitute for having or expressing feelings that run counter to social norms.[45] Shane Sharp suggests from studying victims of intimate partner violence and reviewing numerous other studies that prayer alters the feeling rules of the situations in which people find themselves by essentially redefining and thus relocating them in a different perceived situation. Fear, anger, and anxiety are reduced as the situation shifts toward social interaction between the person and God, thereby reducing the perceived threat and increasing the person's sense of efficacy and self-esteem.[46]

These examples illustrate the argument in religious self-help literature that prayer is an anti-anxiety device—a device that may function effectively in situations mostly controllable in other respects and requiring only an occasional reminder to ask for divine comfort. Everyday life provides a backdrop of constancy against which an emotion-inducing irruption can be experienced as unusual. However, there is also the reality of daily life that defies regularity. It is the unpredictable daily turmoil of the refugee camp, the uncertain aftermath of a terrorist strike, and the scrambling irregularity of life as a fugitive. Against such instability a yearning for solid, unchanging religious verities is not the only possibility. Another is to embrace the dynamics of displacement. Rafael Sánchez, commenting on the María Lionza possession cult in Venezuela, for

---

43. Todd Starnes, *God Bless America: Real Stories from the Front Lines of the Attack on Traditional Values* (Lake Mary, FL: Charisma Media, 2014), 23.

44. Lindsay, *Faith in the Halls of Power*, 171–72.

45. Of some relevance are studies such as those presented and discussed in Jennifer N. Belding et al., "Social Buffering by God: Prayer and Measures of Stress," *Journal of Religion and Health* 49, 2 (2010), 179–87.

46. Shane Sharp, "How Does Prayer Help Manage Emotions?" *Social Psychology Quarterly* 73, 4 (2010), 417–37.

example, says its members seemed almost addicted to displacement as a "means of enjoying and reinventing themselves in circumstances where the vagaries of the job market, the indeterminacies of space, the telegraphics of power, and the media all intimate that if you stay put or stay the same, you might as well give up." The cultists Sánchez observed routinized their worship as well as their subsistence work lives by traveling constantly both in reality and on imaginary journeys as much to escape evil as to seek fortune. The sacred was "invaded and even cozily furnished by the sights and sounds of the profane" and at the same time was so placeless, so contingent that it "seemed to pop up out of the blue." The very transience and unpredictability of the spirits the cultists invoked seemed to Sánchez to be entirely congruent with the fleeting emotions and realities of their lives.[47]

The María Lionza example illustrates the situational adaptability that frequently characterizes the display and experience of feelings in practice. Unlike the flight attendant feeling rules that are learned in pre-flight training, feelings are often matters of improvisation that in turn reinforces or modifies the rules. A first-time airline passenger, for instance, may be complicit in the flight attendants' feeling rules by stifling anger or expressing remorse for having failed to stow one's items properly. An expression of feelings in such person-to-person situations is widely understood to be more than only an outpouring of something from inside a person; it is rather an expression that evokes a response from Person B, which in turn affects Person A. Sara Ahmed gives the example of a white person whose affect toward a black person indicates fear and toward whom the black person also registers fear in response to how the interaction may become threatening. Ahmed's example is of course not hypothetical, to which many interracial encounters attest, including ones between police and citizens.[48]

Encounters in religious practice illustrate similar dynamics. White Christian nationalism that expresses disdain for African Americans, Jews, Muslims, and foreigners feeds on the feedback it perceives among those groups in terms of fear and mutual disdain. The emotive rejection of the alien, Ahmed argues, solidifies the feelings of "we-ness" among the insiders who collectively proclaim

---

47. Rafael Sánchez, "Channel Surfing: Media, Mediumship, and State Authority in the María Lionza Possession Cult (Venezuela)," in *Religion and Media*, edited by Hent de Vries and Samuel Weber (Stanford, CA: Stanford University Press, 2001), 415, 422.

48. Sara Ahmed, *The Cultural Politics of Emotion*, 2nd ed. (Edinburgh: Edinburgh University Press, 2014), 62–63.

their "love of country." To the white Christian nationalist, love of country and love of God come together in expressions of fear that both are being subverted by powerful alien outsiders.[49] Less extreme examples are illustrated in survey research studies that recognize the importance of affect by soliciting responses to "feeling thermometer" questions asking, for instance, if Protestants feel "warm" or "cold" toward Catholics or how believers feel toward atheists. Negative feelings toward religiously defined "outsiders" typically coincide with willingness to discriminate, adherence to certain exclusionary doctrinal tenets, and sometimes with overt ostracism. Less readily observed in such studies are the reciprocating emotions and actions that occur among outsiders. These are more amply documented in qualitative research. Leigh Eric Schmidt's historical investigation of "village atheists," for example, gives numerous examples of the disgust atheists felt toward the pomposity and naiveté of firm believers.[50]

Feeling rules are best understood as *relational* norms, not an imposition from an exclusive source but the result of situations in which the persons involved negotiate the appropriate feeling rules by differentiating themselves from other people in other situations. Frequently these negotiations focus directly on how much or how little emotion is appropriate, with arguments emphasizing reason on the one hand and emotion-driven fanaticism on the other hand. Such negotiations played a prominent role along with doctrinal disputes in post-Reformation Europe and continued as the various traditions populated North America. German Baptist immigrants whose revival meetings frequently included intense emotional activity but who found it useful to distinguish themselves in doctrine and name from Anabaptists with similar practices are an interesting case in point. Much the same was evident among Methodists whose revival meetings inspired emotional fervor but whose announcements emphasized speakers' scholarly credentials. Methodists and Catholics alike criticized fringe sects for promoting emotional fervor to the point of adherents going insane and committing acts of violence.[51]

---

49. Sara Ahmed, "Collective Feelings Or, The Impressions Left by Others," *Theory, Culture, and Society* 21, 2 (2004), 25–42; Sara Ahmed, "Affective Economies," *Social Text* 22, 2 (2004), 117–39.

50. Leigh Eric Schmidt, *Village Atheists: How America's Unbelievers Made Their Way in a Godly Nation* (Princeton, NJ: Princeton University Press, 2016).

51. Robert Wuthnow, *American Misfits and the Making of Middle-Class Respectability* (Princeton, NJ: Princeton University Press, 2017).

The relationality of feeling rules is evident in twenty-first-century discussions of religion both in interactions between secularists and religionists and in disputes among religions. Secularists argue that religionists are guided entirely by emotions instead of intellect, while, according to surveys, the majority Christian US population considers the close-minded fanatics in their midst to be Muslims and Hindus.[52] Saba Mahmood observes the extent to which othering of this kind depends on selective emphases on violence, veiling, book burnings, angry mobs, and fiery preaching services. Even among academics, she suggests, passionate defenses of one's own perspective, whether secular or religious, cloud the ability to conduct empirically rigorous and critical investigations. "Our ability to think outside this set of limitations necessarily requires the labor of critique," she writes, "a labor that does not rest on its putative claims to moral or epistemological superiority but in its ability to recognize and parochialize its own affective commitments."[53]

Relationality of this kind is evidence that feeling rules are more than implicit norms hidden in the behind-the-scenes assumptions to which people conform. Feeling rules communicate directly the feelings that are appropriate to display, as Hochschild observes in emphasizing that flight attendants learn not only that they *should* remain calm but also that calmness is a way of feeling and behaving. Jean Comaroff makes a similar point about Pentecostal churches in South Africa. The gospel of happiness they preach extends beyond teachings encouraging people to be happy. It is demonstrated in practice through sound systems playing upbeat music, in joyful testimonials, and with beaming faces participating in arousing worship services.[54]

Authorities

The idea of feeling rules does not *require* that an entity, such as an airline company, imposes rules on the people it controls—conceivably, the rules can have been agreed upon through an egalitarian process. Power differences nevertheless are usually implied, as in gendered, racial, and age-graded expectations

---

52. Robert Wuthnow, *America and the Challenges of Religious Diversity* (Princeton, NJ: Princeton University Press, 2005).

53. Saba Mahmood, "Religious Reason and Secular Affect: An Incommensurable Divide?" *Critical Inquiry* 35, 4 (2009), 836–62; quote on page 861.

54. Jean Comaroff, "The Politics of Conviction: Faith on the Neo-liberal Frontier," *Social Analysis* 53, 1 (2009), 17–38.

about the kinds of emotion that can legitimately be expressed: the same display of religious exuberance by a man or by a woman or by persons of different races may be interpreted quite differently. Feelings are subject to the power dynamics that Foucault describes in discussing speech: who can say what about whom and to whom? Translated: who can *feel* what about whom and to whom? Concretely, when is it not even possible to *feel angry* toward someone, let alone express that anger to that person or to someone else? It is not hard to imagine such instances, such as in religious communities that firmly believe any expression of anger is sinful.

Although individuals are often the final authority in claiming to experience certain feelings ("who are you to question that I feel sad today?"), these claims are nevertheless subject to challenge and interpretation, often in terms of what can be felt or said to be felt in given situations. Besides the feeling rules that may be the tacit norms that people take for granted, organized machineries of emotion management are often present. David Freeman terms these organized efforts to influence the feelings people have, the intensity of these feelings, and how they are interpreted "emotioneering." Emotioneering, he argues, is present in everything from advertising and gaming to performance counseling and is disseminated through seminars, conferences, publications, advice columns, blogs, and consultations, as well as through the commercial manipulation of visual imagery, sounds, and affordances.[55] Its pervasive presence in our lives accounts for many of the feelings we experience intensely—the anxiety of a closely contested athletic event, the elation of a winning buzzer-beater, the heartbreak of a sad movie. It enters the picture when therapeutic help is needed to manage naturally occurring anger, grief, and depression. Its guidance is present especially in times of emotional vulnerability—when the daily routines are interrupted with accidents, illnesses, and bereavement.

Historically, religion has been among the first responders to these events. If its effects in emotioneering daily life are limited to reminders about comfort and joy, its reach is significantly better organized for dealing with the occasional, truly life-altering events. Births, coming of age, marriage, illnesses, and death are the provenance of religion. Time-worn practices swing into action to guide practitioners through the attendant emotions. However, it is not only in the midst of these occasions that religion structures the rules. Religion's authority to define feeling rules extends to numerous other situations, without which its

---

55. David Freeman, *Creating Emotions in Games: The Craft and Art of Emotioneering* (Boston: New Riders, 2004).

effectiveness during the most emotionally intense occasions in life would be weakened. These other situations include ordinary worship services, religion-based habits that parents may wish to instill in their children (or in themselves), home devotional practices, and community meetings. Indeed, as Christian Smith suggests, it may be the depth and range of these emotions that enhance religious traditions' enduring power.[56]

John Corrigan's study of mid-nineteenth-century Bostonian Protestants provides an interesting example of how the churches' cultural authority defined emotions and influenced how they were expressed. "Emotion increasingly was objectified and traded as a commodity between persons, and to God, according to performance rules that were coded in church teachings, marriage contracts, [and] public media," Corrigan writes. Believers did not have to be persuaded that feelings and faith went together; they knew this from biblical instruction and from the revivalist legacy. But feelings were shaped by the contemporary context into business-like transactions in which a petitioner wrote a request on a slip of paper and handed it to God via the church or wept openly in hope of receiving a favor from God. The broader implication, Corrigan suggests, is that feelings are sufficiently fluid and ambiguous that religion plays a strong role in many contexts in molding their meaning and significance.[57]

In instances such as the ones Corrigan examined, religious authority largely works in tandem with feeling rules institutionalized in other settings such as business, families, the law, and daily life. But other studies show how religion's authority is increased by facilitating displays of feelings that are deemed inappropriate in other settings. Joel Robbins's research among the Urapmin in Papua New Guinea, for example, found that feelings were deeply hidden in everyday life, which provided local spirit women opportunities to gain power by offering themselves as specialists in the discernment and resolution of undesirable and otherwise inexpressible feelings of anger, jealousy, and guilt.[58]

Religion's emotional authority is most unrivaled in the spaces popularly designated for the collective practice of religion—churches, mosques,

---

56. Christian Smith, "Why Christianity Works: An Emotions-Focused Phenomenological Account," *Sociology of Religion* 68, 2 (2007), 165–78, the arguments in which seem applicable to other religious traditions as well; see also Penny Edgell, "We Still Don't Know If Christianity 'Works,' Much Less Why: Response to Smith," *Sociology of Religion* 69, 4 (2008), 445–52.

57. John Corrigan, "Religion and Emotions," in *Doing Emotions History*, edited by Susan J. Matt and Peter N. Stearns (Urbana: University of Illinois Press, 2014), 143–62.

58. Joel Robbins, *Becoming Sinners: Christianity and Moral Torment in a Papua New Guinea Society* (Berkeley and Los Angeles: University of California Press, 2004).

synagogues, temples, meditation centers, and other houses of worship. In addition, religion's proximate spaces often fall under its emotional control as well. One such space is the street, park, or public square sufficiently near an established house of worship that special rules apply, as Omar McRoberts notes in discussing the monitoring of frivolity and exuberance near the African American churches he studied in Boston.[59] Other such spaces are the shrines, grottos, paths, and sacralized places that attract spiritual pilgrims. Geoffrey White's term "emotive institutions" applies to these spaces. Emotive institutions are settings in which emotion, social interaction, bodily movement, and self-understandings come together, sometimes resulting in feelings of psychological healing and at other times heightening emotional concerns. In broader terms, White includes the spaces on airplanes that Hochschild associates with feeling rules but argues that more should be considered than only the rules. The notion of an emotive institution, he writes, "pushes for closer attention to the properties of situations, contexts, and institutionalized activities in which emotions obtain social meaning and force." These properties include the scripts with which people talk about their feelings, the persons with whom they interact, the temporality of the event, and its spatial location. An emotive institution differs from a place that may have emotional resonance for an individual (e.g., where a first kiss occurred) in having a known collectively defined valence that contributes to the feelings experienced—the Pearl Harbor World War II memorial, the Ground Zero 9/11 memorial, Gettysburg National Park, or for local communities, a cemetery.[60]

Janneke Peelen and Willy Jansen suggest that pilgrimages on the road (*el camino*) to Santiago de Compostela in the northwest of Spain provide an interesting case study in religious practices as emotive institutions. Over a ten-year period the number of pilgrims multiplied fivefold, reaching nearly a hundred thousand annually by the early twenty-first century. Clearly the practice had become institutionalized. People heard about it from friends, read brochures and popular books about it, and gained information from churches and travel agencies. They came with their own individual motives, some for healing and some for a respite from daily life. They expected from what they had read and

---

59. Omar M. McRoberts, *Streets of Glory: Church and Community in a Black Urban Neighborhood* (Chicago: University of Chicago Press, 2003).

60. Geoffrey M. White, "Emotive Institutions," in *A Companion to Psychological Anthropology*, edited by Conerly Casey and Robert B. Edgerton (Oxford: Blackwell, 2005), 241–54; quote on page 246.

heard to experience exceptional emotions. It was in the journey, though, that the practice and the special feelings they experienced merged. The location and the walking were special, as were the pilgrims they interacted with along the way. The pace itself, walking slowly, in silence, and usually with blisters and sore muscles, further set the journey apart from ordinary life, both mentally and emotionally. In their journals the pilgrims wrote of pain, homesickness, sadness, and fear, all rising from within them as the walking continued. They also wrote of joy—a "good feeling that made me mad with happiness," one wrote.[61]

White's notion of emotive institutions also casts light on saints and martyrs as well as on pilgrimages. Saints, martyrs, angels, and heavenly beings, Orsi reminds us, populate the social interaction in which religious practitioners participate. It is insufficient, though, to emphasize the social interaction without also specifying why it is sometimes emotionally charged to the extent that it is and in unanticipated ways. Much of the daily interaction that may take place with St. Christopher or St. Jude in everyday life is hardly charged with emotion at all. It is merely the habit of wearing a medallion or saying a prayer or looking at an icon, a practice that hardly has to be thought about at all, even though a person might associate it with religion if asked to do so. The saints' emotional potential is not in the daily interaction but in memories of what they have done in the past and anticipation of what they may do in the future. The memories and anticipations are located in situations that structure the emotional resonance. The situations are visits to shrines, pilgrimages, rescues from danger, and small prayers answered or unanswered. The social interaction succeeds, when it does, in yielding emotion as individuals align themselves and their intentions with the saints—and as often as not when the saints disappoint them. "A woman who throws an image of a saint onto the backseat of her car to punish him for not answering her prayers," Orsi writes, "is not feeling the mysterium tremendum. . . . That is the numinous, upside down on the floor of an old Chevy!"[62]

Compelling as such an example may be, care must be taken to avoid neglecting history in focusing on specific situations. Perhaps the numinous was never

---

61. Jenneke Peelen and Willy Jansen, "Emotive Movement on the Road to Santiago de Compostela," *Entofoor* 20, 1 (2007), 75–96; quote on page 91.

62. Robert A. Orsi, "The Problem of the Holy," in *Cambridge Companion to Religious Studies*, edited by Robert A. Orsi (New York: Cambridge University Press, 2016), 84–106, quote on page 98; on emotion and moral alignment with saints and heroes, see Colin Jerolmack and Douglas Porpora, "Religion, Rationality, and Experience: A Response to the New Rational Choice Theory of Religion," *Sociological Theory* 22, 1 (2004), 140–60; and Douglas Porpora, "Heroes, Religion, and Transcendental Metanarratives," *Sociological Forum* 11, 2 (1996), 209–30.

quite the exclusive preserve of feelings about the sacred that academic interpretations supposed, but there were very likely situations in which an icon would not have been treated so dismissively. Understanding twenty-first-century feelings about the holy requires careful attention to the kinds of authority that exist within individual persons and the pluralizing influences of the mass media, among other things. To understand the numinous being upside down on the floor of an old Chevy, attention must be directed not only to the saints but also to the alternatives that represent authority. Would a person interact with a police officer or a therapist in the same way?

The often presumed declining authority of religious organizations needs to be understood in terms of its command over the expression of emotions, and not just as a function of belief. If religion succeeds because it evokes rich emotions, it fails by the same measure. People who feel somewhat loved and supported by their congregations may well feel more deeply loved by their families and friends; uplifted by communing with God, but more uplifted by music and art; calmed by divine presence, but have their anxiety lowered by medications and therapy. If religion has become more therapeutic in its emphasis on good feelings, it is also faced with competing authorities and expectations of all varieties. Therapists, life coaches, and self-help seminars offer authoritative advice based on practical experience. It is the business of many others—customer service representatives, marketing specialists, salespersons, store clerks, and health professionals, to name a few—to engage in emotional labor as well.

The role of art and music as an authority that competes with religion to provide an emotionally rich sense of spirituality is an interesting case in point. The quip that artists are the theologians of our time and the observation that young people are more likely to experience the sacred listening to music than attending religious services illustrate the competition. Philip S. Francis argues in *When Art Disrupts Religion* that a significant number of the American evangelicals he studied became unsettled about their faith through transformative aesthetic experiences with music, film, theater, poetry, and fiction that moved them deeply with feelings of wonder, awe, and mystery. The feelings, he suggests, seemed more real than the doctrines his interviewees had grown up believing, and the emotions were sufficiently unexpected that they prompted new questions and ideas.[63] David Morgan's work on visual art adds the relational piece that Francis's research implies. In *The Embodied Eye*, Morgan argues that the

---

63. Philip S. Francis, *When Art Disrupts Religion: Aesthetic Experience and the Evangelical Mind* (New York: Oxford University Press, 2017).

feelings evoked by an icon or a flag or a theatrical performance are prompted not only by the art but also by the social relations in which it is experienced and about which it communicates. Children's feelings that reciting the Pledge of Allegiance is special, he notes, stem from doing it together at the behest of their teacher as much as from looking at the flag.[64] Similarly, Francis's interviewees experienced art and music where they felt supported and in institutional settings (such as Christian concerts and college choirs) that conferred authority.

The complicity of persons in subordination with those in authority is an important factor in these examples. Just as passengers are complicit in sustaining the authority of flight attendants, religious practitioners interact with religious authorities in ways that demonstrate mutual adherence to the feeling rules in place. The "call and response" motif in many African American churches in which the congregation responds verbally to the preacher ("amen," "yes," "say it") is a notable example. Less evident but present in all such settings is an adherence on the part of the congregation to feeling rules that reinforce the feeling rules adhered to by the person in authority. Speakers who raise their voices in anguish about God's wrath or in elation about God's love are affirmed in doing so by congregants nodding heads in agreement and registering similar emotions in their facial expressions. In contrast, a speaker whose voice is devoid of emotion in the interest of presenting a logical doctrinal brief is affirmed by an attentive but emotionally restrained response.

Conversion is one of the clearest examples of emotional complicity. Among the many things that conversion is—a narrative of awakening, a shift of identity, a change in social relationships—intense feelings are a feature that can rarely be ignored.[65] The convert confesses to feeling cleansed, affirmed, uplifted, sanctified, and while the feelings may be deeply inward, the feeling rules governing the occasion typically provide for public display. "Cold, wet, yet emotionally excited," Ted Olson observes about river baptisms in the Blue Ridge mountains, "the now-baptized person would return to shore, often displaying outward signs of exuberance—shouting, crying, flailing arms, and uncontrollable moving of

---

64. David Morgan, *The Embodied Eye: Religious Visual Culture and the Social Life of Feeling* (Berkeley and Los Angeles: University of California, 2012).

65. For an extensive survey of the literature, see Raymond F. Paloutzian, "Psychology of Religious Conversion and Spiritual Transformation," in *The Oxford Handbook of Religious Conversion*, edited by Lewis R. Rambo and Charles E. Farhadian (New York: Oxford University Press, 2014), 210–48.

the body."[66] Such displays of emotion, Joanna Bourke suggests, *do things*.[67] They have implications for the emotional life of the person's relationships, such as forging bonds with co-religionists, providing a basis for asserting one's independence from others, and altering gender roles.[68] They affirm the authenticity of the conversion, marking (sacralizing) the occasion, prompting self-interrogation, and heightening intentionality. In a study of newly religious orthodox Jews and converts to Islam, Iddo Tavory and Daniel Winchester suggest that the elevated emotions at the time of conversion launched "experiential careers" that motivated converts' successive practices.[69] Emotional displays also affirm the power of the tradition and organization to which the person has converted. In medieval and early modern Europe, for example, highly publicized stories of deeply emotional conversion experiences authenticated Dominicans' legitimacy against critics.[70] In recent decades, the literature on global Christianity has frequently emphasized the emotional intensity of Christian converts in the global South as evidence of its authenticity compared to the waning Christianity of the global north.[71]

Complicity of a different sort needs to be considered when individuals declare, as is commonly the case, to be guided by feelings that seem "true" or

66. Ted Olson, *Blue Ridge Folklife* (Jackson: University of Mississippi Press, 1998), 107.

67. Joanna Bourke, "Fear and Anxiety: Writing about Emotion in Modern History," *History Workshop Journal* 55 (2003), 111–33; and pertaining to conversion, Jacqueline Van Gent and Spencer E. Young, "Introduction: Emotions and Conversion," *Journal of Religious History* 39, 4 (2015), 461–67.

68. For example, Carolyn Chen, "A Self of One's Own: Taiwanese Immigrant Women and Religious Conversion," *Gender and Society* 19, 3 (2005), 336–57; and Kelly H. Chong, "Negotiating Patriarchy: South Korean Evangelical Women and the Politics of Gender," *Gender and Society* 20, 6 (2006), 697–724; Eliza F. Kent, "Feminist Approaches to the Study of Religious Conversion," in *The Oxford Handbook of Religious Conversion*, edited by Lewis R. Rambo and Charles E. Farhadian (New York: Oxford University Press, 2014), 298–321.

69. Iddo Tavory and Daniel Winchester, "Experiential Careers: The Routinization and Deroutinization of Religious Life," *Theory and Society* 41 (2012), 351–73.

70. Spencer E. Young, "Faith, Favour, and Fervour: Emotions and Conversion among the Early Dominicans," *Journal of Religious History* 39, 4 (2015), 468–83; a similar argument is made about Muslims converting to Christianity in Francois Soyer, "The Public Baptism of Muslims in Early Modern Spain and Portugal: Forging Communal Identity through Collective Emotional Display," *Journal of Religious History* 39, 4 (2015), 506–23.

71. For a discussion of this literature, see Robert Wuthnow, *Boundless Faith: The Global Outreach of American Churches* (Berkeley and Los Angeles: University of California Press, 2009).

"authentic" while denying the social and cultural conditions that shape these feelings. Feeling rules, Hochschild suggests, regulate not only how we behave as good employees and parents, but also how we protect ourselves from the estrangement of those rules and, indeed, from what she considers to be the inevitable alienation of living in a commodified consumerist economy. We fall back on "emotional labor," she says, that is as staged and commodified as everything else but that gives us a false sense of feeling in charge. For instance, we hire a party planner in hopes of achieving an exceptional moment of happiness or study a sex manual to cultivate feelings of intimacy, and if the anticipated feelings fall short, we are left not only with disappointment but also with questions about whether they were worth wanting in the first place.[72]

Might something similar be an aspect of practicing religion? A notable feature of twenty-first-century religion in the United States is its criticism of materialism—the false gods of fine homes, expensive cars, and luxury consumer goods—in favor of feeling in touch with the sacred. How to understand the joy of those uplifting moments while at a high-priced spa or in the comfort of a well-appointed mega-church, though, suggests that the orchestrated contexts of these practices necessitate consideration. Hochschild would probably argue that the situations are at least complex, offering respite and an enlivened sense of one's core self but also leaving room for doubt about how competent we truly are in managing our emotions.

But Hochschild also suggests that these ways of being interested in feelings have been institutionalized to such an extent that we comply with them without having to think much about what we are doing. If a feelings-oriented, self-interested "expressive individualism" of the kind Bellah and his co-authors argue now dominates our "habits of the heart," she asks, how did all this become a *habit*? Is it that feeling rules are guided enough by language that over an extended period we respond to ordinary situations such as a family crisis or a career decision in certain ways? To find out, Hochschild and collaborator Sarah Garrett analyzed sermons, sermon titles, and religious announcements in three major newspapers (the *New York Times, Chicago Tribune,* and *Los Angeles Times*) in 1900 and a century later in 2000. The shift toward individual needs and emotions, they concluded, was notable: up from 2 percent to 16 percent and overall with nearly a third of the recent items focusing on individuals' emotional,

---

72. Arlie Russell Hochschild, "Emotional Life on the Market Frontier," *Annual Review of Sociology* 37 (2011), 20–33.

physical, and spiritual well-being. There was also a corresponding decline in references to community, duty, sympathy, and sacrifice.[73]

Shifts of this sort have been speculated about and documented enough in other sources that the trend itself is not surprising. Its sources, about which several possibilities have been suggested, are harder to determine. One possibility is that the rugged individualism of the nineteenth century gradually morphed into an individualism of feelings as people became better educated, more affluent, and more often employed in secure white-collar bureaucratic jobs that required greater interpersonal skills. Another possibility is that the rapid expansion of mental health concerns and funding and the growth of professional counseling during and in part as a response to the Cold War contributed directly to a therapeutic culture focused on feelings and increasingly mixed with shifts in theological orientations toward individual spirituality. Hochschild's emphasis on commodification prompts her to posit another source: branding and the competition among branded consumer products, she suggests, have focused less on instrumental subsistence needs and increasingly on emotional gratification, as evidenced in advertising for automobiles, clothing, food, and soft drinks. Whether or not religious practices have been shielded from these influences within places of worship, their role in daily life is hard to deny.

Feelings in Ritual

It is the distinctive power of ritual, Durkheim suggests, to move us with such intense emotion that we feel stronger from having been in the presence of the supernatural. Countless writers have followed Durkheim's lead in emphasizing that religion's staying power lies less in its doctrines than in its success in orchestrating rituals in which participants are emotionally energized. How ritual induces such feelings, though, and whether it does, is less clear. Durkheim emphasizes both the physical coordination of action and the physical co-presence of the enactors, the former manifesting the collectivity's power over the individual and the latter communicating in speech and gestures the appropriate emotions. Without the latter, collective effervescence would be no more likely than among students whose coordinated activity consisted of working on mathematics problems. Following Durkheim, Randall Collins also emphasizes physical co-presence, as in crowd behavior at a football game and the

---

73. Arlie Russell Hochschild and Sarah Garrett, *So How's the Family? And Other Essays* (Berkeley and Los Angeles: University of California Press, 2013), 93–110.

rhythmic synchronicity of a dance troupe. Bodily proximity, Collins argues, combines with the crowd's mutual focus of attention and shared mood to heighten the emotional energy experienced by the individuals present.[74] Collins also notes two contributing factors. One, which received greater attention in Victor Turner's work, is that ritual saturates the group's norms and values with emotion, thus giving the emotion a positive valence and casting negative valence on non-participants.[75] The other is that "practical knowledge," as Catherine Bell calls it, informs participants about what to do, what to feel, and how to interpret their feelings.[76] Practical knowledge, or as Neal Krause and R. David Hayward call it, "practical wisdom," may also be the kind of life-informing information that participants gain from repetitive ritual involvement, such as learning from one's mistakes, being cooperative, having patience, and knowing one's limitations, which in turn may be associated with feelings of awe and transcendence.[77]

Agreement that more than feelings alone are present leaves open the question of whether physical co-presence is necessary, and if it is, what its relation is with feelings. A partial answer is given in studies of mirror neurons, which suggest that expressions of feelings such as sadness, anger, or fear automatically prompt empathic feelings in observers of these feelings.[78] Mirror neuron

---

74. Randall Collins, *Interaction Ritual Chains* (Princeton, NJ: Princeton University Press, 2004), 47–140; and for an application to religion, Joel Robbins, "Pentecostal Networks and the Spirit of Globalization: On the Social Productivity of Ritual Forms," *Social Analysis* 53, 1 (2009), 55–66, and Jason Wollschleger, "Interaction Ritual Chains and Religious Participation," *Sociological Forum* 27, 4 (2012), 896–912.

75. Victor Turner, *Forest of Symbols: Aspects of Ndembu Ritual* (Ithaca, NY: Cornell University Press, 1967).

76. Bell, *Ritual Theory, Ritual Practice*, 216; Bell's emphasis on practical knowledge, like Hochschild's focus on feeling rules, contrasts sharply with arguments attributing emotion in ritual to the co-presence and number of participants, duration of participation, common focus, and interdependence, an example of which is J. David Knottnerus, "Religion, Ritual, and Collective Emotion," in *Collective Emotions*, edited by Christian von Scheve and Mikko Salmela (New York: Oxford University Press, 2014), 312–25.

77. Neal Krause and R. David Hayward, "Assessing Whether Practical Wisdom and Awe of God Are Associated with Life Satisfaction," *Psychology of Religion and Spirituality* 7, 1 (2015), 51–59; or, alternatively formulated as virtue attained through practice, Alasdair MacIntyre, *After Virtue: A Study in Moral Theory*, 2nd ed. (Notre Dame, IN: University of Notre Dame Press, 1984).

78. J. M. Kilner and R. N. Lemon, "What We Know Currently about Mirror Neurons," *Current Biology* 23, 23 (2013), R1057–R1062; Marco Iacoboni, "Imitation, Empathy, and Mirror Neurons," *Annual Review of Psychology* 60 (2009), 653–70.

research demonstrates that feelings are communicated vicariously in images and from situational cues that bring memories to mind, as well as from in-person interaction. And yet, physical co-presence is an important contributing factor because of somatic signals that would otherwise be missed, as well as the effects of coordination among multiple individuals and the likely duration and repetition of such action in ritual.[79] Research conducted in controlled experimental-design settings also attests to the importance of shared focus of attention: even when subjects are not physically co-present, knowing or imagining that others are attending to the same task results in higher levels of emotional intensification.[80]

A harder question is whether the emotions present in ritual can justifiably be termed *collective*, as Durkheim and Collins suggest, or whether emotions can ever be anything but individual attributes. Margaret Gilbert argues that this question has not been satisfactorily addressed by suggesting, as phenomenological approaches do, that collective emotion is merely the summation of individual emotions. A satisfactory understanding of collective emotions, she says, must include an "obligation criterion." Evidence of an obligation criterion is present when the parties involved feel that they *should* share certain emotions and feel they have a right to rebuke someone who does not share those emotions. If three friends are collectively excited about a fourth winning a prize, Gilbert suggests, and a fifth expresses anger toward the prize winner, the first three are likely to feel they have a right to rebuke the friend expressing anger. That right stems from their standing as joint members of a collectivity. In short, collective emotion reflects a sense of commitment to the group.[81]

---

79. Elaine Hatfield, John T. Cacioppo, and Richard L. Rapson, *Emotional Contagion* (New York: Cambridge University Press, 1994), provide evidence of the effects of physical proximity on participants' perceptions and mimicry of one another's emotions; the likelihood that ritual participants already know each other and share similar beliefs and demographic characteristics may also enhance emotional contagion, suggestive evidence of which is given in Joseph Chancellor et al., "Clustering by Well-Being in Workplace Social Networks: Homophily and Social Contagion," *Emotion* 17, 3 (2017), 553–67. Phillippe Verduyn, Iven Van Mechelen, and Francis Tuerlinckx, "The Relation Between Event Processing and the Duration of Emotional Experience," *Emotion* 11, 1 (2011), 20–28, provide evidence supporting the idea that social sharing behavior prolongs the duration of emotions.

80. Garriy Shteynberg et al., "Feeling More Together: Group Attention Intensifies Emotion," *Emotion* 14, 6 (2014), 1102–14.

81. Margaret Gilbert, "How We Feel: Understanding Everyday Collective Emotion Ascription," in *Collective Emotions*, edited by Christian von Scheve and Mikko Salmela (New York: Oxford University Press, 2014), 18–36.

Commitment to the group in this example is reinforced by the feelings the three friends express as well as by the fact that they were friends already. Sharing the feelings communicates that they are indeed a group, as does their sense that the angry friend has violated the common bond. In ritual, the sharing of feelings may function similarly; however, ritual also reinforces commitment to the collectivity apart from shared emotions. The collectivity's identity and individuals' commitment to the collectivity is shared behaviorally through the mere act of assembling. It is further expressed through the language that refers to the collectivity by name and that speaks on behalf of it. It is this sense of obligation that renders the ritual's feeling rules operative. The feeling rules do not have to generate the "torrential," "outlandish," "unleashed" frenzy that Durkheim's description of collective effervescence illustrates.[82] The feeling rules can just as well encourage the ritual participants to sit with bowed heads and folded hands.

The feelings felt and displayed in ritual are thus situational, governed by feeling rules and guided by expectations and acts that quiet the soul in some instances and in others, as Birgit Meyer observes of Pentecostal churches in Ghana, "heat up and intensify religious feelings."[83] The places in which ritual occurs, the affordances present, and the expectations people bring from having been in similar situations communicate the rules that guide the feelings experienced. The experience can be thought of as a kind of first-order and second-order event, Timothy Nelson suggests. The first order consists of the spatial, temporal, and formulaic aspects of the situation that predispose people to have certain feelings or to think that having them will be appropriate. The second order occurs as the event unfolds and includes an intensification of feelings or a display of feelings, perhaps magnified by the presence of others, and given additional spiritual meaning by the words and gestures included in the ritual.[84]

---

82. Émile Durkheim, *The Elementary Forms of Religious Life*, trans. Karen E. Fields (New York: Free Press, 1995 [1912]), 218–20; valuable background on emotion in Durkheim's earlier work is given in Jonathan S. Fish, "Religion and the Changing Intensity of Emotional Solidarities in Durkheim's *The Division of Labor in Society* (1893)," *Journal of Classical Sociology* 2, 2 (2002), 203–23.

83. Birgit Meyer, "Religious Sensations: Why Media, Aesthetics, and Power Matter in the Study of Contemporary Religion," in *Religion: Beyond a Concept*, edited by Hent de Vries (New York: Fordham University Press, 2008), 704–23, quote on page 709.

84. Timothy J. Nelson, "Transformations: The Social Construction of Religious Ritual," in *Understanding Religious Ritual: Theoretical Approaches and Innovations*, edited by John P. Hoffman (New York: Routledge, 2012), 9–31.

Ritual conceived of as situational may evoke intense emotion when it is part of an emotive institution that facilitates the expectations, interaction, scripts, and feeling rules that encourage people to have and to express certain feelings. Pamela Klassen suggests that "ritual weeping," for example, is so thoroughly scripted as to the timing and manner in which it occurs that critical outsiders are often tempted to view it as inauthentic, but argues that the feeling rules nevertheless enable expressions of authentic emotion. Much depends on differences in expectations.[85] Religious rituals are emotional in some situations and devoid of emotion in others. The same gathering that sheds tears at a christening or wedding may be as stoic as stones during a high mass. The situational variability of ritual is also the basis for arguments separating events that include "spiritually moving" emotions from religion. The familiar story of Sheila that Bellah and his co-authors describe as a person who is not sufficiently rooted in a religious community, for instance, has prompted studies questioning whether Sheila may have been mischaracterized. She was a nurse caring for dying children, after all, which suggested that she must have had some moral strength from somewhere even if she was not formally religious.

Don Grant, Kathleen O'Neil, and Laura Stephens conducted a study of nurses caring for dying patients to see what may have been missed in the Sheila story. The answer was that the hospital in which the nurses worked included ritual situations in which deep emotions could be expressed. The rituals were not religious or formalized but were, as Nelson suggests, situations that predisposed people toward certain feelings and then were magnified and given spiritual meaning. The hospital and the frequency with which the nurses dealt with dying patients provided context. The nurses struggled with their own grief. "In a backward way I have learned to live and love in the moment," one nurse explained. "There are many good things to be found in sadness and pain—like tenderness and hope and kindness. It centers me spiritually. It gives me a window to look into the best of what humanity has to offer. No books. No interpretation. Just the constancy of what is right in the world."[86]

---

85. Pamela E. Klassen, "Ritual," in *The Oxford Handbook of Religion and Emotion*, edited by John Corrigan (New York: Oxford University Press, 2007), 144–68; see also Pamela E. Klassen, "Ritual Appropriation and Appropriate Ritual: Christian Healing and Adaptations of Asian Religions," *History and Anthropology* 16, 3 (2005), 377–91.

86. Don Grant, Kathleen O'Neil, and Laura Stephens, "Spirituality in the Workplace: New Empirical Directions in the Study of the Sacred," *Sociology of Religion* 65, 3 (2004), 265–83; quote on page 276.

An important caveat to the emphasis on rituals as distinct situations in which intense emotions occur is the fact that people bring ideas to these situations about what they expect to experience. These expectations include ideas not only about what they will feel during the ritual but also about how long these feelings will last, such as feeling a warm glow in the coming days from having communed with fellow believers or from having helped someone in need. Social psychologists call these expectations *affective forecasts*. And social psychological studies show that people systematically overestimate how long the feelings will last: how long they will feel good after a positive experience or bad after a negative one. This is called the *durability bias*. Further research suggests that durability bias is shaped by feeling rules. For instance, a television commercial may proclaim that a prescription medication will bring "lasting relief," or a movie may suggest that a bereaved person will be overwhelmed with grief for years.[87]

Religious practices include feeling rules with similar implications. Insofar as religious practices are to be taken seriously, feeling rules may suggest that a sacred experience will be not only intense but also life-transforming, much more so than worldly pleasures ("disappointing ports of call"), or that a sinful act will bring a lifetime of guilt and shame.[88] Religious organizations also compete with one another by communicating different feeling rules. For instance, a congregation in which people hear repeatedly that the faithful can expect all their days to be filled with joy is quite different from one that encourages believers to expect good days and bad days. The one may provide ritual occasions for people to express (and thus reinforce) their happy feelings, while the other's events are likely to focus more on acknowledging dismay. As with other feeling rules, the disjuncture between what people expect to feel and what they do feel poses an organizational challenge.

The fact that religious organizations compete with one another and with nonreligious sources of authority is an important connection with Durkheim's emphasis on ritual's role in drawing cultural distinctions (i.e., setting things

---

87. Stacy L. Wood and James R. Bettman, "Predicting Happiness: How Normative Feeling Rules Influence (and Even Reverse) Durability Bias," *Journal of Consumer Psychology* 17, 3 (2007), 188–201.

88. "Disappointing ports of call" is one of the many phrases distinguishing worldly pleasures from life-transforming spiritual experience in the Prodigal Son sermons discussed in Marsha Witten, *All Is Forgiven: The Secular Message in American Protestantism* (Princeton, NJ: Princeton University Press, 1993), 67; examples of religious arguments against transitory good feelings are also given in Paul Froese, *On Purpose: How We Create the Meaning of Life* (New York: Oxford University Press, 2016).

apart). Differentiation of this sort is based less on rational calculation than on distinctions between "us" and "them," which in turn reflect bonds of in-group solidarity.[89] These bonds are emotive as well as cognitive and behavioral. An emotional valence differentiates insiders from outsiders. Christian Smith, for example, argues that late-twentieth-century American evangelicals maintained their sense of subcultural identity, despite largely having embraced mainstream culture, by emphasizing feelings of being culturally threatened.[90] Jason Bivins's *Religion of Fear: The Politics of Horror in Conservative Evangelicalism* takes the argument a step further, showing how feeling threatened is reinforced by teachings about evil, demons, violence, and the apocalypse.[91] Rules about the expression of feelings also distinguish between insiders and outsiders. Fanaticism in eighteenth- and nineteenth-century America, for example, was an allegation toward marginalized religious groups that charged them with displaying too much emotion and with substituting impulse for reasoned theological argument.[92]

Perhaps the clearest challenge to research emphasizing the feeling rules that are imposed by authorities such as airline companies and religious organizations is the fact that many people seek and claim to find emotionally moving experiences of the sacred in hybrid contexts in which the rules are neither known nor established authoritatively in advance. In these situations, practice theory draws attention to the processes through which leaders and non-leaders negotiate how to interpret sensory cues. Stories about what to expect, what has been experienced in the past, and how to share these experiences provide the grist with which rituals become or fail to become efficacious. In an interesting study of Christian and neo-Pagan rituals, for instance, Beth Dougherty describes the uncertainties that emerge in ritualized liminal spaces that through small interpretive narratives serve to create "moments of sensory ritual entrainment."[93]

---

89. See Elisa Heinämäki, "Durkheim, Bataille, and Girard on the Ambiguity of the Sacred: Reconsidering Saints and Demoniacs," *Journal of the American Academy of Religion* 83, 2 (2015), 513–36, on this emphasis in Durkheim.

90. Christian Smith, *American Evangelicals: Embattled and Thriving* (Chicago: University of Chicago Press, 1998).

91. Jason C. Bivins, *Religion of Fear: The Politics of Horror in Conservative Evangelicalism* (New York: Oxford University Press, 2008).

92. Numerous instances of accusations of fanaticism that illustrate the relational dynamics of feeling rules are discussed in Wuthnow, *American Misfits*.

93. Beth L. Dougherty, "Somatic Coordination: An Ethnography of Religious Entrainment in Christian and Neo-Pagan Rituals," *Sociology of Religion* 79, 1 (March 2018), 108–28, quote on page 125.

Feelings as Culture

The situational structuring of feelings includes input from the wider context in which these situations occur. Nurses having received training in spiritual and emotional as well as physical care and being part of a healthcare system that furthers the medicalization of suffering and pain are a case in point. The feelings we somatically experience also serve as cultural representations that inform our understandings of what is appropriate to feel. These representations, communicated in feeling words, interpretations of feelings, and emotion-laden visual images, provide scripts that prime our expectations. Not having experienced an apocalypse ourselves, we are invited to imagine what the experience might feel like by watching a horror film. We anticipate grief by reading novels, frustration by watching reality television, anger by listening to talk radio, and divine reverie by hearing it described in sermons. These are features of the emotioneering to which we are routinely exposed.

Among the several approaches to feelings as cultural representations, one that has been prominent in discussions of religion treats culture as a *zeitgeist* or worldview. It is instructive, for example, to think of the many ways in which American culture—and thus religion—is therapeutic in its emphasis on good feelings and self-fulfillment. It is similarly instructive to suggest that the contemporary *zeitgeist* is morally relativistic to the point of decisions being guided principally by feelings and for guilt, joy, anger, and fear to be ephemeral. Of course these generalizations are subject to the criticism "who is the we" when "we" is the object to which they are said to apply. All Americans? Only middle-class Americans? Only white middle-class Americans? Whose lives, Judith Butler asks, are grievable and whose lives are ungrievable?[94] Does a worship service pause to lament the plight of refugees, the victims of war, or only the death of a long-time member?

The fact that cultural representations differentially apply in terms of social class, race, gender, and region is further reason to emphasize that feelings are produced and, as Hochschild suggests, commercialized. Commercialization in turn suggests that markets and competition merit special consideration. As

---

94. Judith Butler, *Precarious Life: The Powers of Mourning and Violence* (London: Verso, 2005); Martha C. Nussbaum, *Upheavals of Thought: The Intelligence of Emotions* (New York: Cambridge University Press, 2001), who poses the same question, emphasizes the extent to which emotions are conditioned by the persons and objects relevant to the pursuit of personal goals.

Patricia Fernandez-Kelly posits, "expressive entrepreneurship" may increasingly be the means through which affective experience is marketed to consumers saturated with ordinary goods and services. An experience economy of this kind clearly exists in high-end arts consumption and in the posh ambience of upscale coffee shops. It may also be an impetus for religious organizations marketing aesthetically rich worship experiences and uplifting messages of purpose and happiness.[95]

In this respect, it also bears considering whether studies of religious experience, ritual, and spiritual support pay enough attention to the fear and trembling that accompanies practicing religion.[96] The feeling most akin to experiences deemed sacred is awe. Awe occurs when we witness something that we cannot imagine ourselves or anyone like us doing, such as a painting that makes us wonder how the artist accomplished it or a spectacular pass caught by a wide receiver. Mountains fill us with awe not only because of their beauty but also because they are more magnificent than any humanly constructed edifice. Durkheim's understanding of the sacred as the ritual symbolization of power on such an encompassing scale resembles awe in these respects. Whether an awe-inspiring work of art is deemed sacred or only special, though, depends on the interpretive framework the observer discovers in the situation.

Awe and dread are often interchangeable, both registering something about the relative insubstantiality of ordinary life. The two are conjoined in the phrase "fear of the sublime." The instinct is both to exalt and to flee. "In the nativity story," Paul Velde observes, "all nature rejoiced at the birth of the Incarnate God that the course of that night might not pass without wonders"—an instance of the sublime toward which it was inevitable both to marvel and to feel unworthy.[97] Schutz's meditation on Goethe's *Wilhelm Meister's Years of Travel* similarly emphasizes the shift from astonishment to fear of insignificance in the face of

---

95. Patricia Fernandez-Kelly, "A Howl to the Heavens: Art in the Life of First- and Second-Generation Cuban Americans," in *Art in the Lives of Immigrant Communities in the United States*, edited by Paul DiMaggio and Patricia Fernandez-Kelly (New Brunswick, NJ: Rutgers University Press, 2010), 52–71; on the experience economy, see B. Joseph Pine and James H. Gilmore, *The Experience Economy*, rev. ed. (Boston: Harvard Business School Press, 2011) and Daniel Hjorth and Monika Kostera, eds., *Entrepreneurship and the Experience Economy* (Fredericksberg, DK: Copenhagen Business School Press, 2014).

96. For a valuable reflection on religious studies' over-emphasis on upbeat religion, see Mark Larrimore, "Religion and the Promise of Happiness," *Social Research* 77, 2 (2010), 569–94.

97. Paul Velde, "Fear of the Sublime," *The Antioch Review* 68 (Spring 2010), 217–31, 395; quote on page 220.

that which transcends our mental capacity.[98] Geertz refers to it as bafflement.[99] Bafflement may be defined functionally as an essential and universal aspect of the sacred. But it, too, can be only special in the sense of something to ponder amid the many puzzlements of ordinary life.

It was to these puzzlements that Geertz returned years later in an essay on William James. Writing as much as a practice theorist as a cultural analyst, if Sherry Ortner's observations are correct, Geertz begins with James's own misgivings about how much *The Varieties of Religious Experience* dwelt on feelings. "I am almost appalled at the amount of emotionality which I find in it," James wrote. It was "literally bathed in sentiment," focusing on "secret selves" and "palpitating documents." James was aware that he was a creature of his times, Geertz suggests. The book reflected the Emersonian individualism of the period and the belief among intellectuals that religion was becoming subjectivized and its authority privatized. A century later, Geertz says, James's emphasis on interiority remains relevant. "Without some 'bathed in sentiment' sense that belief matters, [religion] is hardly worthy of the name." But Geertz argues that things are also quite different. Feelings have become dramatically public, inscribed with identity and power, which implies that they are not only inward ways of struggling with bafflement but also expressions of who one is and how one wants to be treated. Consider the case of modern Muslim women choosing to wear the *jilbab* (headscarf and long gown), Geertz suggests. The habit of wearing traditional Islamic clothing, they tell researchers, quiets their anxieties, allays their self-doubt, produces a sense of calm, and induces feelings of spiritual renewal. Wearing the *jilbab* is thus personal, but it is also public. The feelings are shared, discussed, and experienced in practice. They are part of the women's identity and a signifier of their place in society.[100]

Whether in the heights of divine elation, the depths of fear, or the small intersections of emotion and action in daily life, feelings then are significant aspects of the situations, habits, and rituals that constitute practicing religion. The point of thinking about feelings as practices is that they do not arise

---

98. Alfred Schutz, *Collected Papers VI. Literary Reality and Relationships*, edited by Michael Barber (New York: Springer, 2013), 345–46.

99. Clifford Geertz, *The Interpretation of Cultures: Selected Essays* (New York: Basic Books, 1973), 101.

100. Clifford Geertz, "'The Pinch of Destiny': Religion as Experience, Meaning, Identity, Power," *Raritan* 18, 3 (1999), 1–19; the quotes from James are included in Geertz's essay; Geertz's discussion of Muslim women is based on Suzanne Brenner, "Reconstructing Self and Society: Javanese Muslim Women and 'The Veil,'" *American Ethnologist* 23, 4 (1996), 673–97.

entirely unbidden from within, as we often think, but from social interaction governed by feeling rules. We reveal our conformity to these rules when we express emotion in one situation and suppress it in another. Religion is but one of the contexts in which these rules are learned. They may differ from the rules that guide our emotions in other situations, serving as a refuge from the world—even facilitating emotion in such intensity that it seems sacred. Whether that is the case, religion's contribution to the complex messages that govern the experience and display of feelings is one of its most important societal roles.

5

Bodies

TO SAY that practices are embodied is to say that they are materially constituted in the physical structures and movements of the human body and through the somatic learning that inhabits the body, as well as in bodily appearances and performances that are enacted through posture, facial expressions, grooming, and dress.[1] Interest among social scientists in the role of embodiment in religious practice builds on theoretical work in the Durkheimian tradition and is based on anthropological studies of ritual, healing, and sacrifice. Although *Elementary Forms* provided precedent for studies of religion to focus on mental systems of classification, Durkheim remarked extensively on the tattooing and painting of bodies, the sacralization of hair and blood, the co-presence of bodies in rituals, and the mythic vitality of bodily symbolism. Sacred power

---

1. Theoretical treatments of the role of bodies and embodiment in relation to human personhood, self-concepts, agentic action, consciousness, and practice are discussed from various perspectives in Arthur W. Frank, "For a Sociology of the Body: An Analytical Review," in *The Body: Social Process and Cultural Theory*, edited by Mike Featherstone, Mike Hepworth, and Bryan S. Turner (London: Sage, 1991), 36–101; Rom Harré, *Physical Being: A Theory for a Corporeal Psychology* (Cambridge, MA: Basil Blackwell, 1991); Tim Ingold, *Being Alive: Essays on Movement, Knowledge and Description* (New York: Routledge, 2011); Willis F. Overton, "Embodiment from a Relational Perspective," in *Developmental Perspectives on Embodiment and Consciousness*, edited by Willis F. Overton, Ulrich Müller, and Judith L. Newman (New York: Lawrence Erlbaum, 2008), 1–18; Christian Smith, *What Is a Person? Rethinking Humanity, Social Life, and the Moral Good from the Person Up* (Chicago: University of Chicago Press, 2010); Dennis S. Waskul and Phillip Vannini, "Introduction: The Body in Symbolic Interaction," in *Body/Embodiment: Symbolic Interaction and the Sociology of the Body*, edited by Dennis S. Waskul and Phillip Vannini (New York: Routledge, 2006), 1–20; and Frances Mascia-Lees, "The Body and Embodiment in the History of Feminist Anthropology," in *Mapping Feminist Anthropology in the Twenty-First Century*, edited by Ellen Lewin and Leni M. Silverstein (New Brunswick, NJ: Rutgers University Press, 2016), 146–67.

resided not only in collective representations but also in the flesh of ritual participants.[2] Marcel Mauss's work contributed not only to the study of primitive classification but also to the investigation of embodied practices. In "Techniques of the Body," Mauss posited that variation in bodily activities, such as swimming, marching, digging, running, sitting, sleeping, eating, weaning, and even positioning of the hands was a significant indication of variation in cultural practices, styles of learning, and understandings of efficiency. These, he suggested, were matters of social authority as well as of individual mastery. At the bottom of all our "mystical states," our means of entering into "communication with God," he wrote, "are techniques of the body."[3]

Maurice Merleau-Ponty's writing, grounded in Husserl's phenomenology, furthered an interest in the embodied character of human behavior. Unlike the relatively sparse attention embodiment received in semiotic and social psychological discussions, Merleau-Ponty emphasized that social theory could be advanced by attending to the Cartesian split between mind and body and between subject and object from the standpoint of embodiment. This perspective, he argued, provided greater understanding of persons' awareness and experience of their own body and its physical positioning in space, the habits that constitute the body's being toward the world, and the body's changing relationships with its environment. For Merleau-Ponty, the body was thus the site for investigating situational perception and intentionality in movement and positioning as well as its expression in gestures and speech.[4]

Although none were quite as pronounced as Merleau-Ponty's, other phenomenological inquiries seeking to transcend Cartesian distinctions included considerations of embodiment in work that otherwise became known for its contributions to the cultural turn. Building on Henri Bergson's interest in specifying the accessible realities of ordinary life, Alfred Schutz devoted attention to the bodily expressions exemplified in gestures, music, dance, and erotic relations. Schutz's concern with the cultural construction of reality included extensive remarks about actors' awareness of their bodies and their bodies' image

---

2. Émile Durkheim, *The Elementary Forms of Religious Life*, trans. Karen E. Fields (New York: Free Press, 1995 [1912]).

3. Marcel Mauss, "Techniques of the Body," *Economy and Society* 2 (1973 [1934], 70–88, quote on page 87.

4. Maurice Merleau-Ponty, *Phenomenology of Perception*, trans. Donald Landes (London: Routledge, 2012 [1945]); Edmund Husserl, *On the Phenomenology of the Consciousness of Internal Time* (New York: Springer, 1917 [1893]).

in the outer world. In both the actor's inner awareness and the responses from interlocutors, the body, Schutz argued, served uniquely as a source of duration that provided steadiness to social relations.[5] Berger and Luckmann's extension of Schutz's interest in the life-world similarly identified the body as the focal point around which the here and now of everyday reality was organized. Facial expressions and bodily movements were, in their analysis, means of communication, although of less interest than language, signs, and meanings.[6]

The influence of Mauss and Merleau-Ponty on practice theory has been a matter of interest in discussions tracing the etiology of Bourdieu's emphasis on habitus.[7] Mauss's references to Aristotle's discussion of habitus treated it as the culturally shaped bodily dispositions that manifested themselves in patterned ways of moving and gesturing. Merleau-Ponty's focus on embodiment offered Bourdieu insights about the mutual influences of structure and agency, habits and improvisation, ideas and materiality, and dispositions and intentions. Bourdieu argues that the corporeality of bodies serves as a focal point of persons' experience and action and at the same time is in constant adaptation to its dynamic situations. Judith Butler in an essay on Merleau-Ponty captures this relational quality of embodiment in observing: "The flesh is not something one has, but, rather, the web in which one lives; it is not simply what I touch of the other, or of myself, but the condition of possibility of touch, a tactility that exceeds any given touch, and that cannot be reducible to a unilateral action performed by a subject."[8] Bourdieu includes as examples of the embodiment of habitus the bodily movements, corporeal dispositions, rituals, embodied history, and generative adaptations of which action and interaction are constituted. A person learns to behave intuitively according to the manner the situation requires: the pace at which to walk and talk, the position of one's hands and the direction of one's gaze, the proper gendering of attire, and the range of

---

5. Alfred Schutz, *Collected Papers VI. Literary Reality and Relationships*, edited by Michael Barber (Dordrecht: Springer, 2013); on Bergeson's influence, see Helmut R. Wagner, "The Bergsonian Period of Alfred Schutz," *Philosophy and Phenomenological Research* 38 (1977), 187–99.

6. Peter L. Berger and Thomas Luckmann, *The Social Construction of Reality: A Treatise in the Sociology of Knowledge* (Garden City, NY: Doubleday, 1966).

7. See especially Carrie Noland, *Agency and Embodiment: Performing Gestures/Producing Culture* (Cambridge, MA: Harvard University Press, 2009), 18–54, and Herman Roodenburg, "Pierre Bourdieu: Issues of Embodiment and Authenticity," *Etnofoor* 17 1/2 (2004), 215–26.

8. Judith Butler, "Merleau-Ponty and the Touch of Malebranche," in *The Cambridge Companion to Merleau-Ponty*, edited by Taylor Carman and Mark B. N. Hansen (New York: Cambridge University Press, 2005), 181–205, quote on page 181.

tolerable deviations. The habitus, he says, is evident in posture and demeanor and in laughter and tears. It is inscribed in the bodies of prophets, kings, heirs, and infants, and in the gods made flesh.[9]

Interest in bodies and embodiment as aspects of religious practice has increased significantly in recent years. The empirical literature has emphasized the role of bodies in rituals of worship and devotion and the inescapable connections between religious practice and the physical realities of death, illness, and suffering. Studies of religion's materiality in icons, visual art, and the built environment have necessitated consideration of the gaze from which these artifacts are viewed and the haptic relationships that are frequently present. The theoretical literature has drawn extensively on phenomenology and practice theory, bringing bodies to center stage as the perceivers and shapers of reality. It has also registered continuing concern, sometimes at the expense of romanticization, in transcending Cartesian mind-body dualism. Holistic epistemologies evident in non-Western spiritual practices have been of particular interest, as has greater attention to the role of bodies in historical studies of Western traditions, and intersections in the study of religion and art. Once it is understood that religious beliefs, knowledge, teachings, rituals, and experiences are *practiced*, then it has become necessary to include consideration of the bodies of those who practice.[10]

---

9. Pierre Bourdieu, *The Logic of Practice*, trans. Richard Nice (Stanford, CA: Stanford University Press, 1990 [1980]), especially 66–79; for an excellent theoretical overview, see also Dimitri Ginev, "Conceptualizing the Human Body within Practice Theory," *Social Science Information* 58 (March 2019), 1–20.

10. Martha L. Finch, "Rehabilitating Materiality: Bodies, Gods, and Religion," *Religion* 42, 4 (2012), 625–31, offers qualitative and some quantitative evidence of the growth of interest in bodies and embodiment in religious studies. The work of Thomas J. Csordas played a particularly significant role in these developments; see especially Thomas J. Csordas, "Embodiment as a Paradigm for Anthropology," *Ethos* 18, 1 (1990), 5–47; Thomas J. Csordas, *The Sacred Self: A Cultural Phenomenology of Charismatic Healing* (Berkeley and Los Angeles: University of California Press, 1997); Thomas J. Csordas, "Prophecy and the Performance of Metaphor," *American Anthropologist* 99, 2 (1997), 321–32; and Thomas J. Csordas, "Toward a Cultural Phenomenology of Body-World Relations," in *Phenomenology in Anthropology*, edited by Kalpana Ram and Christopher Houston (Bloomington: Indiana University Press, 2015), 50–67. Contributions in sociology of religion are discussed in Meredith McGuire, "Embodied Practices: Negotiation and Resistance," in *Everyday Religion Observing Modern Religious Lives*, edited by Nancy Tatom Ammerman (New York: Oxford University Press, 2007), 187–200; and Nancy Tatom Ammerman, "Bodies and Spirits: Health, Illness, and Mortality," in *Sacred Stories, Spiritual Tribes: Finding Religion in Everyday Life*, edited by Nancy Tatom Ammerman (New York: Oxford University

In this chapter I discuss recent directions in the study of bodies and embodiment as features of religious practice. I suggest that treatments of these topics have matured beyond the discussions of a quarter century ago in which embodiment was advanced as an epistemological move from which to question the centrality of ideas, propositional knowledge, and beliefs. The lament that could be expressed in those years about the lack of concrete empirical examples—"the body that eats, that works, that dies, that is afraid—that body just isn't there"—no longer applies.[11] Those bodies are now everywhere, so much so in fact that they seem to run off in all directions, offering plenty of rich case material from which to argue that bodies matter, but needing to be brought into some kind of organization. It is the case that bodies are present when people engage in religious rituals and when healing services are performed and when religious membership is signified by distinctive attire; and yet, there is much more to be learned about *how* bodies matter.

I identify five directions that have been particularly productive of new insights: body routines, body rituals, body disciplines, bodies as representations, and "exceptional" bodies (ones that differ in important ways from the bodies we normally take for granted in ordinary life). Each of these lines of investigation demonstrates the value of contextualizing the study of religion in the situations in ordinary life in which they occur. The diversity of these situations requires attending to their substantive particularities rather than seeking abstract generalizations. The role of empirical investigation is to identify and refine the heuristic tools necessary to understand religious practices under further changing and further diversifying conditions. Studies reflect differing disciplinary orientations that prompt varying questions about the relevance of bodies in treatments of cognition, affect, and semiotic relationships.[12] However, there is agreement that bodies are a source of self-knowledge and intentionality. There

---

Press, 2013), 251–300; and for an earlier discussion, see Bryan S. Turner, *The Body and Society: Explorations in Social Theory* (New York: Oxford University Press, 1984). Interesting convergences with performance studies and sociology of science are described in Ben Spatz, "Embodiment as First Affordance: Tinkering, Tuning, and Tracking," *Performance Philosophy* 2, 2 (2017), 257–71; and Ben Spatz, *What a Body Can Do: Technique as Knowledge, Practice as Research* (New York: Routledge, 2015).

11. As discussed in Caroline Bynum, "Why All the Fuss about the Body? A Medievalist's Perspective," *Critical Inquiry* 22, 1 (1995), 1–33; quote on page 1.

12. Saba Mahmood, *Politics of Piety: The Islamic Revival and the Feminist Subject* (Princeton, NJ: Princeton University Press, 2005), especially chapter 5, provides a valuable discussion of alternative theoretical perspectives on embodiment.

is also general agreement that bodies are socially constructed in terms of norms about demeanor, gender, sexuality, and attire, and that bodies in these respects also play a significant role in communicating information about shared intentions and goals. To focus on bodies and embodiment, then, is not to emphasize only that bodies move or are the source of somatic sensations, but to investigate how movement and sensations are structured by the contexts in which they occur. Bodies in these approaches are understood to be relational, connected to and differentiated from other objects and persons and serving as interfaces in these relationships. A key emphasis, evident especially in studies of body routines, is that bodies must be understood as dynamic participants in the temporality of ongoing practices.

Body Routines

In 1862, a month after he died of tuberculosis, the *Atlantic Monthly* published Thoreau's essay "Walking," which ended with these words: "So we saunter toward the Holy Land, till one day the sun shall shine more brightly than ever he has done, shall perchance shine into our minds and hearts, and light up our whole lives with a great awakening light, as warm and serene and golden as on a bankside in autumn."[13] Walking was clearly a practice to which Thoreau attributed transcendent meaning.

Walking is the quintessential example of a body routine; indeed, few of the activities in which the human body engages are quite as routine as walking. Once it is learned and unless a mishap occurs, walking takes us from place to place without having to think much about it at all. Most of the activities Mauss

---

13. Henry David Thoreau, "Walking," *Atlantic Monthly* 9, 56 (June 1862), 657–74, quote on page 674; among the numerous discussions of Thoreau's essay, see Andrew Menard, "Nationalism and the Nature of Thoreau's 'Walking,'" *New England Quarterly* 85, 4 (2012), 591–621; G. Douglas Atkins, *Reading Essays: An Invitation* (Athens: University of Georgia Press, 2008), 93–102; Peter A. Fritzell, *Nature Writing and America: Essays Upon a Cultural Type* (Ames: Iowa State University Press, 1990); and Caroline Crosson Gilpin and Sarah Gross, "Text to Text: Henry David Thoreau's 'Walking' and 'Time to Write? Go Outside,'" *New York Times*, May 10, 2017; on the history of walking and of literary references to walking, see especially Joseph Amato, *On Foot: A History of Walking* (New York: NYU Press, 2004); Nicholas Blomley, *Rights of Passage: Sidewalks and the Regulation of Public Flow* (London: Routledge, 2011); Stephen Miller, *Walking New York: Reflections of American Writers from Walt Whitman to Teju Cole* (New York: Fordham University Press, 2015); and Rebecca Solnit, *Wanderlust: A History of Walking* (New York: Viking, 2000).

enumerates are similar: sitting, running, standing, eating, touching. Body routines are for the most part non-deliberative; though walking is intentional, it is the prior intention that directs it toward its goal (to meet a friend, to attend a class, to tour a garden, to let off steam), whereas the intention in action is indicated in the motion itself, which the body has learned and remembers how to perform automatically. Moreover, its automaticity propels the body in situationally appropriate ways—striding, sauntering, marching, hurrying, ambling, idling, transgressing—that communicate its meaning. Michel de Certeau refers to "pedestrian speech acts" through which the body signals its location of being at home, at ease, engaged, among strangers, or lost—"pedestrian" notably being the term that came into usage in the eighteenth century to connote the commonplace, prosaic, ordinary person who goes on foot. Cities, Certeau writes, are practices in which the ordinary practitioners are "walkers, Wandersmänner, whose bodies follow the thicks and thins of an urban 'text' they write without being able to read it."[14]

Walking is notably present in accounts of religious practice and meditative experience. Nearly all of the accounts William James includes in *Varieties of Religious Experience* mention walking, often in the woods, along a beach, or in some special solitary location.[15] Mircea Eliade writes, "Even the most habitual gesture can signify a spiritual act. The road and walking can be transfigured into religious values, for every road can symbolize the 'road of life,' and any walk a 'pilgrimage,' a peregrination to the Center of the World."[16] Thoreau's allusion to the Holy Land is steeped in the lineages of romanticism and biblical narrative. "I can only meditate when I am walking," Rousseau asserted, "When I stop, I cease to think; my mind only works with my legs."[17] Walking is a frequent topic in contemporary discussions of spirituality as well. Don DeLillo in *White Noise* treats walking both in the routines of everyday life and in an imagined encounter with a bear in the woods as a metaphor for examining the characters' transformative terror of their own death and quest for symbolic

---

14. Michael de Certeau, *The Practice of Everyday Life* (Berkeley and Los Angeles: University of California Press, 1984), 93–94; on pedestrians and urban walking, see Jo Vergunst, "Key Figure of Mobility: The Pedestrian," *Social Anthropology* 25, 1 (2017), 13–27.

15. William James, *The Varieties of Religious Experience: A Study in Human Nature* (Adelaide, South Australia: University of Adelaide Library, 2005 [1902]).

16. Mircea Eliade, *The Sacred and the Profane: The Nature of Religion* (New York: Harcourt, Brace & World, 1959), 183.

17. Jean-Jacques Rousseau, *The Confessions*, trans J. M. Cohen (New York: Penguin Books, 1953 [1765]), 382.

immortality.[18] Buddhist walking meditation has gained popular appeal as a method of achieving mindfulness, as has labyrinth walking.[19] Sauntering in nature, as Thoreau did, seems particularly conducive to spiritual associations. As one of Nancy Tatom Ammerman's interviewees remarked, "I am always amazed when I take a walk at what's around us. What was created. And so that kind of helps center you, I think, and gives you some calm." Elizabeth Drescher's research among religiously unaffiliated Americans found that a few even considered routine dog walking a spiritual practice.[20]

There are several levels at which walking with or without a dog as a spiritual practice might be analyzed. In many accounts such as those of Ammerman's and Drescher's interviewees, observing that someone *considers* walking a spiritual practice is sufficiently interesting, apparently because walking is an instance demonstrating that people connect spirituality with activities that occur in daily life and have no obvious connections with religious organizations. Walking is thus "spiritual" because someone says it is, and if further evidence were needed as to why it might be, the argument would rest on statements about walking being a time to relax, reflect, and ponder the meaning of life. A more complex and interesting argument would bring social interaction into the picture, even when spiritual walking occurs alone, by suggesting that the person may have heard walking described as a spiritual practice from a parent or friend or observed a person walking who somehow appeared to be in a meditative state. Having heard it described this way might further suggest possible circuitous connections with organized religion; for example, in statements about walking in the wilderness, walking to the promised land, and walking with God. How these metaphoric connections relate to body routines, though, necessitates additional explication.

One connection is relatively straightforward once walking is conceived of as a practice. Practice theory suggests that walking is not only a set of movements that the body performs automatically, but is better understood as an iterative process in which information about the body, the situation, thoughts,

---

18. Don DeLillo, *White Noise* (New York: Penguin, 1984).

19. Maddy Cunningham, *Integrating Spirituality in Clinical Social Work Practice: Walking the Labyrinth* (Boston: Pearson Education, 2012).

20. Nancy Tatom Ammerman, "Spiritual Practices in Everyday Life," in *Sacred Stories, Spiritual Tribes: Finding Religion in Everyday Life*, edited by Nancy Tatom Ammerman (New York: Oxford University Press, 2013), 57–104, quote on page 84; Elizabeth Drescher, *Choosing Our Religion: The Spiritual Lives of America's Nones* (New York: Oxford University Press, 2016), 140.

and goals interact. A person who says walking is a spiritual practice, and means it, is likely referring to interpretations that happened not only after the fact but also in real time, as in passing a magnificent tree and having one's memory cued to think about other moments of being awed with grandeur, or noticing fatigue and reflecting on one's passing years and the need to slow down. Understood this way, walking is of interest as a routine because routines occur in time and space and recur in familiar places that prompt memories of the thoughts and feelings that happen in those places. In its physical manifestations, walking is a way of being, of moving, a source of aches and pains, a sensation of strength or weakness, an upright stance that affects what a person sees and how the body touches its environment. Significantly, Ammerman's interviewee not only walks but *sees*.

An additional connection requires considering the manner in which language about spirituality and routine acts of walking may be linked. Courtney Handman's ethnographic research among Christians in Papua New Guinea provides insights into these links. The remote community Handman studied had become Christian in the 1970s based on a New Testament translation that convinced the believers of having a direct relationship with God. After several decades, though, the community was left with doubts about that relationship and focused more on the religious implications of having to walk to the nearest urban center because of lacking a vehicular road. Handman was interested in how this transition from a linguistic to a bodily link with religion had taken place. Homologies between linguistic movement and physical movement are common, she acknowledges. Both are media that convey something from here to there. Religious language is replete with metaphors both of physical movement and of infrastructure. Pilgrims walk through the valley of the shadow of death, forgive those who trespass against them, seek to avoid the wide path that leads to destruction, and so on. But different religions and different experiences posit different relationships. Metaphoric homologies are more commonly Protestant, she argues, whereas pilgrimages that literally take place along specific geographic paths are more commonly Catholic. For the Papua New Guineans she studied, Handman found that walking's spiritual connotations were grounded in their physical walking, which was arduous and seemed to them to not get anywhere. The vehicular road they did not have seemed heavenly, whereas the laborious walking they did connoted being forsaken of God.[21]

---

21. Courtney Handman, "Walking Like a Christian: Roads, Translation, and Gendered Bodies as Religious Infrastructure in Papua New Guinea," *American Ethnologist* 44, 2 (2017), 315–27.

Handman's study is instructive for thinking about other ways in which walking can be understood as more than simply a physical activity with potential spiritual meaning. The manner in which routine walking ordinarily takes place interacts with the spiritual meanings with which it is possibly associated. There is no one-to-one connection of the kind that suggests a deterministic influence of bodily activities on beliefs. However, a person whose spiritual practice includes walking the dog would probably be less inclined to consider workplace treks from cubicle to cubicle and from work station to coffee machine and back the same way. A person walking a labyrinth isn't expecting to "get somewhere," only to be mindful in the moment precisely because of not having a destination to achieve. In contrast, a person schooled in Bunyan's *Pilgrim's Progress* walks toward a celestial destination with temptation and forbearance along the way. Unlike the Papua New Guineans Handman studied, spiritual practitioners in affluent industrialized contexts have greater freedom in deciding to walk or ride or to drive the fast road or the slow route and to think about where and when it might be most appropriate to assign spiritual meanings to these activities. There is nevertheless congruence in thinking that a person who feels spiritual walking the dog might be imagining it to be spiritually refreshing because it is not laborious and that commuting on a busy toll road might be less conducive to such associations.

The fact that, in contrast to Handman's subjects, much more of persons' who live in industrialized societies time is spent driving and "passengering" than walking underscores the importance of considering body routines in the ordinary contexts in which they occur and not as romanticized practices that happen in distant places. The woman Orsi describes throwing a saint onto the back seat of her old Chevy for failing to answer her prayers is engaged in a body routine—driving—as much as a person walking in the woods.[22] "Manspreading" (sitting with one's legs positioned to prevent someone else from being seated) is a meaningful trope in writing about gendered dominance and submission because passengering is a familiar body routine. Nigel Thrift, drawing on Jack Katz's ethnographic observations of driving in Los Angeles, suggests that "automobility" can be considered a body routine in the same way that de Certeau did walking.[23] Katz found that drivers experienced cars as extensions

---

22. Robert A. Orsi, "The Problem of the Holy," in *Cambridge Companion to Religious Studies*, edited by Robert A. Orsi (New York: Cambridge University Press, 2016), 84–106, quote on page 98.

23. Nigel Thrift, "Driving in the City," *Theory, Culture & Society* 21, 4/5 (2004), 41–59; see also the related discussion of "automobilised time-space" in John Urry, "The 'System' of Automobility," *Theory, Culture & Society* 21, 4/5 (2004), 25–39.

of their bodies both in physically taking them from place to place and in supplying the prosthetics with which to signal intentions and to express rage. The body routines that became automatic included the drivers' posture for driving, gripping the steering wheel, becoming familiar with road noise and bumps, and swaying around curves.[24] Understood this way, automobiles are more than symbols of social status and more than symptoms of living in a culture of conspicuous consumption. They are practices that function as body routines. And as such, automobiling is a body routine in which spirituality may be inscribed, as in feeling the protective hand of an angel when automobiling safely on a crowded expressway or when experiencing a near accident. Susan Harding's much-cited example of feeling spoken to by the holy spirit when nearly having an automobile collision after a lengthy interview with a fundamentalist pastor takes on additional meaning in this light. It was not only that the words penetrated her disbelieving psyche but also that the body routine of automobiling established the immediate context for the unanticipated response she experienced.[25]

Body routines other than walking that appear frequently in discussions of religion include kneeling, bowing, genuflecting, lifting one's hands, and of course sitting. The difference between these routines and walking the dog is that they may be even less intentional as sources of spiritual meaning, performed non-deliberatively in acts of prayer and worship simply as what the body has grown accustomed to doing. They vary in meaning and intentionality depending on the situation, how distinct it is from non-religious settings, and what the religious tradition teaches about the scriptural significance of bodies.[26] The bodily movement involved in kneeling and bowing is familiar and versatile, yet perhaps is rarely practiced except in religious devotion, whereas sitting is sufficiently common that a person sitting in a worship service may not consider it important even though it would be recognized as such upon reflection. Attire is another aspect of body routines that often has religious meaning, either

---

24. Jack Katz, *How Emotions Work* (Chicago: University of Chicago Press, 2000).

25. Susan Friend Harding, *The Book of Jerry Falwell: Fundamentalist Language and Politics* (Princeton, NJ: Princeton University Press, 2000), 33–60.

26. Samir Ben-Layashi, "'Muslim Body' versus 'Jewish Body': The Invention of a Division," in *A History of Jewish-Muslim Relations: From the Origins to the Present Day*, edited by Abdelwahab Meddeb and Benjamin Stora (Princeton, NJ: Princeton University Press, 2013), 1042–51, offers the interesting observation that literature by and about Muslims drew close connections between bodies and religious texts, whereas Jewish bodies were discussed apart from scripture.

because it is literally the habit that religious practitioners wear or because an adornment, item of jewelry, or style of clothing has come to be associated with a religious practice. What constitutes something as a body routine, what gives it religious relevance, and how it differs from disciplines, rituals, and symbols, though, requires consideration. Routine bodily motions rarely require conscious thought, and yet it is clear that reflection and interpretation are an important part of what makes some body routines meaningful as religious practices. And, while they may be personally meaningful, they are also social in how they are understood and in what they communicate.

Mauss's observation that walking, weaning, swimming, and other bodily movements take differing forms in differing cultures provides the basis for identifying two important characteristics of body routines: they are mimetic and versatile. Basic bodily routines are learned by mimicry, as in the case of infants learning to walk by imitating what they see older children and adults doing. This is the reason similar patterns can be identified widely in a society despite local variations in many other beliefs and practices. Versatility means that unlike many other activities they are not situation-specific. They instead consist of simple skills that can be effectively applied in many different situations.[27] They are thus routine in the sense of in fact being repeated in many different contexts. A further characteristic is that they are for the most part internally repetitive (e.g., walking as compared with playing a sonata), which adds to their automaticity. Body routines are thus one of the prime examples of habit: a person walks, sits, defecates, dresses, and eats largely by habit. The cues that prompt each activity are situational and include somatic sensations (feeling hungry, tired, restless) as well as external signals (the arrival of a friend for a visit, a phone call from the dentist's office). The responses are nevertheless bundled such that the cognitive schematization that takes place consists of overarching terms such as "walking" or "eating" rather than focusing on each of the muscular actions involved.

Body routines that acquire religious meaning include these characteristics of being mimetic, versatile, simple, and internally repetitive. Practitioners who meditate as they walk already know how to walk, as do those who kneel in prayer

---

27. Thomas Fuchs, "The Phenomenology of Body Memory," in *Body Memory, Metaphor and Movement*, edited by Sabine C. Koch et al. (Philadelphia: John Benjamins, 2012), 9–22, refers to this versatility as the *plasticity* of body memory; see also Thomas Fuchs, "Body Memory and the Unconscious," in *Founding Psychoanalysis: Phenomenological Theory of Subjectivity and the Psychoanalytical Experience*, edited by Dieter Lohmar and Jagna Brudzinska (Dordrecht: Kluwer, 2011), 69–82, on repressed body memory.

already know how to kneel or who listen to homilies having learned to listen at home or in school.[28] Special body routines such as making the sign of the cross are easily learned by watching and imitating the few simple motions involved. Although the emphasis in most discussions of embodied routines is on the practitioner, these routines also sometimes affect persons merely observing them. In one study, for example, a woman who had been raised Catholic recalled, "I would look at the little old ladies on either side of me and I'd see their lips moving. I'd see the rosary beads going and there was something that they connected to. It wasn't something that I felt at that point but I knew that there was something to feel. The lights, the candles, it was very, very powerful. It was very visceral. It was very much in my body."[29]

Helena Kupari's study of the daily religious practices of Karelian Orthodox women examined the body routines that meaningfully contributed to their faith. Now in their seventies, the women lived in the part of Finland ceded to the Soviet Union after World War II. Their practices were ones they had learned during childhood from their mothers and were sufficiently simple and versatile that they had continued unbroken throughout their lives, during the war, under Soviet rule, and after the collapse of the Soviet Union. Invoking Bourdieu, Kupari says the practices constituted the "native layer of the women's habitus"; they were "sedimented into the body" as habits that their bodies knew how to do without conscious thought. The daily rhythm started with a brief silent prayer while bathing, continued with a mealtime prayer, making the sign of the cross when leaving the table, and making it again whenever leaving the house; it included blessing the dough when making bread and crossing oneself when passing an icon. Their bodies knew the appropriate situations in which to pray.[30]

---

28. Mundane bodily practices such as walking, kneeling, sitting, and listening are important reminders that embodiment in religion is not restricted to highly differentiated practices such as distinctive attire, grooming, and ritual performance; on listening, see especially Charles Hirschkind, *The Ethical Soundscape: Cassette Sermons and Islamic Counterpublics* (New York: Columbia University Press, 2006), and on the "desensualized" bodies present in many secular settings, Charles Hirschkind, "Is There a Secular Body?" *Cultural Anthropology* 26, 4 (2011), 633–47; Talal Asad, "Thinking about the Secular Body, Pain, and Liberal Politics," in *Words: Religious Language Matters*, edited by Ernst Van den Hemel and Asja Szafraniec (New York: Fordham University Press, 2016), 348–63.

29. Robert Wuthnow, *All in Sync: How Music and Art Are Revitalizing American Religion* (Berkeley and Los Angeles: University of California Press, 2003), 83.

30. Helena Kupari, "'Remembering God' through Religious Habits: The Daily Religious Practices of Evacuee Karelian Orthodox Women," *Temenos* 47, 2 (2011), 197–222, quote on page 199.

What it means to say that "bodies knew" requires distinguishing the act itself from the situation in which it occurs. The habitual motion of crossing oneself, kneeling, or bowing one's head—what Merleau-Ponty called the "corporeal schema"—is implicit knowledge that governs the positioning and exertion of the relevant muscles. This implicit knowledge is what the literature typically refers to as "body memory."[31] It does not require conscious thought even though it is sufficiently adaptable that a person does not walk, sit, or kneel the same way every time. Its regularity allows it to be performed as habit rather than having to be learned anew each time. The situations that cue these routine movements are in the case of the Karelian women sufficiently recurring— embedded mostly in the private domestic rhythms of daily life—that the repetition also contributes to their automaticity. The same is true of acts that are not as selective as routine prayers. Judith Butler, for instance, argues that gender is constituted through a "stylized repetition of acts." It is the bodily gestures, movements, and stylized performances—"styles of the flesh"—that become taken for granted as common definitions of gender.[32] Butler's argument resembles Frantz Fanon's claim that bodies are similarly racialized through implicit adaptations—"a definitive structuring of my self and the world"—to the recurring details the situations supply.[33] On these accounts, gender and race are constituted in routine religious practices just as they are in other stylized acts.

The religion-based body routines that most publicly and enduringly function as "styles of the flesh" are structured both in the acts that people perform and in the responses those acts elicit. The distinctive attire worn among religious practitioners is a familiar example. Just as Fanon found himself responding viscerally to being pointed out as a black man, so do Catholic and Buddhist nuns in habit, the Amish, Sikhs, Muslims, Orthodox Jews, and others who become bodily structured through the comments, looks, and body language of those they encounter. Clothing, beards, hairstyles, jewelry, veiling, and other adornments mark the body, setting it apart in the eyes of onlookers who shape its meaning by responding in ways that variously suggest respect or derision, or, in the case of verbal and physical attacks, are meant to threaten and intimidate.

---

31. Edward S. Casey, *Remembering: A Phenomenological Study* (Bloomington: Indiana University Press, 2000), 146–80, is a good discussion of body memory; Casey distinguishes three kinds of body memory: performance remembering (driving a car), traumatic memory (a toothache), and erotic memory (orgasm).

32. Judith Butler, *Gender Trouble* (New York: Routledge, 2002), 177, 179.

33. Frantz Fanon, *Black Skin, White Masks*, trans. Richard Philcox (New York: Grove Press, 2008 [1952]), 89–118, quote on page 91.

The subjective connotations of adornments for the devotee vary similarly, ranging from rejection and fear to pride, spiritual conviction, and well-being. A study of Muslim women in the Netherlands that asked about face veiling, for example, demonstrated how the garb that seemed peculiar to outsiders felt right to the persons wearing it. The veil felt good, the women said. They felt inner peace and strength wearing it. The tactility of how it felt reminded them that they were engaging in a religious practice through which they expressed their love of God. The veil also affected their behavior. As one explained, "You should not hang around and talk loudly, that does not go together with wearing a face veil."[34] It was, in short, a practice in which virtue was embodied.

Bodily affordances' affective power reflects practitioners' submission to religious authority. Voluntary submission is evident not only in matters of adornment but also in choices about sex, birth control, pregnancy, and abortion. Pamela Klassen's study of women choosing to give birth at home, for example, found that the choice for some represented a decision to let a religious organization supply the event with sacred meaning, while for others the decision constituted a desire to resist the authority of the medical industry.[35] Extreme instances of involuntary submission include genital mutilation and the withholding of blood transfusions and other medical treatments from children. The authority under which bodily submission is sustained is in turn subject to cultural and political influences and to conflicting interpretations within religious communities. Among Palestinian women during the last quarter of the twentieth century, for example, Annelies Moors found that the customary purchase, receipt, and wearing of gold jewelry became highly contested in conjunction with its changing origins and availability. Traditionally valued as both an economic resource and a religious symbol, the jewelry continued to be prominently related to marriage and kinship, but whether it came from Russia, Italy, or India was as important as how it looked. Women worried about the social statuses it signaled to the point that some eschewed wearing it at all.[36]

---

34. Annelies Moors, "The Affective Power of the Face Veil: Between Disgust and Fascination," in *Things: Religion and the Question of Materiality*, edited by Dick Houtman and Birgit Meyer (New York: Fordham University Press, 2012), 287.

35. Pamela E. Klassen, *Blessed Events: Religion and Home Birth in America* (Princeton, NJ: Princeton University Press, 2001).

36. Annelies Moors, "Wearing Gold, Owning Gold: The Multiple Meanings of Gold Jewelry," *Etnofoor* 25, 1 (2013), 78–89.

How religiously adorned bodies are strategically engaged in social relationships is further evidenced in studies of subversion. Evelyn Brooks Higginbotham's study of late-nineteenth-century urban African American women's churchgoing practices offers a striking example of attire purposefully deployed to subvert class-based racial exclusion and the self-images associated with it. With encouragement from prominent women church leaders, women *dressed up*, wearing Sunday dresses and hats that contrasted with weekday garb and communicated higher status in the community.[37]

Nearly the opposite kind of subversion was evident in Gerardo Marti and Gladys Ganiel's study of young adults' participation in "emerging church" worship services. Besides favoring services that differed from established churches in musical selections and liturgical styles, practitioners subverted traditional norms of "Sunday best" attire by wearing tank tops, T-shirts, blue jeans, and cutoffs. Worshipping in clothing they wore at home and on other occasions whenever they could made them feel more authentic, they said, and thus closer to God.[38] In a wider context, Daniel Miller and Sophie Woodward argue that blue jeans are the adornment through which ordinariness is achieved, which is a way of subverting ethnic, racial, and national subcultural categories, most notably among young adults who wish to disguise their class-based backgrounds and among second-generation immigrants distancing themselves from parents and countries of origin. Ordinariness is a universal adornment that signals identity with no group other than perhaps one's age cohort and in its invisibility also provides a space with which to assert individuality by other means such as piercings and tattoos.[39]

There is a more radical kind of subversion too that not only contrasts with convention but mocks it in a way that brings it into awareness as the cultural construction that it is. This is the subversion that theater and masquerade accomplish: the actor that masquerades as a priest or a witch, and the impersonator, mime, or cross-dresser. Subversion works, Butler suggests, not only by deviating from the taken-for-granted norms but also by revealing them through imitation. Drag subverts gender norms, she says, by demonstrating that gender

---

37. Evelyn Brooks Higginbotham, *Righteous Discontent: The Women's Movement in the Black Baptist Church, 1880–1920* (Cambridge, MA: Harvard University Press, 1994).

38. Gerardo Marti and Gladys Ganiel, *The Deconstructed Church: Understanding Emerging Christianity* (New York: Oxford University Press, 2014).

39. Daniel Miller and Sophie Woodward, *Blue Jeans: The Art of the Ordinary* (Berkeley and Los Angeles: University of California Press, 2012).

is a performance. It creates a picture of a woman that can be compared with what otherwise is accepted implicitly as what a woman naturally is.[40] Peter Morey and Amina Yaqin follow Butler's lead in their analysis of post-9/11 comedic performances that sought to subvert popular Western misconceptions of Islam. Britain's most prominent Muslim comedian, Shazia Mirza, for example, "troubled existing categories and dividing lines" by wearing the traditional hijab during her performances in the "macho beer-swilling world of London's pubs and clubs from which 'Good Muslims' were by definition self-excluded." The hijab at one level dramatized the distance between Islam and these Western settings, while at another level functioned as a kind of masquerade that challenged audiences to re-examine taken-for-granted images of Muslim women.[41]

The intentional rejection and setting aside of body routines differs from subversion in the extent of necessary adaptation that ensues. To permanently abandon a body routine is to leave part of oneself behind. Lynn Davidman's interviews with ex-Orthodox Jewish women, for example, found that they sometimes felt as if a limb had been amputated. They felt uncomfortable wearing ordinary clothes and didn't quite know how to stand or talk in the presence of strangers. Situational cues prompted their bodies to respond in the ways they always had. But wearing clothing that no longer set them apart, styling their hair differently, and no longer following a kosher diet was profoundly unsettling. Davidman's research also disclosed another important aspect of body routines that she figured would be evident among practitioners of other traditions. As non-deliberative action that largely perpetuates itself from month to month and from year to year, body routines are the locus of action that may prompt people to question their religion. Before ever intending to become unorthodox, the women told her, they temporarily disrupted their familiar routines, usually in small ways such as trying on ordinary clothing at a friend's house or smoking a cigarette. The temporary disruption broke the "taken-for-granted-ness" of the routine, which in turn opened a path toward questioning the tradition's beliefs and practices. They became in their own minds a person who had broken a commandment and who now needed to reaffirm her commitment or who with external support stepped further away with each new infraction.[42]

---

40. Butler, *Gender Trouble*, 175.

41. Peter Morey and Amina Yaqin, *Framing Muslims: Stereotyping and Representation after 9/11* (Cambridge, MA: Harvard University Press, 2011), 194–95.

42. Lynn Davidman, *Becoming Un-Orthodox: Stories of Ex-Hasidic Jews* (New York: Oxford University Press, 2014).

Unintentional disruptions of body routines resulting from tragic events also leave lasting marks. The Buffalo Creek flood that swept through Logan County, West Virginia, in 1972, when a coal slurry impoundment dam broke, killed 125 people, injured more than a thousand, and left more than four thousand homeless. Kai T. Erikson's *Everything in Its Path* examined the disaster's social and emotional impact on the survivors' lives. The body routines the devastation of their community disrupted were truly the stuff of ordinary life: sitting on the porch watching it rain, going to the shed out back of their house to fetch a tool, walking to the store without having to think for a moment about where the store was, standing to sing the familiar hymns during the Sunday service at church. The flood carried away the situational markers that told their bodies what to do. The shock of losing their homes and some of their friends diminished with time, but even when the school reopened and the stores and churches were back in business—even when life returned to "normal" two or three years later—the people's body routines registered the effects. "We find ourselves standing, not knowing exactly which way to go or where to turn," said one. "I go places, I don't even know where in the hell I'm at," said another. "I have to sit down and think, 'What the hell am I doing.'" It was the "spiritual mood of the hollow," Erikson concluded, that had been devastated most drastically.[43]

The disorientation in this case was compounded by the erasure of familiar places. Physical injury and impairment of an individual may have similar consequences because the person has to negotiate the body-place relationship anew. Rebecca Seligman refers to "hyperembodiment" as the condition that results. Stroke patients, for example, have to focus on simple acts such as walking and eating that previously required no conscious attention. Increased bodily awareness disturbs the person's accustomed thought processes and fractures the self-continuity that has been taken for granted. Seligman's study of trance possession among Candomblé mediums in northeastern Brazil found hyperembodiment to be a critical aspect of their devotional practices. Hyperembodiment was present prior to initiation as a result of having experienced physical trauma and then was present again as practitioners learned trance possession. A woman in her early sixties, for example, had been traumatized under Brazil's military dictatorship and by subsequent suffering that nearly caused her to commit suicide. Trance possession induced a new kind of dissociation from her body that

---

43. Kai T. Erikson, *Everything in Its Path: Destruction of Community in the Buffalo Creek Flood* (New York: Simon & Schuster, 1976), quotes on pages 210–12.

over time developed into a spiritual practice that contributed to greater control over the relationship between her bodily awareness and sense of self.[44]

Body Rituals

The body routines in which we engage privately are often said to be performed "ritualistically" because they occur repeatedly in stylized ways and with intentionality but without conscious decision making in the moment. This kind of ritualistic behavior, though, is different from body rituals. *Rituals* are collective—performed in the company of others—and thus demonstrate aspects of bodily presence, movement, coordination, and communication with greater complexity than do privately performed body routines. While debate exists as to the necessity of physical co-presence for evoking the intense feelings that frequently occur in rituals, many rituals, perhaps especially those performed in religious settings, do include physical co-presence. It is common in discussions of rituals, therefore, to emphasize the manifold ways in which bodies matter: in movements, dress, coordination, and interaction.

The coordinated interaction of which body rituals consist is necessarily performative, meaning that the actions are staged to produce an effect on those who observe as well as on participants. The staging sets body rituals apart from ordinary situations in which instrumental tasks take precedence over expressive performance. Staging implies planning, practice, and in many instances rehearsal, all of which are done in anticipation of the "main event," which perforce happens at times and in places deemed special. Although rituals vary in emotional intensity, the mere fact of being staged as coordinated performances implies that bodies are taught, moved, adorned, and managed in specialized ways. The most dramatic examples of bodily management occur in rituals that include feats of skill, such as carefully choreographed dancing, but rituals ostensibly as mental as a Bible memorization contest also necessitate the practiced arrangement of bodies.

---

44. Rebecca Seligman, "The Unmaking and Making of Self: Embodied Suffering and Mind-Body Healing in Brazilian Candomblé," *Ethos* 38, 3 (2010), 297–320; see also Rebecca Seligman, "Distress, Dissociation, and Embodied Experience: Reconsidering the Pathways to Mediumship and Mental Health," *Ethos* 33, 1 (2005), 71–99; and Rebecca Seligman and Laurence J. Kirmayer, "Dissociative Experience and Cultural Neuroscience: Narrative, Metaphor and Mechanism," *Culture, Medicine, Psychiatry* 32, 1 (2008), 31–64.

Body rituals benefit from the meanings and interpretations that the collectivities in which they occur supply. Unlike body routines that acquire and sustain religious meanings through socialization and repetition, body rituals are subject to real-time verbal instruction and after-the-fact verbal interpretation. These verbalizations turn bodily acts into symbolic expressions of shared devotion. Eleanor Sanderson's field research with Christian groups in Fiji and Tanzania, for example, illustrates the significant meanings that attach to small gestures that are repeated and interpreted in collective gatherings. The theology of hope among the participants in these communities, she argues, was embodied through the layered meanings of hands being held, hands being placed on the sick, and hands being associated with spiritual meaning. As the woman leading one of the groups "touches her hands together in prayer, joining the similarly held hands of other group members," Sanderson observes, "their actions explicitly relate to the touching hands of God (an action to 'place things in the hands of God')."[45]

The performative aspect of body ritual is also featured in Omri Elisha's study of Latino neo-Pentecostals' participation in the annual New York Dance Parade held each spring in festive celebration of dance and the city's performing arts. The challenge the dancers faced in view of the artistic festival in which they participated was precisely to define *their* performance as something different, namely, as "ministry." They accomplished this definitional task, Elisha suggests, through rigorous training and special garments worn by the dancers who bonded during the training and danced regularly on stage during worship services. The dancing included explanations both during training to the dancers and during worship services to the congregation about the biblical basis of timbrels, ephods, the colors of garments and banners, and dancing itself. In preparation for the parade, dancers were further instructed in how to think critically about the performances they would see in the parade by viewing and discussing videos of "sinful" practices such as belly dancing and booty shaking. The larger point, Elisha argues, is that body rituals work at the intersection of religious and non-religious practices by adapting to changing situations and by training bodies not only to perform but also to "see" antithetical performances in critical ways.[46]

---

45. Eleanor Sanderson, "Eschatology and Development: Embodying Messianic Spaces of Hope," *Space and Culture* 11, 2 (2008), 93–108, quote on page 100.

46. Omri Elisha, "Proximations of Public Religion: Worship, Spiritual Warfare, and the Ritualization of Christian Dance," *American Anthropologist* 119, 1 (March 2017), 73–85.

Like the dancers Elisha studied, many of the body rituals that take place in religious settings are structured by the informal norms, habits, and improvisations of the community. The norms become pragmatic adaptations to the local realities of the situation. For example, one of the bodily impositions of religious authorities is traditionally exercised at weddings, over which a pastor or priest will not preside unless certain conditions are met, such as the parties having been celibate, not having been married or divorced before, not being closely related, and holding official membership in the same religion or denomination. Yet, in practice, congregations have fudged these rules to accommodate local situations, such as authorizing weddings for religiously exogenous couples as long as they are from "similar" traditions or make certain promises concerning the religious upbringing of children.

Body rituals in religious communities vary in how formal or informal they are and in how rigidly they are enforced. Studies seeking to differentiate religious communities in terms of "strictness" typically refer to the formality and rigidity with which body rules are defined and collectively expressed. Examples include rules against blood transfusions, vaccinations, and palliative medical treatment; teachings about contraception and abortion; practices of genital mutilation; prohibitions against smoking and consuming alcohol; and expectations about clothing and jewelry. Strict enforcement may take the form of expulsion from the community or in lesser degrees consist of "degradation ceremonies," as Goffman termed them. For instance, an unmarried woman who is a member of a conservative Christian congregation in twenty-first-century America and who becomes pregnant may be publicly condemned during a worship service and asked to confess her sin, and if she happens to be a student at a Christian high school or college, may be excluded from formal graduation ceremonies.[47]

The value of thinking about strictness as a practice rather than as a set of formalized rules is that the manner in which enforcement occurs, to whom it applies, whether it happens publicly or in private, and how it changes over time and varies from situation to situation are more clearly taken into account. The formal prohibition among nineteenth-century German Baptists against marrying non-members, for instance, remained on the books, but was gradually abandoned among immigrant congregations in the United States as a response

---

47. Jessica Schladerbeck, "Pregnant Maryland Teen Barred from Christian School Graduation," *New York Daily News*, May 24, 2017.

to the limited marriage markets available in sparsely populated areas and on grounds that Baptist teachings, after all, placed authority over such matters in the hands of local congregations.[48] Liza Steele's study in a quite different setting showed that Pentecostal congregations in Brazilian *favelas* formally condemned sexual intercourse outside of marriage but embraced and actively supported single women who were pregnant or had children.[49]

In their study of food taboos among African American Muslims, Carolyn Rouse and Janet Hoskins underscore the importance of understanding body rituals "in an historical—rather than simply a classificatory—framework" and further nuance this perspective by showing how gender roles influence the timing and negotiations involved as practices change. The food taboos they observed mostly followed formal halal rules but included "soul food" about which there were ongoing debates as to whether its signification of race and oppression should be eschewed or embraced. Because food purchasing and preparation largely remained in the domestic sphere, women played the decisive role in determining which of the formal and informal norms to follow and shaping how the practices evolved.[50]

Rouse and Hoskins's study is one of many that demonstrate the ways in which power is expressed in body rituals. Participants' willingness to participate in rituals according to specified rules attests, as Durkheim argued, to the collectivity's power. As their limbs move in certain ways and as they perceive one another doing the same things, they sense the collectivity's authority over them. Durkheim claims that the person whose individuality is weakened in this manner nevertheless feels stronger, empowered by believing that individual movements amount to something greater. The presence of collective power also offers the possibility for individuals to exert their own power through acts of resistance. The pregnant teen subjected to a degradation ceremony, for instance, can use the occasion to call out the father or testify against the congregation's hypocrisy. The women Rouse and Hoskins observed exercised power both in making decisions about food that deviated from the ideas of male leaders and

---

48. Robert Wuthnow, *American Misfits and the Making of Middle-Class Respectability* (Princeton, NJ: Princeton University Press, 2017).

49. Liza G. Steele, "'A Gift from God': Adolescent Motherhood and Religion in Brazilian Favelas," *Sociology of Religion* 72, 1 (2011), 4–27.

50. Carolyn Rouse and Janet Hoskins, "Purity, Soul Food, and Sunni Islam: Explorations at the Intersection of Consumption and Resistance," *Cultural Anthropology* 19, 2 (2004), 226–49.

in honoring Muslim norms in the presence of non-Muslim family members.[51]

In seeking new lines of inquiry about body rituals, researchers have returned to earlier work on funerary rites. Much of that work emphasized the affective functions of ritual participation among the bereaved. However, archaeological and anthropological investigations focusing on practices of mummification, embalmment, and burial of the bodies of the deceased have given rise to renewed interest in these aspects of contemporary body rituals as well. Shannon Novak, for example, extends the notion of physical co-presence to consideration of the fact that a graveyard's bodies also constitute a kind of co-present "community." Taking the early twenty-first-century exhumation of a mid-nineteenth-century cemetery in New York City as a case study, she considers what it means for bodies whose paths mostly did not cross in life to be placed together in death. The answer, she argues, is that cemeteries are quintessential "catchment zones" in which people who in the main are strangers are placed together and thus must be periodically reimagined for some semblance of commonness to emerge. As material infrastructure located in geographic space, cemeteries still require this sort of reimagining, as Novak discovered in tracing how the church with which the cemetery was associated told stories of charismatic leaders, anti-slavery agitation, reunions, and family histories that served to reanimate personal relations. Asynchronous relations of this kind among strangers, Novak suggests, are the essence of cities and indeed of many other "communities." Among the dead just as among the living, bodies are reimagined to bring non-existent physical co-presence into being. Reconceiving physical resemblances among distant relatives, recalling common speech patterns and modes of dress, displaying photos of the deceased, and participating in common meals are among such means of reimagining.[52]

---

51. These themes are developed further in Carolyn Rouse, *Engaged Surrender: African American Women and Islam* (Berkeley and Los Angeles: University of California Press, 2004); gendered situational adaptations of food taboos are also the focus of Elsa Mescoli, "Islamic Food Practices in a Migration Context: An Ethnography Among Moroccan Women in Milan (Italy)," in *Everyday Life Practices of Muslims in Europe*, edited by Erkan Toguslu (Leuven: Leuven University Press, 2015), 9–39.

52. Shannon A. Novak, "Corporeal Congregations and Asynchronous Lives: Unpacking the Pews at Spring Street," *American Anthropologist* 119, 2 (2017), 236–52.

Disciplining the Body

Body disciplines differ from body routines and body rituals in the mastery, deliberation, skill, and extent of temporal engagement required. A person may routinely recite a rote prayer at mealtime or participate passively in a worship service, but to discipline the body over a long period to meditate or to serve one's country by performing military service is a different matter. To discipline oneself requires the decision to do something, the desire to keep doing it, the willpower to stick with it, and a learning process that extends over time and succeeds in developing greater skills. Disciplining the body consists of somatic developments that condition the body toward greater accomplishments as practice continues, whether in being able to sit quietly and concentrate longer, as schoolchildren are expected to do, or in becoming progressively skilled at sports.

Theoretical sources of interest in body disciplines include developmental psychology, in which theories of socialization, the body's changing physical capacities, and the cultivation of desirable habits and avoidance of undesirable habits supply the primary focus of investigation. A second source is virtue ethics as expressed especially in Alasdair MacIntyre's reflections on mental and physical practices (such as chess and soccer) as means of learning patience, courage, and cooperation. MacIntyre conceives of discipline less in terms of prior intention and more as complex skilled activities in which motivation is sustained through intrinsic rewards and the desire for mastery is an emergent property of the practice.[53] Interest in discipline is grounded in Weberian concerns about the ethical meaning systems supplying motivation for rationally ascetic economic behavior and acquisition. Weber's work, like Durkheim's, has contributed to lineages of inquiry focusing on the role of social support in maintaining discipline and, as illustrated by Foucault, the state's role in imposing discipline through the training, assembling, and imprisonment of bodies. Foucault's focus on the external imposition of bodily discipline parallels Goffman's observations on total institutions, although Foucault's is more encompassing in arguing that the distinctive feature of modernity was the rise of a disciplinary epoch in which schools, factories, prisons, and the state exercised unceasing discipline over the lives of individuals. The ascetic discipline that interested Weber was instituted, as Philip Gorski shows, in the Calvinist conventicles and was prefigured,

---

53. Alasdair MacIntyre, *After Virtue*, 2nd ed. (Notre Dame, IN: University of Notre Dame Press, 1984), 181–203.

Randall Collins suggests, during the High Middle Ages in the monastic regimen of wakening the body at regular intervals for prayer, requiring it to eat and refrain from eating according to specified rules, and putting it to work at communal chores.[54]

Much of this literature emphasizes the kinds of discipline—mental, spiritual, ethical, and bodily—that accompanied the industrial revolution, either as internalized regimens of personal control or as the consequence of mechanization and large-scale bureaucratic methods of dictating how workers and soldiers used their bodies. Discipline no longer inhered only in the stern personal control implied in heroic notions of willpower but descended over large numbers of bodies through organized mechanisms of supervision. Industrial laborers' bodies became accustomed to a different daily rhythm governed by clocks and factory whistles and street noise.[55] Bodies became "docile," in Foucault's memorable phrasing, as their physical power became harnessed to utilitarian ends. And whether those utilitarian ends were accomplished, the institutional mechanisms of controlling bodies prevailed. Militaries turned individuals into undifferentiated fighting units, and mental institutions classified bodies that suffered from chronic diarrhea or that spoke too enthusiastically about religion as lunatics. Moreover, institutional disciplines extended over time well beyond their immediate spaces of employment and residence. The indigent and sick found their eating habits, daily schedules, and movements increasingly constrained by the appointments, recordkeeping, and surveillance imposed on them.[56]

---

54. Max Weber, *The Protestant Ethic and the Spirit of Capitalism*, trans. Talcott Parsons (New York: Charles Scribner's Sons, 1958 [1920]); references to Weber's "iron cage" metaphor as an image of internally or externally imposed discipline should be reassessed in relation to discussions that view the metaphor as a mistranslation grounded in Parsons's familiarity with Bunyan's *Pilgrim's Progress* (see especially Stephen A. Kent, "Weber, Goethe, and the Nietzschean Allusion: Capturing the Source of the 'Iron Cage' Metaphor," *Sociological Analysis* 44, 4, 1983, 297–319); Michel Foucault, *Discipline and Punish: The Birth of the Prison*, trans. Alan Sheridan (New York: Vintage Books, 1976); Philip S. Gorski, *Disciplinary Revolution: Calvinism and the Rise of the State in Early Modern Europe* (Chicago: University of Chicago Press, 2003); Randall Collins, *Weberian Sociological Theory* (New York: Cambridge University Press, 1986), 45–76; and besides Collins, of course, see also Talal Asad, *Genealogies of Religion: Discipline and Reasons of Power in Christianity and Islam* (Baltimore, MD: Johns Hopkins University Press, 1993).

55. The classic treatment of these changes is E. P. Thompson, "Time, Work-Discipline, and Industrial Capitalism," *Past & Present* 38 (1967), 56–97.

56. See for instance Amy Cooper, "Time Seizures and the Self: Institutional Temporalities and Self-preservation Among Homeless Women," *Culture, Medicine, and Psychiatry* 39, 1 (2015),

In a commentary on Foucault, Gilles Deleuze argues that the disciplinary order of early industrial and military organization has been replaced by a more subtle form of social control that gives the individual an illusion of voluntary submission. The prisons, hospitals, factories, schools, and armed forces that interested Foucault, Deleuze says, functioned as enclosures, operating from birth to death in a succession of spaces punctuated by baptisms at the start and last rites at the end. But rapid social change, migration, differentiated labor markets, and information technology have rendered those modes of discipline obsolete compared to free-floating methods of control. These methods maneuver with the individual through improvisational settings in the form of pharmaceuticals, genetic manipulations, resumés, salary determinations, television, and, one would presume, social media. The discipline these methods of control require consists of training the body to adapt within constraints to new situations rather than mastering a specified skill. Surfing, Deleuze says, has replaced sports.[57]

The difference between learning a versatile skill that accedes to personal fulfillment instead of the community's mandates does not elide the fact that individually cultivated disciplines are socially grounded. Tim Dant and Belinda Wheaton's study of windsurfing, for instance, emphasizes the subculture in which individual skills are learned and rewarded. As Deleuze would anticipate, the subculture is quite different from yacht sailing in which status and expectations of achievement bear on the wider societies that sailors represent. The windsurfing subculture focuses instead on individual achievements realized in experiences of thrill, whiz, flow, buzz, and excitement, and these experiences are *shared* in the small talk that sensitizes the windsurfers to value them.[58] A subculture of this kind encourages conformity to certain standards of performance; and yet, those standards can include individual variation as an ideal. In an ethnographic study of body builders at a multicultural gym, for instance, Alexis Sossa found that everyone talked to everyone else, thus creating a

---

162–85, which documents the extent to which homeless women's everyday lives were controlled by bureaucratic regulations; and Sarah Brayne, "Surveillance and System Avoidance: Criminal Justice Contact and Institutional Attachment," *American Sociological Review* 79, 3 (2014), 367–91, and Sarah Brayne, *Policed: Surveillance and Prediction in the Age of Big Data* (New York: Oxford University Press, 2018), on recent extensions of institutional control through surveillance.

57. Gilles Deleuze, "Postscript on the Societies of Control," *October* 59 (1992), 3–7, quote on page 7.

58. Tim Dant and Belinda Wheaton, "Windsurfing: An Extreme Form of Material and Embodied Interaction?" *Anthropology Today* 23 (December 2007), 8–12.

supportive subculture, but that nobody ever criticized anyone else, which enabled the participants to focus on their individual selves.[59]

Insofar as Deleuze is correct, the body disciplines that supply religious meanings must be considered to have shifted as well. Unlike the Benedictine whose practice was enclosed within a lifetime of collective devotion, the twenty-first-century practitioner of body disciplines experiences the freedom to pick and choose which discipline to practice. The two characteristics that follow are, first, selecting disciplines that can be picked up, abandoned, and transferred to new situations, and, second, evaluating disciplines in terms of what they are expected to contribute to the individual's well-being.

These characteristics are evident in many of the disciplines that have been examined in studies of contemporary religious practice. Erin Johnston's research among Integral Yoga Institute practitioners documents the spiritual devotion with which many of the practitioners disciplined their bodies in conformity with physical postures, breathing, silence, and mantra repetition, all of which were transportable to daily life and which, despite being learned in classes, focused on each person's individuality. The practitioners, Johnston concludes, "sought to uncover and reveal their truest, most authentic (and divine) self."[60] Marie Griffith in *Born Again Bodies* identifies a similar emphasis among American Christians on self-improvement in body disciplines as diverse as fasting, dieting, participating in church-based weight-loss programs, and abstaining from sex. These practices, she suggests, have deep roots in biblical traditions about subduing the flesh and in specific teachings about holiness and perfection, and yet have adapted to the more commercialized contemporary setting in which norms are shaped by popular music, self-help movements, motivational speakers, and a flourishing subculture within conservative Protestant mega-churches.[61]

The training through which these disciplines are learned varies enormously. Abstinence programs, for instance, range from learning techniques of distraction that stifle prurient desires to overcoming physical addictions through a combination of therapy and medication. Practices that consist of long hours

---

59. Alexis Sossa, "'Yeah, and What's the Problem?' Embodiment, Cultural Practices and Working Out in a Dutch Gym," *Social Sciences* 6, 44 (2017), 1–15.

60. Erin Johnston, "The Enlightened Self: Identity and Aspiration in Two Communities of Practice," *Religions* 7, 7 (2016), 1–15.

61. R. Marie Griffith, *Born Again Bodies: Flesh and Spirit in American Christianity* (Berkeley and Los Angeles: University of California Press, 2004).

of walking, chanting, sitting, and meditating are more like learning to play tennis or sing opera in the extent of somatic skill needing to be acquired. In a study of Vipassana Buddhist meditation practitioners, for example, Michal Pagis suggests that learning to meditate eleven hours a day over a period of several months imposes the kind of body discipline that assists meditators to understand more clearly the practice's abstract tenets. Aching legs, hunger, and focusing on their breathing separated practitioners' minds from the usual taken-for-grantedness of their bodies and sharpened their awareness of the distinction between the ordinary reality of their stable everyday self and the impermanent reality of what they learned to call their "true self" or "not self." Pagis argues that the bodily experiences the practitioners felt somatically were like tools that drove home the meaning of the practice's concepts. The two interacted, just as the concept of driving interacts with learning to drive or the concept of love does with love-making. Pagis further suggests that for some meditators the conceptual apparatus eventually disappeared entirely, just as it does for a ballet performer, while for others it became increasingly active, much as scientific concepts do for lab scientists.[62]

The relationship between bodily discipline and conceptual apparatus is further illustrated in studies associating mental discipline with physical training. Loïc Wacquant, for example, found that boxers considered mental toughness to be as essential to becoming a champion fighter as physical skill. Mental discipline especially meant learning to control emotions, as one boxer explained, learning "to stay calm and relaxed though you know this guy's tryin' to knock yer head off."[63] Studies of military training demonstrate similar connections between the mental control of aggression and fear. The "body callusing" that hardens the soldier's capacity to endure pain facilitates the soldier's mental focus during combat as well.[64]

Examples in which bodily discipline consists of extreme physical conditioning, though, miss an important aspect of discipline that may be more

---

62. Michal Pagis, "From Abstract Concepts to Experiential Knowledge: Embodying Enlightenment in a Meditation Center," *Qualitative Sociology* 33 (2010), 469–89.

63. Loïc Wacquant, *Body and Soul: Notebooks of an Apprentice Boxer* (New York: Oxford University Press, 2006), 93; Wacquant elaborates, "Failure to tame the sensory experience of punches flying at you amputates your ability to act and by the same token alters your corporeal state. Conversely, to be at the height of physical fitness allows you to be mentally ready and therefore to better master the feelings triggered by the flow of blows."

64. Limor Samimian-Darash, "Rebuilding the Body through Violence and Control," *Ethnography* 14, 1 (2013), 46–63.

characteristic of Western religious practices. Peter Collins's ethnographic study of Quaker worship meetings provides an interesting case in point. Quaker worship as a non-creedal tradition in which discipline is nevertheless emphasized and that currently attracts participants who may identify as Buddhists, Hindus, or Humanists rather than as Christians, Collins argues, can be understood through the lens of practice theory. The Quakers Collins studied met in silence for an hour each Sunday morning, after which they socialized over tea and biscuits. It would have been hard to imagine them as an instance of bodily discipline. On the surface, the quasi-canonic text, *Quaker Faith and Practice*, that set forth the meaning of Quaker discipline did so in terms of mental habits to be cultivated, such as love of God and respect for truth. But in practice, the meetings served as ritual reinforcement for personal acts of bodily discipline. Participants refrained from alcohol and tobacco, according to Quaker principles; most were vegetarians; the meetings adhered to strict arrangements of seating and of breaking the silence with brief moments of spoken ministry; members sometimes found ways to include visual messages (such as one participant whose T-shirt read "Walk for the World"); and participants shared stories after the meeting about peace rallies, arrests, and helping the poor. While Quaker discipline was not physically demanding, it was thus an engagement of bodies as well as of minds. They learned to act, Collins concluded, "by a feel for the game rather than by constant reference to the rules of the game."[65]

Bodily discipline includes not only the physical training of the body in terms of musculature and nutrition but also the disciplining of the situations in which the body is present. Meditation centers, Pagis says, are "labscapes" that provide a semi-sterile environment in which ordinary life is excluded through spatial isolation, turning off the phone, dimming the lights, and playing music.[66] In other instances, spatial discipline consists of advice to alcoholics to stay away from bars and to adolescents to steer clear of bad company. Less obvious is how material space may also be disciplined. Cities are disciplined, for instance, by maps, surveys, zoning regulations, tax codes, and elections. Personal space is similarly disciplined. Mary Douglas, for example, writes that tidying one's living quarters can be a kind of ritual that rids the space of distractions so that work

---

65. Peter Collins, "The Practice of Discipline and the Discipline of Practice," in *Exploring Regimes of Discipline: The Dynamics of Restraint*, edited by Noel Dyck (New York: Berghahn Books, 2008), 135–55; quote on page 146.

66. The term "labscapes" is from Robert K. Kohler, *Landscapes and Labscapes: Exploring the Lab-Field Border in Biology* (Chicago: University of Chicago Press, 2002).

can be done more efficiently.⁶⁷ Other examples include the cues and affordances previously discussed, such as the presence of a sacred book or icon in clear view as a means of disciplining the ethical decisions that may be made in that space.

Locating bodily disciplines in disciplined situations suggests the value of considering the ways in which these situations may function. One is protected space in which an activity that can only be performed there takes place, as in the case of a scientific lab or a tennis court. Bodily practices that have religious implications rarely fall into this category (except among monastics) since the aim is to pervade and inform other aspects of life. The more likely function is as training ground. Pagis found that even though vipassana practitioners meditated in silence and hoped to transfer meditation into daily life, they were enabled to better do so by cultivating relationships with other practitioners in other venues.⁶⁸ The idea of "cocoon work" has been adopted in studies of new religious movements to suggest that initiates experiment in these set-apart spaces with novel ways of speaking, touching, and experiencing physical intimacy.⁶⁹ Yet another function is suggested by the fact that *travel* is often what makes it possible for people to practice bodily disciplines in disciplined situations. John Urry suggests that the world of "hypermobility" in which we live facilitates being "face-to-face" with people who share certain practices (e.g., a gathering of wiccans), "face-to-place" where the physical location matters (e.g., pilgrimages), and "face-the-moment," which involves travel to attend special events (e.g., a lecture by a prominent religious leader). The implication for understanding bodily disciplines is that being disciplined is often a matter of having the luxury to exit temporarily from the demands of ordinary life.⁷⁰

67. Mary Douglas, *Purity and Danger: An Analysis of the Concepts of Pollution and Taboo* (London: Routledge, 1966), 2–6.

68. Michal Pagis, "Producing Intersubjectivity in Silence: An Ethnographic Study of Meditation Practice," *Ethnography* 11, 2 (2010), 309–28.

69. Susan J. Palmer, "Women's 'Cocoon Work' in New Religious Movements: Sexual Experimentation and Feminine Rites of Passage," *Journal for the Scientific Study of Religion* 32, 4 (1993), 343–55.

70. John Urry, *The Tourist Gaze: Leisure and Travel in Contemporary Societies* (London: Sage, 1990); applications to pilgrimages are discussed in Ellen Badone, "Conventional and Unconventional Pilgrimages: Conceptualizing Sacred Travel in the Twenty-First Century," in *Redefining Pilgrimage: New Perspectives on Historical and Contemporary Pilgrimages*, edited by Antón M. Pazos (New York: Routledge, 2014), 7–32.

Disciplining the situation includes disciplining one's body in such a way that others know what to expect and can respond accordingly. Discussions of religious ritual often follow Durkheim's lead in suggesting that coordination in the sense of everyone doing the same thing is key. But that is not the case in rituals involving a division of labor, such as one praying, followed by another reading a scripture, and another lighting a candle. Here, bodily comportment consists not of imitation but of each person moving in a way that cues the next person's actions. Rituals that have been repeated many times include strong expectations about these movements and cues. Practices in which improvisation is present require subtler cues to be read into bodily movements. A discussion of how best to stage a protest, for example, requires participants to "read" the body language of fellow participants in facial expressions and gestures as well as in words. A further instance of bodily coordination occurs when physical danger is present unless each person performs in exactly the right way. Religious practices rarely involve this level of danger, although deaths resulting from improper snake handling might be considered. Athletics is the arena in which danger is often present, as in pair skating. Matthew Desmond's gripping study of wilderness firefighters, which draws on practice theory, provides striking examples of the need for disciplined bodily coordination.[71]

Practices such as pair skating in which bodily coordination is essential to the performance highlight the importance of body disciplines that fall short of the collective enactments associated with religious rituals and yet may be governed by religious institutions. Religious strictures on sexual activity are probably the clearest example. While it is possible to consider strictures on nonmarital sex and same-sex relationships, for example, as matters pertaining only to individuals, these activities are of course social. Moreover, they are frequently the focus of social monitoring in the form of abstinence groups, congregations, and in some contexts by the state. Accusations of sexual harassment and inappropriate sexual conduct illustrate the complexities of subtle relationships among physical contact, words, intentions, and situations.[72]

---

71. Matthew Desmond, *On the Fireline: Living and Dying with Wildland Firefighters* (Chicago: University of Chicago Press, 2008).

72. Among numerous studies, see especially Christine J. Gardner, *Making Chastity Sexy: The Rhetoric of Evangelical Abstinence Campaigns* (Berkeley and Los Angeles: University of California Press, 2011); Gillian A. Frank, "'Ideals of Stability, Order and Fidelity': The Love Dare Phenomenon, Convergence Culture and the Marriage Movement," *Journal of Religion and Popular Culture* 23, 3 (2011), 118–38; and for a non-US example, James Bourk Hoestery, "Vicissitudes

The lack of bodily coordination among multiple persons is one of the principal considerations differentiating the kind of individualistic body disciplines that Deleuze emphasizes from the highly regimented ones that interested Foucault. A person praying, meditating, or doing yoga alone is free to tinker, making adjustments to changing situations that assist in conducting the practice without having to worry about somehow fitting in and adhering strictly to prespecified rules.[73] The discipline involved takes the form of "tuning" one's body or "attuning" oneself to the conditions at hand, much as an artist does. The body acquires skills in the process and discovers more about what it can and cannot do with the affordances at hand. The body is agentic rather than docile.[74] However, even in highly regimented contexts bodies are less docile than Foucault's wording might suggest. Persons in prison, mental institutions, and the military also engage actively in attuning their bodies to the demands placed upon them. To be disciplined is to attain the physical skills required, to know how to protect one's back, and to decide when to acquiesce and when to resist. Religious practice is sometimes part of the process. The Brazilian prisoners Andrew Johnson studied, for example, frequently came in bloodied and broken from gang fights, were ill-nourished, and had to rely on visitors for clean clothing, but learned to hug one another in symbols of acceptance and healing as they embraced the disciplines of Pentecostal submission.[75] Physical adaptation through religious practice was no less significant among the inmates Joshua Dubler studied in Pennsylvania. "Chapel religion does one thing

---

of Vision: Piety, Pornography, and Shaming the State in Indonesia," *Visual Anthropology Review* 32, 2 (2016), 133–43.

73. On tinkering, see Karin D. Knorr, "Tinkering toward Success: Prelude to a Theory of Scientific Practice," *Theory and Society* 8, 3 (1979), 347–76, who describes it as "a progressive selection of what works by using what has worked in the past and what is likely to work under the present, idiosyncratic circumstances" (page 369), to which might be added that skill derived from training is essential to the improvisational adaptions required; on tinkering in religious practice, see Wuthnow, *All in Sync*.

74. Spatz, "Embodiment as First Affordance." See also Andrew Pickering, *The Mangle of Practice: Time, Agency, and Science* (Chicago: University of Chicago Press, 1995), who describes "disciplined human agency" as a practice that is tuned and interactively stabilized" (page 17). Pickering's usage of "tuning" is from Ludwik Fleck, *Genesis and Development of a Scientific Fact* (Chicago: University of Chicago Press, 1979 [1935]), 86, whose examples implied adaptation to the material conditions at hand as well as coordination among co-investigators.

75. Andrew Johnson, *If I Give My Soul: Faith Behind Bars in Rio de Janeiro* (New York: Oxford University Press, 2017).

principally," Dubler writes. "It helps to transform convicts into prisoners—by which we mean those with the embodied know-how to survive prison."[76]

The common feature of body disciplines that are voluntarily embraced, on the one hand, or institutionally imposed, on the other hand, is that the body serves as a tool through which important aspects of a person's identity are communicated. A cult leader who rapes the women and children of its members manifests their subjection to his control. A totalitarian state that has no other use for the identities of its individual subjects can brand serial numbers onto their bodies, thus demonstrating its power over them, and an "egalitarian" state can establish racially segregated restrooms or set up separate hospitals for religious minorities, ostensibly for their own protection as well as the public's.[77] But studies acknowledging these enforcements of power document acts of defiance and resistance as well. Tattoos that display individualized messages, attire that differentiates high school students from the dress codes of their institutions, colorful hijabs that symbolize fashion as much as tradition, and prosthetics that demonstrate incredible endurance in athletic events are among the many examples. They enhance what Caroline Bynum calls "my particularity," which includes the individuality of unique bodily appearance, height, weight, movement, and how one's body feels from the inside.[78] To have disciplined the body is also to know the means through which to tamper with the identity the discipline conveys. Indeed, mastery of a discipline—religious or otherwise—is demonstrated by intentionally defying the rules from time to time as much as by dutifully adhering to them.[79] Susan Leigh Foster, for instance, suggests in her study of yoga that practitioners learn over time to follow their bodies'

---

76. Joshua Dubler, *Down in the Chapel: Religious Life in an American Prison* (New York: Farrar, Straus and Giroux, 2013), 309.

77. The establishment of separate hospital facilities in France for North African immigrant Muslims is an interesting case in point; see Naomi Davidson, *Only Muslim: Embodying Islam in Twentieth-Century France* (Ithaca, NY: Cornell University Press, 2012).

78. Bynum, "Why All the Fuss," 32.

79. Rudolph M. Bell, *Holy Anorexia* (Chicago: University of Chicago Press, 1985), offers a suggestive analysis of the relationships of gender, patriarchy, monastic life, and fasting as conformity, over-conformity, and deviance among medieval women. Defiance and deviation may be less apt as descriptions of twenty-first-century ascetic disciplines than ritualized ascetic cleansing that occurs within and indeed legitimates excessive materiality and consumption; a point amply illustrated in the discussion of fitness and eating detoxes in Dana W. Logan, "The Lean Closet: Asceticism in Postindustrial Consumer Culture," *Journal of the American Academy of Religion* 85, 3 (2017), 600–28.

"suggestions" and improvise instead of adhering to habitual techniques, thus asserting the uniqueness of their selfhood.[80] Moreover, defiance as an act of self-assertion is as possible to accomplish through over-conformity as through under-conformity. Especially when disciplines are instituted in the inherited identities of religious traditions, becoming *more* devout by praying longer, attending services more often, adopting a more differentiated style of clothing, performing more extreme cleansing rituals, and engaging in greater acts of heroism and sacrifice serve as ways to *achieve* an identity that has heretofore been only ascribed.[81]

Bodies as Representations

As illuminating as it is, a difficulty with much of the recent work on embodiment is that the bodies at issue are assumed to be corporeally engaged. Yet this emphasis occurs against the backdrop of what we know to be untrue. Much of our social interaction does not occur in person at all. It takes place via the images we see on digital screens. The bodies we interact with are distantly connected rather than physically present. We send emails, post and reply to posted

---

80. Susan Leigh Foster, "Improvising Yoga," in *The Oxford Handbook of Critical Improvisation Studies, vol. 1*, edited by George E. Lewis and Benjamin Piekut (New York: Oxford University Press, 2016), 217–25, quote on page 218; situating her discussion in Foucault's work, Foster describes improvisation in this context as a way of resisting the "docilization" of the body. On disciplined physical and mental training, see also Sandra Foster, Paul J. Lloyd, and Sara Kamin, "Mental Preparation, Memorization, and Improvisation," in *Performance Psychology in Action: A Casebook for Working with Athletes, Performing Artists, Business Leaders, and Professionals in High-Risk Occupations*, edited by K. F. Hays (Washington, DC: American Psychological Association, 2009), 77–97.

81. Robert Garot and Jack Katz, "Provocative Looks: Gang Appearance and Dress Codes in an Inner-City Alternative School," *Ethnography* 4, 3 (2003), 421–54, is essential reading on bodily acts of resistance. Amanda K. Booher, "Docile Bodies, Supercrips, and the Plays of Prosthetics," *International Journal of Feminist Approaches to Bioethics* 3, 2 (2010), 63–89, offers a Foucauldian analysis of prosthetics. Wendy Cadge and Lynn Davidman, "Ascription, Choice, and the Construction of Religious Identities in the Contemporary United States," *Journal for the Scientific Study of Religion* 45, 1 (2006), 23–38, presents examples in Judaism and Buddhism of persons engaged in practices that enable an ascribed religion to also be achieved; see also Maheshvari Naidu, "Seeing (through) the Gaze: Marking Religious and Cultural Differences onto Muslim Female Bodies," *Journal for the Study of Religion* 22, 2 (2009), 23–42; and Khairudin Aljunied, *Muslim Cosmopolitanism: Southeast Asian Islam in Comparative Perspective* (Edinburgh: Edinburgh University Press, 2017), 102–30.

photos on social media, watch short videos online, and speak across great distances on Internet hookups.

How to think about these digitally mediated bodily encounters requires a shift in focus from thinking about bodies engaged in physical action and interaction. Bodies are corporeal realities, but they are also images that populate our experience visually and discursively. We speak metaphorically of the body politic. We form mental images of racial and sexual variations from what we think is important about phenotypical characteristics and attire. The person whose photo we respond to on social media has a body. Bodies in these ways are representations. They serve metaphorically and literally in organizing and communicating ideas and beliefs about the world in which we live. Moreover, they organize and guide lived experience by connecting the dots, as it were, between what we know to be true from the sensations in our own body and how we imagine other bodies to act and feel. Hearing that the "body politic is under siege" or that the "community is dying" prompts a visceral reaction that suggests a need to take action without specifying precisely what is wrong or what action should be taken.[82]

As a representation, the body ceases to be an object of the kind to which a person dieting or doing workouts aspires—a specific body or an idealized image of a material body—and becomes a symbol of a broader social reality that is in many instances well-institutionalized. "The symbol," David Morgan writes in discussing Roman Catholic teachings about the sacred heart, "refers to and endorses dogmas, a corpus of authorized ideas that exerts a powerful structuring effect among large numbers of people [and] promotes mass movements."[83] The sacred heart symbolizes the community's essential commonality and the life-giving force that sustains it. So it is with bodily substances that flow in and out of bodies and thereby serve readily as symbols of social exchange. Studies of kinship, for instance, emphasize the attachments that are expressed through

---

82. Steven Van Wolputte, "Hang on to Your Self: Of Bodies, Embodiment, and Selves," *Annual Review of Anthropology* 33 (2004), 252–69, reviews a number of ways in which the anthropological literature in the 1980s and 1990s addressed the metaphoric aspects of bodies and embodiment.

83. David Morgan, "Rhetoric of the Heart: Figuring the Body in Devotion to the Sacred Heart of Jesus," in *Things: Religion and the Question of Materiality*, edited by Dick Houtman and Birgit Meyer (New York: Fordham University Press, 2012), 100. The powerful structuring effect of bodily representations about sex is amply documented in R. Marie Griffith, *Moral Combat: How Sex Divided American Christians and Fractured American Politics* (New York: Basic Books, 2017).

the exchange of fluids in sexual relations, the transmission of milk from mother to infant, and the transfer of genetic material from one generation to the next. In religious contexts, blood is the bodily fluid that frequently is given special significance. Protestants and Catholics understand the Eucharist to be a reminder of the blood of Christ. Muslims' Feast of Immolation includes the blood sacrifice of an animal. It is not simply the presence of blood that matters, however, but what is done with it, particularly its movement and how that expresses something about relationships. By symbolically drinking of Christ's blood, Christians bring God into their lives. And by participating ritually in the event, they symbolize their solidarity as a community. The same is true of the Feast of Immolation for Muslims.[84]

Interest in the symbolic aspects of bodies is evident in Durkheim's emphasis on collective representations. The rituals in which tribal peoples participate, Durkheim argues, make sense as representations of societal power not only during and within the rituals themselves but also as mythic constructions revelatory of how the society originated and what its members hold in common. The bodies in rituals become signifiers of the collectivity's organic unity. Collective representations of this sort are all the more important in large, complex, modern societies. Indeed, Durkheim's interest in tracing religion's elementary forms stemmed in large measure from concerns about the limitations of other sources of societal solidarity.

Discussions in the Durkheimian tradition of bodies as representations have emphasized their symbolic role in discursive formulations. The trajectory of Mary Douglas's influential work runs from considerations of bodily fluids and transgressions to the cultural placement of spaces and lines. The double mapping of descriptive and evaluative distinctions in structuralist approaches further emphasizes the body's discursive representations. Less tendentiously, the focus on metaphoric communication in George Lakoff's work suggests that many of these distinctions—near and far, up and down, hot and cold—take the body as the basic point of reference. Religious references to the body appear prominently in these discussions. Treatments in Leviticus of food, fluids, and animal bodies figure as exemplary constructions in Douglas's discussion of cultural order. Lakoff suggests that basic theological differences in contemporary American religion can be understood in terms of acceptance or rejection of rigid,

---

84. Willy Jansen and Grietje Dresen, "Fluid Matters: Gendering Holy Blood and Holy Milk," in *Things: Religion and the Question of Materiality*, edited by Dick Houtman and Birgit Meyer (New York: Fordham University Press, 2012), 215–31.

tightly controlled paternalistic bodily metaphors. Other applications draw parallels between teachings about Christ's body and understandings of congregational dynamics and codes of personal conduct.[85] At issue throughout is the fact that bodies are both bounded, serving as symbols of lines, separation, and enclosure, and porous, evoking images of transgression, receptiveness, and invasion.[86]

The strongest connections between physical bodies and representational bodies occur in arguments suggesting that the one corresponds almost exactly to the other. Asha Persson terms this relationship "somatopoesis," in which practitioners seek to align their physical bodies with their understanding of the universe. Satyananda Yoga practitioners, for instance, imaginatively seek an embodied empathy in which the expansion and contraction of breathing corresponds with cosmic pulsations. Standing tall and taking up space is understood to alleviate depression because the body is better aligned with the universe. Further correspondences, Persson suggests, are evident in teachings about forces and dimensions of the universe being incarnated in embodied energy centers, in spiritual practitioners telling stories about the bodily impact of their journeys, and in metaphors likening the body and the world.[87]

The tight one-on-one parallels between bodily parts or functions and their symbolic representations are present in some situations but absent in many others. Indeed, the notion that uplifted hands have a single meaning or that eating or abstaining from a certain food connotes membership in a community suggests more about the power of an institutionalized authority structure to enforce that interpretation than it does the inevitability of such correspondences. Metaphoric references to bodily parts and functions do not occur automatically but through a structuring practice—"metaphorization," as Michael Jackson calls it—that thematizes what a person does and suggests

---

85. Douglas, *Purity and Danger*; George Lakoff and Mark Johnson, *Metaphors We Live By* (Chicago: University of Chicago Press, 1980); George Lakoff, *Women, Fire, and Dangerous Things* (Chicago: University of Chicago Press, 1987).

86. Sophie Bjork-James, "Training the Porous Body: Evangelicals and the Ex-Gay Movement," *American Anthropologist* 120, 4 (December 2018), 547–58, develops an interesting connection between porous bodies and evangelical belief in the indwelling of the Holy Spirit.

87. Asha Persson, "Embodied Worlds: A Semiotic Phenomenology of Satyananda Yoga," *Journal of the Royal Anthropological Institute* 16, 4 (2010), 797–815; Persson's emphasis on metaphor draws from Jackson as well as from Lakoff; see Michael Jackson, *Paths Toward a Clearing: Radical Empiricism and Ethnographic Inquiry* (Bloomington: Indiana University Press, 1989).

what the person is supposed to feel.[88] Morgan's discussion of the sacred heart, for example, associates changes in its meaning from penitential practices to teachings about Jesus' compassion for humanity to specific papal interpretations, each lending both the authority of the pope and the church's capacity for instructing members to each new interpretation.[89] The important feature of bodies as symbols is that their applicability and potential versatility increase. The obdurate physical limitations of bodies as corporeal realities become less important because the ideas they symbolize can be more easily challenged, translated, interpreted, and misinterpreted. Body symbolism, Norman Brown suggests in *Love's Body*, can be "polysymbolic," rendering it open to playfulness, to a kind of "polymorphous perversity" that deals imaginatively with the intersection of bodies, senses, sensuality, and meanings.[90]

Where Brown envisions playfulness, even suggesting that Pentecostal speaking in tongues might be interpreted as a kind of imaginative freedom in fusing bodily expression and meaning, an alternative approach emphasizes the discursive *structuring* of body representations. Discursive structuring refers to the fact that much of the time bodies are not a material presence at all, notwithstanding claims about embodiment being a departure from semiotic approaches, but are present only as elements of speech and as such are shaped primarily by who has the power to make authoritative claims about them. Lyn Spillman and Brian Conway illustrate this perspective in discussing the embodied practices of Catholics and Protestants in Northern Ireland as they commemorated the 1972 event that became known as Bloody Sunday in which thirteen people were killed and fourteen injured by British paratroopers. Against the notion that acts of violence and their ritual commemoration in annual marches perpetuated a somatically engrained embodied memory of each side's identity, Spillman and Conway argue that the memories at issue were as much textual as they were embodied. To be sure, performances based on bodily habits were present, but these performances, they argue, were sufficiently ambiguous that how they were

---

88. Michael Jackson, "Introduction: Phenomenology, Radical Empiricism, and Anthropological Critique," in *Things as They Are: New Directions in Phenomenological Anthropology*, edited by Michael Jackson (Bloomington: Indiana University Press, 1996), 1–50.

89. Morgan, "Rhetoric of the Heart."

90. Norman O. Brown, *Love's Body* (Berkeley and Los Angeles: University of California Press, 1996 [1966]), 249–54.

interpreted depended on verbalizations that communicated interpretations across generations in families, at religious services, and via the mass media.[91]

Although Spillman and Conway's argument disputes a singular emphasis on bodily aspects of commemorative rituals, the Bloody Sunday example offers several specific ways in which to think about body representations that take on collective significance. First, it does matter that bodies were killed and that the horror of the event is remembered in periodic marches in which people physically participate. Bodies are central in these respects, just as they are in many religious and nationalistic rituals. Second, the periodic marches include not only the marchers' bodies but also the changing meanings of participation that in turn reflect memories of previous marches and cues provided by changing personal and political situations. Third, these cues include information that extends beyond the marches and the participants in the form of testimonials, books, and news stories, all of which communicate to a wider public. Fourth, organizations supply leadership and resources (as Sinn Féin did in the case of Bloody Sunday) that shape how commemorative events are interpreted. And fifth, the interpretations may be shaped but often are subject to competing interpretations that reflect the presence of alternative organizations and contested political circumstances.

The manner in which competing interpretations occur is attributable to bodily representations being multivalent, as in the case of a brutalized body that leaves open questions about who was to blame. Body representations, like other images, are also relational, as in male and female being defined by their relation to each other. Claire Sponsler provides an interesting example of the relational character of body imagery in her study of "devoted bodies" in late medieval devotional books: one commissioned insertion in a wealthy French family's book showing the father and son, mother and daughter kneeling in prayer surrounded by elegant furnishings; the other portraying the same family members dressed in the same clothing but outdoors on desolate ground in a barren landscape. Together, more than had only one or the other been included, the two representations showed the benevolence of God and the saints providing safety amid danger and docility amid threat.[92] An interview study among ordinary twenty-first-century Americans illustrated a different kind of relational

---

91. Lyn Spillman and Brian Conway, "Texts, Bodies, and the Memory of Bloody Sunday," *Symbolic Interaction* 30, 1 (2007), 79–103.

92. Claire Sponsler, *Drama and Resistance: Bodies, Goods, and Theatricality in Late Medieval England* (Minneapolis: University of Minnesota Press, 1997), 104–35.

imagery. When asked to say what they thought God was like, interviewees relied less on scriptural descriptions and more on contrasts with human frailty, such as stories about children whose illnesses, weaknesses, or size suggested by implication that God was whole, strong, or large.[93]

The fact that represented bodies come to public attention from a distance, rather than in direct ritual participation, poses the additional question of what the collective response may be, especially in situations in which a physically victimized body would generate sympathy or indignation if the event depicted was close at hand. The discursive structuring here may have significant consequences for subsequent action. Luc Boltanski suggests that a decisive factor is whether both the perpetrator and the victim or only the victim are represented. The Rodney King case, he argues, generated indignation because the perpetrators were shown, whereas a photo of a homeless person may not because the agency that has evicted the person is out of sight in a real estate office or bank in another city. Boltanski further suggests that an image of the homeless person being assisted directly by a compassionate person may be sufficiently powerful that it becomes harder to visualize the connection between the distraught person and the bank.[94]

A related line of inquiry pursues the insight that representations and corporeal bodies interact. An interesting case in point are body disciplines that physically strengthen the persons involved and at the same time are understood to represent a symbolic strengthening of the community or nation of which they are a part. Norbert Peabody has examined these connections in an interesting study of anti-Muslim violence among Hindu wrestlers in the north Indian state of Rajasthan. Following a tradition dating at least to the eighteenth century if not earlier, the wrestlers, among whom are women as well as men, participate in a rigorous daily training regime that includes calisthenics, building upper body strength, and learning to wield weapons such as maces and knives. The practice in turn represents a form of "somatic nationalism" for the wrestlers and their supporters who perceive the physical strengthening as a rejection of weakened and effeminate Hinduism. Peabody argues that an important connection also exists with religion. The wrestling specifically draws on Shakta tantrism, which is known for its worship of the "divine feminine" but also for its emphasis

---

93. Robert Wuthnow, *The God Problem: Expressing Faith and Being Reasonable.* (Berkeley and Los Angeles: University of California Press, 2012).

94. Luc Boltanski, *Distant Suffering: Morality, Media and Politics,* trans. Graham Burchell (Cambridge, UK: Cambridge University Press, 2004), 61–62, 77–78.

on blood sacrifice and the use of hand-held weapons, and thus as a cosmology in which the defeat of hypermasculinized Muslim opponents enhances the symbolic superiority of the victors. In the process, Peabody suggests, the elements of the cosmology are "re-weighted and recombined in order to incorporate new orientations deriving from Hindu nationalism." The connection with religion also suggests a surprising aspect of the anti-Muslim violence that periodically erupts, as it did in large-scale rioting in 1989. The rioting was sufficiently understood as ritual set apart from ordinary life that the wrestlers afterward expressed no shame or misgivings for their actions and resumed ordinary and even collegial social interaction with their opponents.[95]

The north Indian example suggests parallels with religion-based body disciplines serving as somatic representations of collective strengthening in other contexts. Studies of Victorian-era "muscular Christianity" draw connections between American and British nationalistic colonial expansion and social movements such as the YMCA and college sports programs encouraging men to engage in athletic competition, recover the physical vigor of agrarian life, and recover from illness through physical exercise and good nutrition. Strengthened bodies were represented not only in physical regimes but also in renewed emphasis on the "manliness" of Christ and the promotion of male leadership in churches.[96] Such connections, the literature suggests, emerge from perceived inadequacies both among men themselves and in broader political and economic arrangements. The north Indian example also points to representations of strength perceived in the "other." Marcia Inhorn, for example, argues that "hegemonic masculinity" is a deeply essentialized Western perception of Middle

---

95. Norbert Peabody, "Disciplining the Body, Disciplining the Body-Politic: Physical Culture and Social Violence among North Indian Wrestlers," *Comparative Studies in Society and History* 52, 2 (2009), 372–400, quote on page 375; the term "somatic nationalism" is from Joseph Alter, *The Wrestler's Body: Identity and Ideology in North India* (Berkeley and Los Angeles: University of California Press, 1992); and on the broader relationship with gender roles, see Sikata Banerjee, *Muscular Nationalism: Gender, Violence, and Empire in India and Ireland, 1914–2004* (New York: NYU Press, 2012).

96. See Clifford Putney, *Muscular Christianity: Manhood and Sports in Protestant America, 1880–1920* (Cambridge, MA: Harvard University Press, 2001); and the essays in Donald E. Hall, ed., *Muscular Christianity: Embodying the Victorian Age* (Cambridge, UK: Cambridge University Press, 1994); and on the later wave of muscular Christianity in the 1950s, James A. Mathisen, "Reviving 'Muscular Christianity': Gil Dodds and the Institutionalization of Sport Evangelism," *Sociological Focus* 23, 3 (1990), 233–49.

Eastern Islam that emphasizes physical appearance (untrimmed beards), strength, heterosexuality, and fertility.[97]

Besides the symbolic enhancement of strength, acts of violence through which strength is expressed underscore the importance and religious connotations of blood sacrifice. These are present in many religious traditions and are prominently featured in teachings about sacrifice in Judaism, Islam, and Christianity. Blood sacrifice and blood atonement also figure importantly in American religious nationalism, as Philip Gorski stresses in his book on the "American Covenant," linking justifications for the American revolution, American Civil War, and US imperialism to biblical traditions of divine justice and punishment.[98] Nor were the connections entirely textual and representational. English colonists' encounters with Indians, Susan Juster writes, "offered a veritable feast of flesh and blood that proved irresistible to Protestants hungry for concrete evidence of their status as God's chosen people."[99] Beyond the obvious fact that bloodshed and blood sacrifice publicize images of societal pain, redemption, and chosenness, though, studies of the topic draw attention to a different implication. While blood sacrifice reminds a nation of its most painful—and heroic—episodes, the raw suffering and inhumanity are not memories that societies readily want to preserve. René Girard suggests that religion contributes directly to this suppression by having accounts of the bloodiest events take place outside of consecrated space and performed by persons other than the accepted leaders of the faith, after which the focus quickly turns to resurrection, solidarity, and glory.[100] Sarah Purcell's work on war, sacrifice, and memory in revolutionary America is especially instructive on this point. The war was scarcely over, she finds, before the bloodshed and fear were submerged beneath a glorified version of war that provided solace and distraction. It is not hard to imagine that the bloodiest aspects of other wars and instances of collective bloodshed have been similarly suppressed.[101]

---

97. Marcia C. Inhorn, *The New Arab Man: Emergent Masculinities, Technologies, and Islam in the Middle East* (Princeton, NJ: Princeton University Press, 2012), 39–62.

98. Philip S. Gorski, *The American Covenant: A History of Civil Religion from the Puritans to the Present* (Princeton, NJ: Princeton University Press, 2017).

99. Susan Juster, *Sacred Violence in Early America* (Philadelphia: University of Pennsylvania Press, 2016), 19.

100. René Girard, *Sacrifice* (East Lansing: Michigan State University Press, 2011 [2003]).

101. Sarah J. Purcell, *Sealed with Blood: War, Sacrifice, and Memory in Revolutionary America* (Philadelphia: University of Pennsylvania Press, 2002); and for a more general treatment of the

Collective responses to bloodshed exemplify the extent to which ritualized religious interpretations intersect with the situations that supply different ways of responding to these events. Mutilated bodies, beheadings, and other evidences of extreme violence are largely shielded from public view through the editorial decisions of print journalism and television news. Motion pictures with graphic violence do less to drive home the bloodshed of war and terror than to depict valor as protection of loved ones. The nation's masculine strength is resurrected after an event such as the 9/11 attacks on New York and Washington without depictions of brutal atrocities. These are images that privileged populations that are not themselves in harm's way can largely escape. They fall less easily into the standard theodicies that religions provide than into the abyss that is simply unthinkable.[102]

The exceptions are images of ordinary people committing heinous acts of bodily injury. The visceral shock is inescapable, demanding an explanation, for which attributions of responsibility to "foreign" religious ideologies supply a ready interpretation. When the perpetrators are "people like us," the search for understanding is more difficult. Mental illness and lax surveillance become the standard explanations for gun violence. Degradation and death committed on behalf of the nation necessarily require political deliberation and on occasion embodied activism as in opposition to the death penalty and protests against police violence. Different responses occur when the injured and degraded bodies represent acts that may be publicly understood, even approved, and yet are necessary to publicly disavow. The images published by CBS News in 2004 of prisoners at Abu Ghraib being tortured by American soldiers evoked international condemnation but also prompted efforts to account for what had happened. Interpretations unsurprisingly placed blame on the soldiers directly involved and posed questions about who if anyone at higher ranks should be held responsible. The more interesting responses dealt with the management of the images themselves. The most widely publicized photo which became emblematic of the larger event was the image of prisoner Ali Shallal al-Quaisi shrouded and with arms outstretched in a manner impossible for Western viewers to avoid associating with crucifixion. Gruesome photos of short-shackling,

---

horrors of war and the values that nevertheless motivate participation and acceptance, Miguel A. Centeno and Elaine Enriquez, *War and Society* (Cambridge, UK: Polity Press, 2016).

102. Claire Sisco King, *Washed in Blood: Male Sacrifice, Trauma, and the Cinema* (New Brunswick, NJ: Rutgers University Press, 2012), 120–61, develops these conclusions in the context of post-9/11 motion pictures.

nudity, beatings, and rape were generally withheld on grounds that they violated norms of public decency and that narrative descriptions were horrific enough. Some of the accounts found it as troubling that the soldiers took pictures as that they engaged in torture. Advocates for wider circulation of the photos argued that the shock value would shape public opinion sufficiently to affect policy but worried that interest would diminish before that happened. Further discussion also noted how the placement of the event at the distant prison diminished its power and how soon the response turned toward procedural aspects of military regulations and legislation.[103]

Exceptional Bodies

In addition to the practices that pertain to ordinary people, the literature on religion has long included an emphasis on what for lack of a better word can be termed "exceptional" bodies. Exceptional bodies stand out because they are understood to be depraved, ignoble, carnal, or despised; weak, disabled, or dying; exceptionally strong, valorous, or heroic; or in some fashion suprahuman. Roland Barthes famously describes the wrestler in these terms, a body whose grandiloquence in each excessive gesture presents a spectacle of good and evil.[104] Interest in exceptional bodies is evident in religious teachings about miraculous births, angels, spirits, healings, sinless lives, and resurrected bodies.[105] Mircea Eliade says the "dream time" that preceded the world as we know it is populated in tribal mythology with bodies that are larger than life, purer, and holier.[106] These bodies function as out-of-reach models for ordinary bodies to emulate and in so doing to gain greater awareness of human frailty and mortality. They are also of interest in cognitive theories of evolutionary

---

103. Jared Del Rosso, *Talking about Torture: How Political Discourse Shapes the Debate* (New York: Columbia University Press, 2015), 77–94; Anne-Marie Cusac, *Cruel and Unusual: The Culture of Punishment in America* (New Haven, CT: Yale University Press, 2009), 244–52; Jonathan Markovitz, "Art and Abu Ghraib," *Contexts* 8, 3 (2009), 62–64; and Amy Adler, *Punishment and Popular Culture* (New York: NYU Press, 2015), 236–56.

104. Roland Barthes, "The World of Wrestling," in Roland Barthes, *Mythologies,* trans. Annette Lavers (New York: Farrar, Straus, and Giroux, 1972 [1957]), 13–23.

105. See for example Serinity Young, *Women Who Fly: Goddesses, Witches, Mystics, and Other Airborne Females* (New York: Oxford University Press, 2018).

106. Eliade, *The Sacred and the Profane,* 68–114; an allusion to this argument is also present in Bellah's discussion of America's myth of origin in Robert N. Bellah, *The Broken Covenant: American Civil Religion in Time of Trial* (Boston: Seabury, 1975).

psychology which suggest that religion may have gained adherents and perpetuated itself over the millennia through ritual practices devoted to memorable beings who could walk through walls, become invisible, be in more than one place at a time, and perform other suprahuman feats.[107] Further interest in exceptional bodies reflects questions about exclusion and inclusion, ambiguities and transformations of sexual and racial identities, and the cultural ascription of embodied norms. Bodies that are mad, feeble-minded, deranged, promiscuous, cruel, or dangerous serve as stigmatized "others" to be discriminated against or avoided, for instance, while sick, disabled, and suffering bodies provide occasions for compassion.

Robert Orsi's challenge to religion scholars to pay greater attention to the American Catholic cult of pain and suffering directed attention toward the largely neglected normalization and even adulation of bodies in exceptional difficulty. Crippled saints, deformed babies, hunchbacks, persons afflicted with speech defects, and people dying of cancer, Orsi argued, were all among the bodies that religious practices deal with, less in the Weberian sense of providing theodicies, and more in terms of real-life interaction. The crucial point is that these exceptional bodies are less exceptional than their categorization and exclusion from ordinary life implies. It is the exceptional person who does not have to interact with a family member in a nursing home or a friend who has returned from military service permanently disabled or who personally is under treatment for an addiction or a debilitating disease. Acknowledgment of the physical imperfections of life is further reason to insist that the ontologies of religious practice include the undesired and unanticipated.[108] Exceptional bodies serve both as reminders of past or anticipated personal pain and as representations of distant suffering that can be experienced vicariously from afar. Omri Elisha's study of the "persecuted church," for example, provides an interesting discussion of twenty-first-century Americans establishing vicarious connections with martyrs in other countries by donating to charitable

---

107. Pascal Boyer, *Religion Explained: The Human Instincts that Fashion Gods, Spirits, and Ancestors* (London: Heinemann, 2001); Pascal Boyer and Charles Ramble, "Cognitive Templates for Religious Concepts: Cross-Cultural Evidence for Recall of Counter-Intuitive Representations," *Cognitive Science* 25, 4 (2001), 535–64; and Pascal Boyer and Brian Bergstrom, "Evolutionary Perspectives on Religion," *Annual Review of Anthropology* 37 (2008), 111–30.

108. Robert A. Orsi, *Between Heaven and Earth: The Religious Worlds People Make and the Scholars Who Study Them* (Princeton, NJ: Princeton University Press, 2005), 19–46.

organizations, subscribing to newsletters, and wearing commemorative wristbands and bracelets.[109]

Much of the recent work on exceptional bodies has focused on sexual identities. In conventional classificatory treatments, sexual identities posed questions about the phenotypical markers and adornments that prompted persons to be classified as male, female, or transgendered. Practice approaches also emphasize the processes of classification but consider them extending over time and varying in situational selectivity. Brian Morris, for instance, adapts Certeau's discussion of urban walking to highlight how gay couples in 1990s Melbourne consulted "alternative" maps of the city to identify "gay friendly" areas where they would feel safe walking hand-in-hand down the street. It was the interaction between bodily affection and socially defined space that transformed the meaning of exceptionality.[110] Amin Ghaziani makes a theoretically similar observation in a different context, arguing that the suburban dispersal of gay persons in the United States during the same period required a renegotiation of assumptions about where and when same-sex walking was safe. Walking in suburbia did not feel as safe, natural, or "at home" as in a gay neighborhood, and thus occurred less often or with different attire and mannerisms.[111] The comparable adaptation implied in studies of religious settings is that "welcoming," as congregations may assert themselves to be, means not only a doctrinal stance but also a safe space in which ordinary physical gestures of welcoming are present. Elizabeth Grosz terms the recognition of this kind of interaction between bodies and space an "interface" of the body with its environment, each potentially influencing the other, just as living in a city produces urbanized ways of walking and speaking, which in turn collectively create the disparate flows and movements that define the city. Always there is the asymmetry between what the individual experiences and what the collectivity requires.[112]

In the final analysis, exceptional bodies' exceptionality poses one of the most difficult challenges for future studies of religion focusing on practice. Much of practice theory's appeal is that its ontological richness makes the human

---

109. Omri Elisha, "Saved by a Martyr: Evangelical Mediation, Sanctification, and the 'Persecuted Church,'" *Journal of the American Academy of Religion* 84, 4 (2016), 1056–80.

110. Brian Morris, "What We Talk about When We Talk about 'Walking in the City,'" *Cultural Studies* 18, 5 (2004), 675–97.

111. Amin Ghaziani, *There Goes the Gayborhood?* (Princeton, NJ: Princeton University Press, 2014).

112. Elizabeth Grosz, "Bodies-Cities," in *Sexuality and Space*, edited by Beatriz Colomina (New York: Princeton Architectural Press, 1992), 241–54.

sciences more human by emphasizing the person and the personal idiosyncrasies that are enacted in ordinary life. These are the reasons that heuristic tools that can be versatilely applied and that are generalizable in this respect are intellectually preferable to the parsimonious but elusive generalizations that pertain to randomly sampled populations. They are also the source of claims that the value of investigating practice in ordinary life is to disclose the hidden acts, assumptions, and meanings of which it is constituted. The local, immediate, micro textures of ordinary life are thus privileged. Yet, as I have shown in the case of situations, intentions, feelings, and bodies, these inherently personal small-scale habits and improvisations are always nested within larger structures and have implications for those structures. The power arrangements that stigmatize or valorize exceptional bodies also shape the actions of non-exceptional bodies in governing the situations in which they are present and the motions, postures, and positions that are expected. Bodies are acted upon, the passive construction reflecting all that is not under their control, and how they proactively respond both signifies and amplifies certain cultural representations.

The challenge that next-generation studies of religious practice must address is developing more satisfactory analytic tools for connecting the micro textures of ordinary devotion to the large, seemingly intractable forces that are visibly evident in the vast disparities of human freedom and opportunity. The situations, intentions, feelings, and bodies that constitute ordinary life for individual human persons inform the well-publicized narratives that supply interpretations of what it means to be human and what our purposes should be. The assumptions that seem so readily taken for granted in personal affairs are ideas that the privileged few have been able to produce and disseminate. The narratives and ideas form the basis of collective identities and the communities in which we live. These too need to be examined with the same attentiveness to practice.

Conclusion

THE PRACTICE TURN, as I have suggested, has been gathering steam over the past several decades to the point that much of what it says about religion in general terms can now be taken for granted. Indeed, in conversations with colleagues and students, the point about considering religion as a practice seems to be accepted as given. And this is as it should be. The more we know about religion, the more we realize that its presence in the world is not only about tradition and belief but also about the messiness of everyday life that requires constant adaptation and recurrent improvisation. In brief, religion is best understood as practice. Still, this is a much more significant development than is often realized. It profoundly challenges the notion that vast generalizations about religion can be attained from preconceived scientific investigations that seek to test variables and hypotheses. It calls for closer attention to the details of religious practice in all its complexity and for heuristic concepts to be used that illuminate the particularities of those details. It especially emphasizes the situated specificity of practice and the fact that practices unfold over time. What I have tried to do is pull together observations from the strands of empirical research that have been moving the study of religious practice in these directions toward greater detail and with closer attention to the complexities and nuances involved. This second generation of scholarship, building as it has on significant insights from mid-twentieth-century epistemological explorations, has produced a rich trove of literature that contributes not only to substantive descriptions of religion's many manifestations but also to an enhanced toolkit of concepts and topics for future studies.

My experience in helping to guide the work of younger scholars of religion across the several disciplinary traditions they represent is that conceptual insights are too often drawn only from within particular disciplines and, for that matter, too often limited to remarks about suggestive ideas from a single book or article that happens to be in vogue. Despite reading widely, scholars of religion, just as in other fields, have limited time to explore what has been a burgeoning literature specifically on religion, let alone on related topics. I've tried in the foregoing pages to be brief and at the same time to identify significant arguments and observations in this emerging literature. I am confident that the next generation of scholarship on religious practice will be enriched by asking in even greater detail how the convictions and activities that bring a sense of sacredness into our lives are cobbled together with the ordinary stuff of daily experience.

Stepping away from the interesting details of the many contributions that scholars of religion have made in recent years, the main arguments I have tried to develop are these: First, the most familiar theoretical works—from Durkheim forward—that have guided scholarship on religion remain of enormous value but need to be revisited to see that the central arguments were not about cognitive categories and classifications but about practices, whether instantiated in rituals, conversations, meetings, and other varieties of social interaction. Second, religious practice occurs in concrete situations and must be investigated taking account of the constraints, cues, affordances, habits, improvisations, and power dynamics in those situations, despite the fact that conclusions from such investigations necessitate a focus on contingencies and variations to a greater extent than on universals and generalizations. Third, the intentionality that has long been considered an elemental feature of religious practice needs to be rediscovered and recast away from discussions of psychological states and goal orientations toward intentions in action that are both observable and provisional. Fourth, feelings also must be considered anew less as the awe and ecstasy typically associated with profound religious experience and more as the features of ordinary life that are carried into religious practice in conformity with implicit rules about expressing and interpreting feelings. And fifth, the rich inquiries that have focused on bodies and embodiment in recent years need to be enhanced in conversation with research on body memory, kinesthetics, habit, and adornment.

The challenge but also the opportunity for scholarship on religion going forward is to probe more deeply into the nuances of religious practice by pulling insights from the literature on these and related topics. Field experiments, audit studies, lab studies, surveys, and big data from social media will continue to provide quantifiable evidence, but it has been notable in recent years that scholars working with the best quantitative methods have also turned toward qualitative research to gain greater purchase on the meanings and implications of quantitative results. The basic demographics of religion are of continuing interest, and yet the measurement problems associated with even such rudimentary religious practices as worship service attendance are sufficiently complex that applications of statistical precision are often impossible or at best disappointing. Religious practice that emphasizes the complexities of situations, intentions, feelings, and bodies is likely to be investigated with greater insight by qualitative methods than by quantitative methods. Qualitative studies bring possibilities of closer attention to *how* people talk about and enact religious practices and how those practices intersect with ordinary life.

Scholarly studies of religion bear the burden of focusing on topics that only for the most dedicated few can be said to dominate the daily lives of ordinary people and, for this reason, will continue to focus, on the one hand, on exceptional communities and places and events through which religion's power is known and, on the other hand, to require attention to the influences of nonreligious activities on institutional religious practices and the disparate manifestations of religious practice in settings as diverse as corporate boardrooms and refugee relocation camps. It will always remain disputable whether religion is truly of sufficient importance in the contemporary world to bear as much inquiry as studies of business, politics, and families. Yet it remains true that religious practices continue to play significant roles in the lives of vast numbers of people and indeed to be topics about which much can be learned, both by those who specialize in the study of religion and by those who consider it mostly in reference to other topics.

What is notable about the ever-widening and ever-diversifying scholarship on religious practice is that it has benefited greatly from intensive engagement on the part of specialists whose work focuses squarely on religion, often within a single tradition or context, and at the same time from insights drawn from wider inquiries in multiple disciplines such as anthropology, history, literature, and sociology. I am confident that will continue to be true. Indeed, one can hardly imagine understanding conceptions of sacred space or sacred experience, for instance, without paying close attention to the various literatures on place, situated social interaction, materiality, and affordances, just as scholarship on intentions, feelings, bodies, and other topics also necessitates asking what can be known about these matters in settings having nothing to do with religion. To be sure, much of what is desired to be known about religion will be driven by current events at least as long as religion is a matter of journalistic interest. The challenge for academic scholarship nevertheless is also to work in the crevices, asking questions that both address and transcend the immediate concerns of the day. To that end, delving deeply into the constituent dynamics of practice will be an endeavor of enduring value.

BIBLIOGRAPHY

Abreu, Maria José A. de. "The FedEx Saints: Patrons of Mobility and Speed in a Neoliberal City." In *Things: Religion and the Question of Materiality*, edited by Dick Houtman and Birgit Meyer, 321–35. New York: Fordham University Press, 2012.

Abu-Lughod, Lila and Catherine A. Lutz. "Introduction: Emotion, Discourse, and the Politics of Everyday Life." In *Language and the Politics of Emotion*, edited by Catherine A. Lutz and Lila Abu-Lughod, 1–23. New York: Cambridge University Press, 1990.

Abu-Raiya, Hisham, Kenneth I. Pargament, Neal Krause, and Gail Ironson. "Robust Links Between Religious/Spiritual Struggles, Psychological Distress, and Well-Being in a National Sample of American Adults." *American Journal of Orthopsychiatry* 85, 6 (2015), 565–75.

Adams, Will. "Discovering the Sacred in Everyday Life: An Empirical Phenomenological Study." *Humanistic Psychologist* 24, 1 (1996), 28–54.

Adler, Amy. *Punishment and Popular Culture*. New York: NYU Press, 2015.

Ahmed, Sara. "Affective Economies." *Social Text* 22, 2 (2004), 117–39.

———. "Collective Feelings Or, The Impressions Left by Others." *Theory, Culture, and Society* 21, 2 (2004), 25–42.

———. *The Promise of Happiness*. Durham, NC: Duke University Press, 2010.

———. *The Cultural Politics of Emotion*, 2nd ed. Edinburgh: Edinburgh University Press, 2014.

Aldrich, John H., Jacob M. Montgomery, and Wendy Wood. "Turnout as a Habit." *Political Behavior* 33, 4 (2011), 535–63.

Alexander, Catherine. "The Garden as Occasional Domestic Space." *Signs* 27, 3 (2002), 857–71.

Alexander, Jeffrey. "Citizen and Enemy as Symbolic Classification." In *Cultivating Differences: Symbolic Boundaries and the Making of Inequality*, edited by Michele Lamont and Marcel Fournier, 289–308. Chicago: University of Chicago Press, 1992.

———. "Cultural Pragmatics: Social Performance between Ritual and Strategy." *Sociological Theory* 22, 4 (2004), 527–73.

———. "Iconic Experience in Art and Life: Surface/Depth Beginning with Giacometti's Standing Woman." *Theory, Culture, and Society* 25, 5 (2008), 1–19.

———. "Iconic Consciousness: The Material Feeling of Meaning." *Theory, Culture, and Society* 103, 1 (2010), 10–15.

Aljunied, Khairudin. *Muslim Cosmopolitanism: Southeast Asian Islam in Comparative Perspective*. Edinburgh: Edinburgh University Press, 2017.

Allen, Kieran and Brian O'Boyle. *Durkheim: A Critical Introduction*. London: Pluto Press, 2017.

Almquist, Julka and Julia Lupton. "Affording Meaning: Design-Oriented Research from the Humanities and Social Sciences." *Design Issues* 26, 1 (2010), 3–14.
Alston, William P. "Feelings." *Philosophical Review* 78, 1 (1969), 3–34.
Alter, Joseph. *The Wrestler's Body: Identity and Ideology in North India*. Berkeley and Los Angeles: University of California Press, 1992.
Amato, Joseph. *On Foot: A History of Walking*. New York: NYU Press, 2004.
Ammerman, Nancy Tatom. "Bodies and Spirits: Health, Illness, and Mortality." In *Sacred Stories, Spiritual Tribes: Finding Religion in Everyday Life*, edited by Nancy Tatom Ammerman, 251–300. New York: Oxford University Press, 2013.
———. "Spiritual Practices in Everyday Life." In *Sacred Stories, Spiritual Tribes: Finding Religion in Everyday Life*, edited by Nancy Tatom Ammerman, 57–94. New York: Oxford University Press, 2013.
———. "From Canopies to Conversations: The Continuing Significance of 'Plausibility Structures.'" In *Peter L. Berger and the Sociology of Religion: 50 Years after The Sacred Canopy*, edited by Titus Hjelm, 45–69. London: Bloomsbury Academic, 2018.
Anscombe, G.E.M. *Intention*. Oxford: Basil Blackwell, 1957.
Appadurai, Arjun. "Introduction: Commodities and the Politics of Value." In *The Social Life of Things: Commodities in Cultural Perspective*, edited by Arjun Appadurai, 3–63. New York: Cambridge University Press, 1986.
Archer, Margaret S. "Routine, Reflexivity, and Realism." *Sociological Theory* 28, 3 (2010), 272–303.
Argyle, Michael. "Causes and Correlates of Happiness." In *Well-Being: Foundations of Hedonic Psychology*, edited by Daniel Kahneman, Ed Diener, and Norbert Schwarz, 353–73. New York: Russell Sage Foundation, 1999.
Asad, Talal. "The Definition of Marriage." *Man* 60 (May 1960), 73–74.
———. "Anthropological Conceptions of Religion: Reflections on Geertz." *Man* 18, 2 (1983), 237–59.
———. "Medieval Heresy: An Anthropological View." *Social History* 11, 3 (1986), 346–62.
———. *Genealogies of Religion: Discipline and Reasons of Power in Christianity and Islam*. Baltimore, MD: Johns Hopkins University Press, 1993.
———. "Thinking about the Secular Body, Pain, and Liberal Politics." In *Words: Religious Language Matters*, edited by Ernst Van den Hemel and Asja Szafraniec, 348–63. New York: Fordham University Press, 2016.
Atkins, G. Douglas. *Reading Essays: An Invitation*. Athens: University of Georgia Press, 2008.
Aupers, Stef. "Enchantment, Inc.: Online Gaming Between Spiritual Experience and Commodity Fetishism." In *Things: Religion and the Question of Materiality*, edited by Dick Houtman and Birgit Meyer, 339–55. New York: Fordham University Press, 2012.
Bachelard, Gaston. *The Poetics of Space*. Boston: Beacon Press, 1994.
Badone, Ellen. "Conventional and Unconventional Pilgrimages: Conceptualizing Sacred Travel in the Twenty-First Century." In *Redefining Pilgrimage: New Perspectives on Historical and Contemporary Pilgrimages*, edited by Antón M. Pazos, 7–32. New York: Routledge, 2014.
Bakhtin, Mikhail M. *The Dialogic Imagination: Four Essays*. Austin: University of Texas Press, 1981.
Bandelj, Nina. "Emotions in Economic Action and Interaction." *Theory and Society* 38, 4 (2009), 347–66.

Banerjee, Sikata. *Muscular Nationalism: Gender, Violence, and Empire in India and Ireland, 1914–2004*. New York: NYU Press, 2012.

Bargh, John A. "The Four Horsemen of Automaticity: Awareness, Intention, Efficiency, and Control in Social Cognition." In *Handbook of Social Cognition: Vol. 1 Basic Processes*, edited by Robert S. Wyer and Thomas K. Srull, 1–40. Hove, UK: Erlbaum Associates, 1994.

Barnes, Barry. "Practice as Collective Action." In *The Practice Turn in Contemporary Theory*, edited by Theodore R. Schatzki, Karin Knorr Cetina, and Eike von Savigny, 25–36. New York: Routledge, 2001.

Barreto, Matt A. *Ethnic Cues: The Role of Shared Ethnicity in Latino Political Participation*. Ann Arbor: University of Michigan Press, 2010.

Barro, Robert J. and Rachel M. McCleary. "Religion and Economic Growth Across Countries." *American Sociological Review* 68, 5 (2003), 760–81.

Barthes, Roland. "The World of Wrestling." In Roland Barthes, *Mythologies*, trans. Annette Lavers, 13–23. New York: Farrar, Straus, and Giroux, 1972, originally published 1957.

Bartkowski, John P. and Christopher G. Ellison, eds. *Children and Childhood in American Religions*. New Brunswick, NJ: Rutgers University Press, 2009.

Batson, C. Daniel and W. Larry Ventis. *The Religious Experience*. New York: Oxford University Press, 1982.

Bauch, Nicholas. *A Geography of Digestion: Biotechnology and the Kellogg Cereal Enterprise*. Berkeley and Los Angeles: University of California Press, 2017.

Becker, Howard. "Constructive Typology in the Social Sciences." *American Sociological Review* 5, 1 (1940), 40–55.

——. "Sacred and Secular Societies: Considered with Reference to Folk-State and Similar Classifications." *Social Forces* 28, 4 (1950), 361–76.

Becker, Howard and Robert C. Myers. "Sacred and Secular Aspects of Human Sociation." *Sociometry* 5, 3 (1942), 207–29.

Belding, Jennifer N., Malcolm G. Howard, Anne M. McGuire, Amanda C. Schwartz, and Janie H. Wilson. "Social Buffering by God: Prayer and Measures of Stress." *Journal of Religion and Health* 49, 2 (2010), 179–87.

Bell, Catherine. *Ritual Theory and Ritual Practice*. New York: Oxford University Press, 1992.

Bell, Daniel. "Beyond Modernism, Beyond Self." In *Art, Politics, and Will: Essays in Honor of Lionel Trilling*, edited by Quentin Anderson, Stephen Donadio, and Steven Marcus, 213–53. New York: Basic, 1977.

Bell, Rudolph M. *Holy Anorexia*. Chicago: University of Chicago Press, 1985.

Bellah, Robert N. "Durkheim and History." *American Sociological Review* 24, 4 (1959), 447–61.

——. "Religious Evolution." *American Sociological Review* 29 (June 1964), 358–74.

——. "Transcendence in Contemporary Piety." In *Transcendence*, edited by Herbert W. Richardson and Donald R. Cutler, 85–97. Boston: Beacon Press, 1969.

——. "Confessions of a Former Establishment Fundamentalist." *Bulletin of the Council on the Study of Religion* 1, 3 (1970), 3–6.

——. *Beyond Belief: Essays on Religion in a Post-Traditional World*. New York: Harper & Row, 1970.

——. "Introduction." In *Émile Durkheim on Morality and Society*, edited by Robert N. Bellah, ix–lv. Chicago: University of Chicago, 1973.

———, editor. *Emile Durkheim on Morality and Society*. Chicago: University of Chicago Press, 1973.

———. *The Broken Covenant: American Civil Religion in Time of Trial*. Boston: Seabury, 1975.

———. "Durkheim and Ritual." In *The Cambridge Companion to Durkheim*, edited by Jeffrey C. Alexander and Philip Smith, 183–210. New York: Cambridge University Press, 2005.

———. *Religion in Human Evolution*. Cambridge, MA: Harvard University Press, 2011.

Bellah, Robert N., Richard Madsen, William M. Sullivan, Ann Swidler, and Steven M. Tipton. *Habits of the Heart: Individualism and Commitment in American Life*. Berkeley and Los Angeles: University of California Press, 1984.

Ben-Layashi, Samir. "'Muslim Body' versus 'Jewish Body': The Invention of a Division." In *A History of Jewish-Muslim Relations: From the Origins to the Present Day*, edited by Abdelwahab Meddeb and Benjamin Stora, 1042–51. Princeton, NJ: Princeton University Press, 2013.

Bender, Courtney. *Heaven's Kitchen: Living Religion at God's Love We Deliver*. Chicago: University of Chicago Press, 2003.

———. "Touching the Transcendent: Rethinking Religious Experience in the Sociological Study of Religion." In *Everyday Religion: Observing Modern Religious Lives*, edited by Nancy T. Ammerman, 202–27. New York: Oxford University Press, 2007.

———. *The New Metaphysicals: Spirituality and the American Religious Imagination*. Chicago: University of Chicago Press, 2010.

———. "Practicing Religions." In *The Cambridge Companion to Religious Studies*, edited by Robert A. Orsi, 273–95. New York: Cambridge University Press, 2011.

Bennett, Jane. *The Enchantment of Modern Life: Attachments, Crossings, and Ethics*. Princeton, NJ: Princeton University Press, 2001.

Bereczkei, Tamas, Bela Birkas, and Zsuzsanna Kerekes. "The Presence of Others, Prosocial Traits, Machiavellianism: A Personality x Situation Approach." *Social Psychology* 41, 4 (2010), 238–45.

Berg, Anna Lea. "From Religious to Secular Place-making: How Does the Secular Matter for Religious Place Construction in the Local?" *Social Compass* 66, 1 (March 2019), 35–48.

Berger, Peter L. *The Sacred Canopy: Elements of a Sociological Theory of Religion*. Garden City, NY: Doubleday, 1967.

———. *Adventures of an Accidental Sociologist: How to Explain the World Without Becoming a Bore*. Amherst, NY: Prometheus Books, 2011.

Berger, Peter L. and Hansfried Kellner. "Marriage and the Construction of Reality." In Peter L. Berger, *Facing Up to Modernity: Excursions in Society, Politics, and Religion*, 5–22. New York: Basic Books, 1977.

Berger, Peter L. and Thomas Luckmann. *The Social Construction of Reality: A Treatise in the Sociology of Knowledge*. Garden City, NY: Doubleday, 1966.

Berkowitz, Aaron L. *The Improvising Mind: Cognition and Creativity in the Musical Moment*. New York: Oxford University Press, 2010.

Berryman, Phillip. *The Religious Roots of Rebellion: Christians in Central American Revolutions*. Maryknoll, NY: Orbis Books, 1984.

Biehl, João and Peter Locke. "Foreword." In *Unfinished: The Anthropology of Becoming*, edited by João Biehl and Peter Locke, ix–xiii. Durham, NC: Duke University Press, 2017.

Biel, Anders and Andreas Nilsson. "Religious Values and Environmental Concern: Harmony and Detachment." *Social Science Quarterly* 86, 1 (2005), 178–91.
Bierman, Alex. "The Effects of Childhood Maltreatment on Adult Religiosity and Spirituality: Rejecting God the Father Because of Abusive Fathers?" *Journal for the Scientific Study of Religion* 44, 3 (2005), 349–59.
Bivens, Jason C. *Religion of Fear: The Politics of Horror in Conservative Evangelicalism*. New York: Oxford University Press, 2008.
Bjork-James, Sophie. "Training the Porous Body: Evangelicals and the Ex-Gay Movement." *American Anthropologist* 120, 4 (December 2018), 547–58.
Bloch, Maurice. "Language, Anthropology and Cognitive Science." *Man* 26, 2 (1991), 183–98.
Blomley, Nicholas. *Rights of Passage: Sidewalks and the Regulation of Public Flow*. London: Routledge, 2011.
Bobker, Danielle. "The Literature and Culture of the Closet in the Eighteenth Century." *Digital Defoe* 6, 1 (2014), 1948–1802.
———. "Coming Out: Closet Rhetoric and Media Publics." *History of the Present* 5, 1 (2015), 31–64.
Boltanski, Luc. *Distant Suffering: Morality, Media and Politics*, trans. Graham Burchell. Cambridge, UK: Cambridge University Press, 2004.
Booher, Amanda K. "Docile Bodies, Supercrips, and the Plays of Prosthetics." *International Journal of Feminist Approaches to Bioethics* 3, 2 (2010), 63–89.
Borsch, Frederick. *Keeping Faith at Princeton: A Brief History of Religious Pluralism at Princeton and Other Universities*. Princeton, NJ: Princeton University Press, 2012.
Bourdieu, Pierre. *Outline of a Theory of Practice*. New York: Cambridge University Press, 1977.
———. *The Logic of Practice*, trans. Richard Nice. Stanford, CA: Stanford University Press, 1990, originally published 1980.
———. "Genesis and Structure of the Religious Field." *Comparative Social Research* 13, 1 (1991), 1–44.
———. *The Field of Cultural Production: Essays on Art and Literature*, edited by Randal Johnson. New York: Columbia University Press, 1993.
———. *The Rules of Art: Genesis and Structure of the Literary Field*. Stanford, CA: Stanford University Press, 1995.
Bourke, Joanna. "Fear and Anxiety: Writing about Emotion in Modern History." *History Workshop Journal* 55 (2003), 111–33.
Boyer, Pascal. *Religion Explained: The Human Instincts that Fashion Gods, Spirits, and Ancestors*. London: Heinemann, 2001.
Boyer, Pascal and Charles Ramble. "Cognitive Templates for Religious Concepts: Cross-Cultural Evidence for Recall of Counter-Intuitive Representations." *Cognitive Science* 25, 4 (2001), 535–64.
Boyer, Pascal and Brian Bergstrom. "Evolutionary Perspectives on Religion." *Annual Review of Anthropology* 37 (2008), 111–30.
Brader, Ted. *Campaigning for Hearts and Minds: How Emotional Appeals in Political Ads Work*. Chicago: University of Chicago Press, 2006.
Brayne, Sarah. "Surveillance and System Avoidance: Criminal Justice Contact and Institutional Attachment." *American Sociological Review* 79, 3 (2014), 367–91.

———. *Policed: Surveillance and Prediction in the Age of Big Data*. New York: Oxford University Press, 2018.
Brekke, Torkel. "Contradiction and the Merit of Giving in Indian Religions." *Numen* 45, 3 (1998), 287–320.
Bremer, Thomas. *Blessed with Tourists: The Borderlands of Religion and Tourism in San Antonio*. Chapel Hill: University of North Carolina Press, 2004.
Brenner, Suzanne. "Reconstructing Self and Society: Javanese Muslim Women and 'The Veil.'" *American Ethnologist* 23, 4 (1996), 673–97.
Brown, Bill. "Thing Theory." *Critical Inquiry* 28, 1 (2001), 1–22.
Brown, Norman O. *Life Against Death: The Psychoanalytical Meaning of History*, 2nd ed. Middletown, CT: Wesleyan University Press, 1985.
———. *Love's Body*. Berkeley and Los Angeles: University of California Press, 1996; originally published 1966.
Brubaker, Rogers and Frederick Cooper. "Beyond 'Identity.'" *Theory and Society* 29, 1 (2000), 1–47.
Brubaker, Rogers, Mara Loveman, and Peter Stamatov. "Ethnicity as Cognition." *Theory and Society* 33, 1 (2004), 31–64.
Bryan, Jennifer L., Sydnee H. Lucas, Michalle C. Quist, Mai-Ly N. Steers, Dawn W. Foster, Chelsie M. Young, and Qian Lu. "God, Can I Tell You Something? The Effect of Religious Coping on the Relationship Between Anxiety Over Emotional Expression, Anxiety, and Depressive Symptoms." *Psychology of Religion and Spirituality* 8, 1 (2016), 46–53.
Buchanan, Ian. *Michel de Certeau: Cultural Theorist*. London: Sage, 2000.
Buggeln, Gretchen. *The Suburban Church: Modernism and Community in Postwar America*. Minneapolis: University of Minnesota Press, 2015.
Burawoy, Michael. "The Extended Case Method." *Sociological Theory* 16, 1 (1998), 4–33.
———. *The Extended Case Method: Four Countries, Four Decades, Four Great Transformations, and One Theoretical Tradition*. Berkeley and Los Angeles: University of California Press, 2009.
Bush, Stephen S. *Visions of Religion: Experience, Meaning, and Power*. New York: Oxford University Press, 2014.
Butler, Judith. *Gender Trouble*. New York: Routledge, 2002.
———. "Merleau-Ponty and the Touch of Malebranche." In *The Cambridge Companion to Merleau-Ponty*, edited by Taylor Carman and Mark B. N. Hansen, 181–205. New York: Cambridge University Press, 2005.
———. *Precarious Life: The Powers of Mourning and Violence*. London: Verso, 2005.
Byford, Jovan and Cristian Tileaga. "Accounts of a Troubled Past: Psychology, History, and Texts of Experience." *Qualitative Psychology* 4, 1 (2017), 101–17.
Bynum, Caroline. "Why All the Fuss about the Body? A Medievalist's Perspective." *Critical Inquiry* 22, 1 (1995), 1–33.
Cadge, Wendy. *Heartwood: The First Generation of Theravada Buddhism in America*. Chicago: University of Chicago Press, 2005.
Cadge, Wendy and Lynn Davidman. "Ascription, Choice, and the Construction of Religious Identities in the Contemporary United States." *Journal for the Scientific Study of Religion* 45, 1 (2006), 23–38.
Calvino, Italo. *Six Memos for the Next Millennium*. Cambridge, MA: Harvard University Press, 1988.

Casasanto, Daniel and Gary Lupyan. "All Concepts Are Ad Hoc Concepts." In *The Conceptual Mind: New Directions in the Study of Concepts*, edited by Eric Margolis and Stephen Laurence, 543–66. Cambridge, MA: MIT Press, 2015.

Casey, Edward S. *Remembering: A Phenomenological Study*. Bloomington: Indiana University Press, 2000.

Centeno, Miguel A. and Elaine Enriquez. *War and Society*. Cambridge, UK: Polity Press, 2016.

Cerulo, Karen A. *Deciphering Violence: The Cognitive Structure of Right and Wrong*. New York: Routledge, 1998.

Cerulo, Karen A. and Andrea Barra. "In the Name of . . . : Legitimate Interactants in the Dialogue of Prayer." *Poetics* 36, 5–6 (2008), 374–88.

Chancellor, Joseph, Kristin Layous, Seth Margolis, and Sonja Lyubomirsky. "Clustering by Well-Being in Workplace Social Networks: Homophily and Social Contagion." *Emotion* 17, 3 (2017), 553–67.

Chaves, Mark. *American Religion: Contemporary Trends*. Princeton, NJ: Princeton University Press, 2011.

Cheah, Joseph. "The Function of Ethnicity in the Adaptation of Burmese Religious Practices." In *Emerging Voices: Experiences of Underrepresented Asian Americans*, edited by Huping Ling, 199–217. New Brunswick, NJ: Rutgers University Press, 2008.

Chen, Carolyn. "A Self of One's Own: Taiwanese Immigrant Women and Religious Conversion." *Gender and Society* 19, 3 (2005), 336–57.

Chong, Kelly H. "Negotiating Patriarchy: South Korean Evangelical Women and the Politics of Gender." *Gender and Society* 20, 6 (2006), 697–724.

Cioffi, Frank. "Intention and Interpretation in Criticism." In *On Literary Intention*, edited by David Newton-DeMolina, 55–73. Edinburgh: Edinburgh University Press, 1976.

Clawson, Laura. "'Blessed Be the Tie that Binds': Community and Spirituality among Sacred Harp Singers." *Poetics* 32, 3–4 (2004), 311–24.

———. *I Belong to This Band, Hallelujah! Community, Spirituality, and Tradition Among Sacred Harp Singers*. Chicago: University of Chicago Press, 2011.

Collins, Peter. "The Practice of Discipline and the Discipline of Practice." In *Exploring Regimes of Discipline: The Dynamics of Restraint*, edited by Noel Dyck, 135–55. New York: Berghahn Books, 2008.

Collins, Randall. *Weberian Sociological Theory*. New York: Cambridge University Press, 1986.

———. *Interaction Ritual Chains*. Princeton, NJ: Princeton University Press, 2004.

———. "The Classical Tradition in Sociology of Religion." In *The Sage Handbook of the Sociology of Religion*, edited by James A. Beckford and N. Jay Demerath, 19–38. Thousand Oaks, CA: Sage, 2007.

Comaroff, Jean. "The Politics of Conviction: Faith on the Neo-liberal Frontier." *Social Analysis* 53, 1 (2009), 17–38.

Comilang, Susan. "Through the Closet: Private Devotion and the Shaping of Female Subjectivity in the Religious Recess." *Renaissance and Reformation* 27, 3 (2003), 79–96.

Connolly, William E. "The Complexity of Intention." *Critical Inquiry* 37, 4 (2011), 792–99.

Cooper, Amy. "Time Seizures and the Self: Institutional Temporalities and Self-preservation Among Homeless Women." *Culture, Medicine, and Psychiatry* 39, 1 (2015), 162–85.

Cooper, M. Lynne. "Toward a Person × Situation Model of Sexual Risk-Taking Behaviors: Illuminating the Conditional Effects of Traits Across Sexual Situations and Relationship Contexts." *Journal of Personality and Social Psychology* 98, 2 (2010), 319–41.
Corrigan, John. "Religion and Emotions." In *Doing Emotions History*, edited by Susan J. Matt and Peter N. Stearns, 143–62. Urbana: University of Illinois Press, 2014.
Crawley, Ashon T. *Blackpentecostal Breath: The Aesthetics of Possibility*. New York: Fordham University Press, 2017.
Csordas, Thomas J. "Embodiment as a Paradigm for Anthropology." *Ethos* 18, 1 (1990), 5–47.
———. "Prophecy and the Performance of Metaphor." *American Anthropologist* 99, 2 (1997), 321–32.
———. *The Sacred Self: A Cultural Phenomenology of Charismatic Healing*. Berkeley and Los Angeles: University of California Press, 1997.
———. "Ritualization of Life." In *Practicing the Faith: The Ritual Life of Pentecostal-Charismatic Christians*, edited by Martin Lindhardt, 129–51. Brooklyn, NY: Berghahn Books, 2011.
———. "Toward a Cultural Phenomenology of Body-World Relations." In *Phenomenology in Anthropology*, edited by Kalpana Ram and Christopher Houston, 50–67. Bloomington: Indiana University Press, 2015.
Cunningham, Maddy. *Integrating Spirituality in Clinical Social Work Practice: Walking the Labyrinth*. Boston: Pearson Education, 2012.
Cusac, Anne-Marie. *Cruel and Unusual: The Culture of Punishment in America*. New Haven, CT: Yale University Press, 2009.
D'Andrade, Roy G. *The Development of Cognitive Anthropology*. New York: Oxford University Press, 1995.
Dant, Tim and Belinda Wheaton. "Windsurfing: An Extreme Form of Material and Embodied Interaction?" *Anthropology Today* 23, 6 (2007), 8–12.
Das, Veena. "Wittgenstein and Anthropology." *Annual Review of Anthropology* 27 (1998), 171–95.
Davidman, Lynn. *Becoming Un-Orthodox: Stories of Ex-Hasidic Jews*. New York: Oxford University Press, 2014.
Davidson, Donald. *Essays on Actions and Events*. New York: Oxford University Press, 1980.
Davidson, Naomi. *Only Muslim: Embodying Islam in Twentieth-Century France*. Ithaca, NY: Cornell University Press, 2012.
Davie, Grace. *The Sociology of Religion*. London: Sage, 2007.
Dawkins, Richard. *The God Delusion*. Boston: Houghton Mifflin, 2006.
De Certeau, Michel. *The Practice of Everyday Life*, trans. Steven Rendall. Berkeley and Los Angeles: University of California Press, 1984.
Deleuze, Gilles. "Postscript on the Societies of Control." *October* 59 (1992), 3–7.
DeLillo, Don. *White Noise*. New York: Penguin, 1984.
Del Rosso, Jared. *Talking about Torture: How Political Discourse Shapes the Debate*. New York: Columbia University Press, 2015.
Del Socorro Castañeda-Liles, Maria. *Our Lady of Everyday Life: La Virgen de Guadalupe and the Catholic Imagination of Mexican Women in America*. New York: Oxford University Press, 2018.
Dennett, Daniel C. *Breaking the Spell: Religion as a Natural Phenomenon*. New York: Penguin, 2006.
DeNora, Tia. *Music in Everyday Life*. New York: Cambridge University Press, 2000.

Derks, Sanne, Willy Jansen, and Catrien Notermans. "Miniatures and Stones in the Spiritual Economy of the Virgin of Urkupiña in Bolivia." In *Things: Religion and the Question of Materiality*, edited by Dick Houtman and Birgit Meyer, 198–211. New York: Fordham University Press, 2012.

Desmond, Matthew. *On the Fireline: Living and Dying with Wildland Firefighters*. Chicago: University of Chicago Press, 2008.

Dewey, John. *Human Nature and Conduct: An Introduction to Social Psychology*. New York: Henry Holt and Company, 1922.

Diehl, David and Daniel McFarland. "Toward a Historical Sociology of Social Situations." *American Journal of Sociology* 115, 6 (2010), 1713–52.

Djupe, Paul A. and Brian R. Calfano. *God Talk: Experimenting with the Religious Causes of Public Opinion*. Philadelphia: Temple University Press, 2013.

Dougherty, Beth L. "Somatic Coordination: An Ethnography of Religious Entrainment in Christian and Neo-Pagan Rituals." *Sociology of Religion* 79, 1 (March 2018), 108–28.

Douglas, Mary. *Purity and Danger: An Analysis of Concepts of Pollution and Taboo*. London: Routledge, 1966.

———. "The Idea of Home: A Kind of Space." *Social Research* 58, 1 (1991), 287–307.

Drescher, Elizabeth. *Choosing Our Religion: The Spiritual Lives of America's Nones*. New York: Oxford University Press, 2016.

Dubler, Joshua. *Down in the Chapel: Religious Life in an American Prison*. New York: Farrar, Straus and Giroux, 2013.

Duranti, Alessandro. "Intentionality." *Journal of Linguistic Anthropology* 9, 1/2 (1999), 134–36.

Durkheim, Émile. *The Rules of Sociological Method*. New York: Free Press, 1964, originally published 1885.

———. *The Elementary Forms of Religious Life*, trans. Karen E. Fields. New York: Free Press, 1995; originally published 1912.

Durkheim, Émile and Marcel Mauss. *Primitive Classification*, trans. Rodney Needham. London: Taylor and Francis, 2009, originally published 1903.

Duschinsky, Robbie. "Recognizing Secular Defilement: Douglas, Durkheim and Housework." *History and Anthropology* 25, 5 (2014), 553–70.

Edgell, Penny. "We Still Don't Know If Christianity 'Works,' Much Less Why: Response to Smith." *Sociology of Religion* 69, 4 (2008), 445–52.

Eliade, Mircea. *The Sacred and the Profane: The Nature of Religion*. New York: Harcourt, Brace and World, 1959.

Elias, Norbert. "On Human Beings and Their Emotions: A Process-Sociological Essay." In *The Body: Social Process and Cultural Theory*, edited by Mike Featherstone, Mike Hepworth, and Bryan S. Turner, 103–25. London: Sage, 1991.

Eliasoph, Nina and Paul Lichterman. "Culture in Interaction." *American Journal of Sociology* 108, 4 (2003), 735–94.

Eliot, T. S. *Murder in the Cathedral*. New York: Harcourt Brace, 1935.

Elisha, Omri. "Saved by a Martyr: Evangelical Mediation, Sanctification, and the 'Persecuted Church.'" *Journal of the American Academy of Religion* 84, 4 (2016), 1056–80.

———. "Proximations of Public Religion: Worship, Spiritual Warfare, and the Ritualization of Christian Dance." *American Anthropologist* 119, 1 (March 2017), 73–85.

Ellison, Christopher G. "Religious Involvement and Subjective Well-Being." *Journal of Health and Social Behavior* 32, 1 (1991), 80–99.

Ellison, Christopher G., Mark A. Musick, and George W. Holden. "Conservative Protestants and Corporal Punishment." *Journal of Marriage and Family* 73, 5 (2011), 946–61.

Emirbayer, Mustafa. "Useful Durkheim." *Sociological Theory* 14, 2 (1996), 109–30.

Emirbayer, Mustafa and Douglas W. Maynard. "Pragmatism and Ethnomethodology." *Qualitative Sociology* 34 (2011), 221–61.

Endres, Kirsten W. "Engaging the Spirits of the Dead: Soul-Calling Rituals and the Performative Construction of Efficacy." *Journal of the Royal Anthropological Institute* 14, 4 (2008), 755–73.

Erikson, Kai T. *Everything in Its Path: Destruction of Community in the Buffalo Creek Flood*. New York: Simon & Schuster, 1976.

Etherington, Laurence. "Canons of Environmental Law: Pollution of Churches and the Regulation of the Medieval 'Environment.'" *Legal Studies* 36, 4 (2016), 566–90.

Evans, Jonathan St. B. T. and Keith E. Stanovich. "Dual-Process Theories of Higher Cognition: Advancing the Debate." *Perspectives on Psychological Science* 8, 3 (2013), 223–41.

Fanon, Frantz. *Black Skin, White Masks*, trans. Richard Philcox. New York: Grove Press, 2008, originally published 1952.

Farrell, Justin. *The Battle for Yellowstone: Morality and the Sacred Roots of Modern Environmental Conflict*. Princeton, NJ: Princeton University Press, 2015.

Fedele, Anna. "Gender, Sexuality and Religious Critique among Mary Magdalene Pilgrims in Southern France." In *Gender, Nation and Religion in European Pilgrimage*, edited by Catrien Notermans and Willy Jansen, 55–70. New York: Routledge, 2012.

Feinberg, Joel. *Doing and Deserving: Essays in the Theory of Responsibility*. Princeton, NJ: Princeton University Press, 1970.

Feodorov, Aleksandar. "Habit Beyond Psychology." *European Journal of Pragmatism and American Philosophy* 9, 1 (2017), 1–18.

Fernandez-Kelly, Patricia. "A Howl to the Heavens: Art in the Life of First- and Second-Generation Cuban Americans." In *Art in the Lives of Immigrant Communities in the United States*, edited by Paul DiMaggio and Patricia Fernandez-Kelly, 52–71. New Brunswick, NJ: Rutgers University Press, 2010.

Finch, Martha L. "Rehabilitating Materiality: Bodies, Gods, and Religion." *Religion* 42, 4 (2012), 625–31.

Fish, Jonathan S. "Religion and the Changing Intensity of Emotional Solidarities in Durkheim's *The Division of Labor in Society* (1893)." *Journal of Classical Sociology* 2, 2 (2002), 203–23.

Fleck, Ludwik. *Genesis and Development of a Scientific Fact*. Chicago: University of Chicago Press, 1979, originally published 1935.

Foster, Sandra, Paul J. Lloyd, and Sara Kamin. "Mental Preparation, Memorization, and Improvisation." In *Performance Psychology in Action: A Casebook for Working with Athletes, Performing Artists, Business Leaders, and Professionals in High-Risk Occupations*, edited by K. F. Hays, 77–97. Washington, DC: American Psychological Association, 2009.

Foster, Susan Leigh. "Improvising Yoga." In *The Oxford Handbook of Critical Improvisation Studies, vol. 1*, edited by George E. Lewis and Benjamin Piekut, 217–25. New York Oxford University Press, 2016.

Foucault, Michel. *Discipline and Punish: The Birth of the Prison*, trans. Alan Sheridan. New York: Vintage Books, 1976.
Fourcade, Marion and Kieran Healy. "Categories All the Way Down." *Historical Social Research* 42, 1 (2017), 286–96.
France, Lisa Respers. "Prince's Last Concert Was a 'Sacred' Experience." *CNN*, April 22, 2016; cnn.com.
Francis, Philip S. *When Art Disrupts Religion: Aesthetic Experience and the Evangelical Mind*. New York: Oxford University Press, 2017.
Frank, Arthur W. "For a Sociology of the Body: An Analytical Review." In *The Body: Social Process and Cultural Theory*, edited by Mike Featherstone, Mike Hepworth, and Bryan S. Turner, 36–101. London: Sage, 1991.
Frank, Gillian A. "'Ideals of Stability, Order and Fidelity': The Love Dare Phenomenon, Convergence Culture and the Marriage Movement." *Journal of Religion and Popular Culture* 23, 3 (2011), 118–38.
Frauley, Jon and Frank Pearce. "Critical Realism and the Social Sciences: Methodological and Epistemological Preliminaries." In *Critical Realism and the Social Sciences: Heterodox Elaborations*, edited by Jon Frauley and Frank Pearce, 3–29. Toronto: University of Toronto Press, 2007.
Freeman, David. *Creating Emotions in Games: The Craft and Art of Emotioneering*. Boston: New Riders, 2004.
Fritzell, Peter A. *Nature Writing and America: Essays Upon a Cultural Type*. Ames: Iowa State University Press, 1990.
Froese, Paul. *On Purpose: How We Create the Meaning of Life*. New York: Oxford University Press, 2016.
Frye, Margaret. "Bright Futures in Malawi's New Dawn: Educational Aspirations as Assertions of Identity." *American Journal of Sociology* 117, 6 (2012), 1565–1624.
Fuchs, Thomas. "Body Memory and the Unconscious." In *Founding Psychoanalysis: Phenomenological Theory of Subjectivity and the Psychoanalytical Experience*, edited by Dieter Lohmar and Jagna Brudzinska, 69–82. Dordrecht: Kluwer, 2011.
———. "The Phenomenology of Body Memory." In *Body Memory, Metaphor and Movement*, edited by Sabine C. Koch, Thomas Fuchs, Michela Summa, and Cornelia Müller, 9–22. Philadelphia: John Benjamins, 2012.
Gallagher, Sally K. *Getting to Church: Narratives of Gender and Joining*. New York: Oxford University Press, 2017.
Gardner, Christine J. *Making Chastity Sexy: The Rhetoric of Evangelical Abstinence Campaigns*. Berkeley and Los Angeles: University of California Press, 2011.
Garot, Robert and Jack Katz. "Provocative Looks: Gang Appearance and Dress Codes in an Inner-City Alternative School." *Ethnography* 4, 3 (2003), 421–54.
Gatta, John. *Spirits of Place in American Literary Culture*. New York: Oxford University Press, 2018.
Geertz, Clifford. "Religion as a Cultural System." In *Anthropological Approaches to the Study of Religion*, edited by Michael Banton, 1–46. London: Tavistock Publications, 1966.
———. *The Interpretation of Cultures: Selected Essays*. New York: Basic Books, 1973.
———. "'The Pinch of Destiny': Religion as Experience, Meaning, Identity, Power." *Raritan* 18, 3 (1999), 1–19.

———. *Available Light*. Princeton, NJ: Princeton University Press, 2000.
Ghaziani, Amin. *There Goes the Gayborhood?* Princeton, NJ: Princeton University Press, 2014.
Gibson, James J. *The Senses Considered as Perceptual Systems*. New York: Houghton Mifflin, 1966.
———. "The Theory of Affordances." In *Perceiving, Acting, and Knowing: Toward an Ecological Psychology*, edited by Robert Shaw and John Bransford, 67–82. Hillsdale, NJ: Lawrence Erlbaum, 1977.
———. *The Ecological Approach to Visual Perception*. New York: Taylor & Francis, 1986.
Giddens, Anthony. *New Rules of Sociological Method: A Positive Critique of Interpretative Sociologies*. London: Hutchinson, 1976.
Giddings, Franklin H. "The Concepts and Methods of Sociology." *American Journal of Sociology* 10, 2 (1904), 161–76.
Gieryn, Thomas F. "A Space for Place in Sociology." *Annual Review of Sociology* 26 (2000), 463–96.
Gilbert, Margaret. "How We Feel." In *Collective Emotions*, edited by Christian von Scheve and Mikko Salmela, 18–32. New York: Oxford University Press, 2014.
Gilpin, Caroline Crosson and Sarah Gross. "Text to Text: Henry David Thoreau's 'Walking' and 'Time to Write? Go Outside.'" *New York Times*, May 10, 2017.
Ginev, Dimitri. "Conceptualizing the Human Body within Practice Theory." *Social Science Information* 58 (March 2019), 1–20.
Girard, René. *Sacrifice*. East Lansing: Michigan State University Press, 2011, originally published 2003.
Glausser, Wayne. "The Rhetoric of New Atheism." *Style* 50, 1 (2016), 1–18.
Gluckman, Max. "The Utility of the Equilibrium Model in the Study of Social Change." *American Anthropologist* 70, 2 (1968), 219–37.
Goffman, Erving. *The Presentation of Self in Everyday Life*. New York: Doubleday, 1959.
———. *Interaction Ritual: Essays on Face-to-Face Behavior*. Garden City, NY: Anchor Books, 1967.
———. *Frame Analysis*. Cambridge, MA: Harvard University Press, 1974.
Goldberg, Amir, Michael T. Hannan, and Balázs Kovács. "What Does It Mean to Span Cultural Boundaries? Variety and Atypicality in Cultural Consumption." *American Sociological Review* 81, 2 (2016), 215–41.
Gollwitzer, Peter M. "Implementation Intentions: Strong Effects of Simple Plans." *American Psychologist* 54, 7 (1999), 493–503.
Gorski, Philip S. *The Disciplinary Revolution: Calvinism and the Rise of the State in Early Modern Europe*. Chicago: University of Chicago Press, 2003.
———. "What Is Critical Realism? And Why Should You Care?" *Contemporary Sociology* 42, 5 (2013), 658–70.
———. *The American Covenant: A History of Civil Religion from the Puritans to the Present*. Princeton, NJ: Princeton University Press, 2017.
Gorski, Philip S. and Jeffrey Guhin. "The Ongoing Plausibility of Peter Berger: Sociological Thoughts on *The Sacred Canopy* at Fifty." *Journal of the American Academy of Religion* 85, 4 (December 2017), 1–14.
Grant, Don, Kathleen O'Neil, and Laura Stephens. "Spirituality in the Workplace: New Empirical Directions in the Study of the Sacred." *Sociology of Religion* 65, 3 (2004), 265–83.

Graybiel, Ann M. "Habits, Rituals, and the Evaluative Brain." *Annual Review of Neuroscience* 31 (2008), 359–87.
Greenawalt, Kent. *Does God Belong in Public Schools?* Princeton, NJ: Princeton University Press, 2005.
Gregg, Melissa. "On Friday Night Drinks: Workplace Affects in the Age of the Cubicle." In *The Affect Theory Reader*, edited by Melissa Gregg and Gregory J. Seigworth, 250–68. Durham, NC: Duke University Press, 2010.
Greitemeyer, Tobias and Dirk Oliver Mügge. "When Bystanders Increase Rather Than Decrease Intentions to Help." *Social Psychology* 46, 2 (2015), 116–19.
Griffith, R. Marie. *Born Again Bodies: Flesh and Spirit in American Christianity*. Berkeley and Los Angeles: University of California Press, 2004.
———. *Moral Combat: How Sex Divided American Christians and Fractured American Politics*. New York: Basic Books, 2017.
Gronow, Antti. *From Habits to Social Structures: Pragmatism and Contemporary Social Theory*. Frankfurt: Peter Lang, 2011.
Gross, Neil. "A Pragmatist Theory of Social Mechanisms." *American Sociological Review* 74, 3 (2009), 358–79.
———. "Pragmatism and the Study of Large-Scale Social Phenomena." *Theory and Society* 47, 1 (February 2018), 87–111.
Grosz, Elizabeth. "Bodies-Cities." In *Sexuality and Space*, edited by Beatriz Colomina. New York: Princeton Architectural Press, 1992.
Hall, Donald E., ed., *Muscular Christianity: Embodying the Victorian Age*. Cambridge, UK: Cambridge University Press, 1994.
Hambrick-Stowe, Charles E. *The Practice of Piety: Puritan Devotional Disciplines in Seventeenth-Century New England*. Chapel Hill: University of North Carolina Press, 1982.
Hamilton, Malcolm. "Rational Choice Theory: A Critique." In *The Oxford Handbook of the Sociology of Religion*, edited by Peter B. Clark, 116–33. New York: Oxford University Press, 2009.
Handman, Courtney. "Walking Like a Christian: Roads, Translation, and Gendered Bodies as Religious Infrastructure in Papua New Guinea." *American Ethnologist* 44, 2 (2017), 315–27.
Hanegraaff, Wouter. *New Age Religion and Western Culture: Esotericism in the Mirror of Secular Thought*. Leiden: Brill, 1996.
Harding, Susan Friend. *The Book of Jerry Falwell: Fundamentalist Language and Politics*. Princeton, NJ: Princeton University Press, 2000.
Hargreaves, David, Dorothy Miell, and Raymond MacDonald, eds. *Musical Imaginations: Multidisciplinary Perspectives on Creativity, Performance and Perception*. New York: Oxford University Press, 2011.
Harman, Gilbert. "Skepticism about Character Traits." *Journal of Ethics* 13, 2/3 (2009), 235–42.
Harré, Rom. *Physical Being: A Theory for a Corporeal Psychology*. Cambridge, MA: Basil Blackwell, 1991.
Harvey, David. *Consciousness and the Urban Experience*. Oxford: Basil Blackwell, 1985.
Hatfield, Elaine, John T. Cacioppo, and Richard L. Rapson. *Emotional Contagion*. New York: Cambridge University Press, 1994.
Hayes, Edward Cary. "The Classification of Social Phenomena." *American Journal of Sociology* 17, 5 (1911), 90–118.

Hechter, Michael, Lynn Nadel, and Richard E. Michod. *The Origin of Values*. New York: Aldine de Gruyter, 1993.

Heinämäki, Elisa. "Durkheim, Bataille, and Girard on the Ambiguity of the Sacred: Reconsidering Saints and Demoniacs." *Journal of the American Academy of Religion* 83, 2 (2015), 513–36.

Heller, Agnes. *Everyday Life*. London: Routledge and Kegan Paul, 1984.

Hervieu-Léger, Danièle. "Religion as Memory: Reference to Tradition and the Constitution of a Heritage of Belief in Modern Societies." In *Religion: Beyond a Concept*, edited by Hent de Vries. New York: Fordham University Press, 2008.

Hickman, Larry A. *Pragmatism as Post-Postmodernism: Lessons from John Dewey*. New York: Fordham University Press, 2007.

Higginbotham, Evelyn Brooks. *Righteous Discontent: The Women's Movement in the Black Baptist Church, 1880–1920*. Cambridge, MA: Harvard University Press, 1994.

Hirschkind, Charles. *The Ethical Soundscape: Cassette Sermons and Islamic Counterpublics*. New York: Columbia University Press, 2006.

———. "Is There a Secular Body?" *Cultural Anthropology* 26, 4 (2011), 633–47.

Hjorth, Daniel and Monika Kostera, eds. *Entrepreneurship and the Experience Economy*. Fredericksberg, DK: Copenhagen Business School Press, 2014.

Hochschild, Arlie Russell. "Emotion Work, Feeling Rules, and Social Structure." *American Journal of Sociology* 85, 3 (1979), 551–75.

———. "Emotional Life on the Market Frontier." *Annual Review of Sociology* 37 (2011), 20–33.

———. *The Managed Heart: Commercialization of Human Feeling*. Berkeley and Los Angeles: University of California Press, 2012, originally published 1979.

Hochschild, Arlie Russell and Sarah Garrett. *So How's the Family? And Other Essays*. Berkeley and Los Angeles: University of California Press, 2013.

Hoestery, James Bourk. "Vicissitudes of Vision: Piety, Pornography, and Shaming the State in Indonesia." *Visual Anthropology Review* 32, 2 (2016), 133–43.

Holmes-Rodman, Paula Elizabeth. "'They Told What Happened on the Road': Narrative and the Construction of Experiential Knowledge on the Pilgrimage to Chimayo, New Mexico." In *Intersecting Journeys: The Anthropology of Pilgrimage and Tourism*, edited by Ellen Badone and Sharon R. Roseman, 24–51. Champaign: University of Illinois Press, 2004.

Hoover, Brett C. *The Shared Parish: Latinos, Anglos, and the Future of U.S. Catholicism*. New York: NYU Press, 2014.

Hout, Michael and Andrew Greeley. "Religion and Happiness." In *Social Trends in American Life: Findings from the General Social Survey since 1972*, edited by Peter V. Marsden, 288–314. Princeton, NJ: Princeton University Press, 2012.

Huang, Julie Y. and John A. Bargh. "The Selfish Goal: Autonomously Operating Motivational Structures as the Proximate Cause of Human Judgment and Behavior." *Behavioral and Brain Sciences* 37 (2014), 121–75.

Hughes, Everett Charrington. "Personality Types and the Division of Labor." *American Journal of Sociology* 33, 5 (1928), 754–68.

Hunter, James Davison. *American Evangelicalism: Conservative Religion and the Quandary of Modernity*. New Brunswick, NJ: Rutgers University Press, 1983.

Husserl, Edmund. *On the Phenomenology of the Consciousness of Internal Time*. New York: Springer, 1917, originally published 1893.

———. *Ideas Pertaining to a Pure Phenomenology and to a Phenomenological Philosophy, First Book*. The Hague: Matinus Nijhoff, 1982.

Hutter, Michael and David Stark. "Pragmatist Perspectives on Valuation: An Introduction." In *Moments of Valuation: Exploring Sites of Dissonance*, edited by Ariane Berthoin Antal, Michael Hutter, and David Stark, 1–12. New York: Oxford University Press, 2015.

Iacoboni, Marco. "Imitation, Empathy, and Mirror Neurons." *Annual Review of Psychology* 60 (2009), 653–70.

Illouz, Eva. *Saving the Modern Soul: Therapy, Emotions, and the Culture of Self-Help*. Berkeley and Los Angeles: University of California Press, 2008.

Ingold, Tim. *Being Alive: Essays on Movement, Knowledge and Description*. New York: Routledge, 2011.

Inhorn, Marcia C. *The New Arab Man: Emergent Masculinities, Technologies, and Islam in the Middle East*. Princeton, NJ: Princeton University Press, 2012.

Jackson, Michael. *Paths Toward a Clearing: Radical Empiricism and Ethnographic Inquiry*. Bloomington: Indiana University Press, 1989.

———. "Introduction: Phenomenology, Radical Empiricism, and Anthropological Critique." In *Things as They Are: New Directions in Phenomenological Anthropology*, edited by Michael Jackson, 1–50. Bloomington: Indiana University Press, 1996.

Jaeger, C. Stephen. *Enchantment: On Charisma and the Sublime in the Arts of the West*. Philadelphia: University of Pennsylvania Press, 2012.

James, William. *The Principles of Psychology*. London: Macmillan, 1890.

———. *The Varieties of Religious Experience: A Study in Human Nature*. Adelaide, South Australia: University of Adelaide Library, 2005, originally published 1902.

Jansen, Willy and Grietje Dresen. "Fluid Matters: Gendering Holy Blood and Holy Milk." In *Things: Religion and the Question of Materiality*, edited by Dick Houtman and Birgit Meyer, 215–31. New York: Fordham University Press, 2012.

Jasso, Guillermina. "Principles of Theoretical Analysis." *Sociological Theory* 6, 1 (1988), 1–20.

Jerolmack, Colin and Douglas Porpora. "Religion, Rationality, and Experience: A Response to the New Rational Choice Theory of Religion." *Sociological Theory* 22, 1 (2004), 140–60.

Jiang, Da, Helene H. Fung, Tamara Sims, Jeanne L. Tsai, and Fan Zhang. "Limited Time Perspective Increases the Value of Calm." *Emotion* 16, 1 (2016), 52–62.

Joas, Hans. *The Creativity of Action*. Cambridge, UK: Polity Press, 1992.

———. "Religious Experience and Its Interpretation: Reflections on James and Royce." In *The Varieties of Transcendence: Pragmatism and the Theory of Religion*, edited by Hermann Deuser, Hans Joas, Matthias Jung, and Magnus Schlette, 291–35. New York: Fordham University Press, 2016.

Johnson, Andrew. *If I Give My Soul: Faith Behind Bars in Rio de Janeiro*. New York: Oxford University Press, 2017.

Johnston, Erin. "The Enlightened Self: Identity and Aspiration in Two Communities of Practice." *Religions* 7 (2016), 1–15.

———. "Failing to Learn, or Learning to Fail? Accounting for Persistence in the Acquisition of Spiritual Disciplines." *Qualitative Sociology* 40, 3 (September 2017), 221–35.

Joselit, Jenna Weissman. *Set in Stone: America's Embrace of the Ten Commandments.* New York: Oxford University Press, 2017.

Juster, Susan. *Sacred Violence in Early America.* Philadelphia: University of Pennsylvania Press, 2016.

Kaell, Hillary. "Seeing the Invisible: Ambient Catholicism on the Side of the Road." *Journal of the American Academy of Religion* 85, 1 (2017), 136–67.

Kahlberg, Stephen. "Max Weber's Types of Rationality: Cornerstones for the Analysis of Rationalization Processes in History." *American Journal of Sociology* 85, 5 (1980), 1145–79.

Kahneman, Daniel. *Thinking, Fast and Slow.* New York: Farrar, Straus and Giroux, 2011.

Kahneman, Daniel and Alan B. Krueger. "Developments in the Measurement of Subjective Well-Being." *Journal of Economic Perspectives* 20, 1 (2006), 3–24.

Kahneman, Daniel, Alan B. Krueger, David A. Schkade, Norbert Schwarz, and Arthur A. Stone. "A Survey Method for Characterizing Daily Life Experience: The Day Reconstruction Method." *Science* 306, 5702 (2004), 1776–80.

Kapferer, Bruce. "Situations, Crisis, and the Anthropology of the Concrete: The Contribution of Max Gluckman." *Social Analysis* 49, 3 (2005), 85–122.

Katz, Jack. *How Emotions Work.* Chicago: University of Chicago Press, 2000.

Keane, Webb. "The Evidence of the Senses and the Materiality of Religion." *Journal of the Royal Anthropological Institute* 14 (2008), S110–S127.

———. "Rotting Bodies: The Clash of Stances toward Materiality and Its Ethical Affordances." *Current Anthropology* 55, S10 (2014), S312–21.

———. *Ethical Life: Its Natural and Social Histories.* Princeton, NJ: Princeton University Press, 2016.

Kent, Eliza F. "Feminist Approaches to the Study of Religious Conversion." In *The Oxford Handbook of Religious Conversion*, edited by Lewis R. Rambo and Charles E. Farhadian, 298–321. New York: Oxford University Press, 2014.

Kent, Stephen A. "Weber, Goethe, and the Nietzschean Allusion: Capturing the Source of the 'Iron Cage' Metaphor. *Sociological Analysis* 44, 4, 1983, 297–319.

Kermani, Zoreh. "Playing with Fire (and Water, Earth, and Air): Ritual Fluency and Improvisation among Contemporary Pagan Children." In *The Study of Children in Religions: A Methods Handbook*, edited by Susan B. Ridgely, 108–20. New York: NYU Press, 2011.

Keys, Jennifer. "Running the Gauntlet: Women's Use of Emotional Management Techniques in the Abortion Experience." *Symbolic Interaction* 33, 1 (2010), 41–70.

Kilner, J. M. and R. N. Lemon. "What We Know Currently about Mirror Neurons." *Current Biology* 23, 23 (2013), R1057–R1062.

King, Claire Sisco. *Washed in Blood: Male Sacrifice, Trauma, and the Cinema.* New Brunswick, NJ: Rutgers University Press, 2012.

Kirsh, David. "The Intelligent Use of Space." *Artificial Intelligence* 73 (1995), 31–68.

Kis-Halas, Judit. "Pilgrims on the Rosary Route." *Material Religion* 14, 1 (March 2018), 148–52.

Klassen, Pamela E. *Blessed Events: Religion and Home Birth in America.* Princeton, NJ: Princeton University Press, 2001.

———. "Ritual Appropriation and Appropriate Ritual: Christian Healing and Adaptations of Asian Religions." *History and Anthropology* 16, 3 (2005), 377–91.

———. "Ritual." In *The Oxford Handbook of Religion and Emotion*, edited by John Corrigan, 144–68. New York: Oxford University Press, 2007.

Klugman, Karen, Jane Kuenz, Shelton Waldrep, and Susan Willis. *Inside the Mouse*. Durham, NC: Duke University Press, 1995.

Knappett, Carl. *Thinking Through Material Culture: An Interdisciplinary Perspective*. Philadelphia: University of Pennsylvania Press, 2005.

Knorr Cetina, Karin D. "Tinkering toward Success: Prelude to a Theory of Scientific Practice." *Theory and Society* 8, 3 (1979), 347–76.

———. "Introduction: The Micro-Sociological Challenge of Macro-Sociology: Towards a Reconstruction of Social Theory and Methodology." In *Advances in Social Theory and Methodology*, edited by Karin Knorr Cetina and Aaron Cicourel, 1–47. Boston and London: Routledge and Kegan Paul, 1981.

———. "The Synthetic Situation: Interactionism for a Global World." *Symbolic Interaction* 32, 1 (2009), 61–87.

Knottnerus, J. David. "Religion, Ritual, and Collective Emotion." In *Collective Emotions*, edited by Christian von Scheve and Mikko Salmela, 312–25. New York: Oxford University Press, 2014.

Kohler, Robert K. *Landscapes and Labscapes: Exploring the Lab-Field Border in Biology*. Chicago: University of Chicago Press, 2002.

Kormina, Jeanne and Sonja Luehrmann. "The Social Nature of Prayer in a Church of the Unchurched: Russian Orthodox Christianity from Its Edges." *Journal of the American Academy of Religion* 86, 2 (June 2018), 394–424.

Kraus, Rachel. "They Danced in the Bible: Identity Integration among Christian Women Who Belly Dance." *Sociology of Religion* 71, 4 (2010), 457–82.

Krause, Neal and R. David Hayward. "Assessing Whether Practical Wisdom and Awe of God Are Associated with Life Satisfaction." *Psychology of Religion and Spirituality* 7, 1 (2015), 51–59.

———. "Humility, Compassion, and Gratitude to God: Assessing the Relationships Among Key Religious Virtues." *Psychology of Religion and Spirituality* 7, 3 (2015), 192–204.

Kress, Gunther and Theo van Leeuwen. *Reading Images: The Grammar of Visual Design*. New York: Routledge, 2006.

Kugelmass, Heather and Alfredo Garcia. "Mental Disorder Among Nonreligious Adolescents." *Mental Health, Religion and Culture* 18, 5 (2015), 368–79.

Kupari, Helena. "'Remembering God' through Religious Habits: The Daily Religious Practices of Evacuee Karelian Orthodox Women." *Temenos* 47, 2 (2011), 197–222.

Kurakin, Dmitry. "Reassembling the Ambiguity of the Sacred: A Neglected Inconsistency in Readings of Durkheim." *Journal of Classical Sociology* 15 (November 2015), 377–95.

Kyttä, Marketta. "Affordances of Children's Environments in the Context of Cities, Small Towns, Suburbs and Rural Villages in Finland and Belarus." *Journal of Environmental Psychology* 22 (2002), 109–23.

Lakoff, George. *Women, Fire, and Dangerous Things*. Chicago: University of Chicago Press, 1987.

Lakoff, George and Mark Johnson. *Metaphors We Live By*. Chicago: University of Chicago Press, 1980.

Lamont, Michèle and Ann Swidler. "Methodological Pluralism and the Possibilities and Limits of Interviewing." *Qualitative Sociology* 37, 2 (2014), 153–71.

Langer, Suzanne K. *Philosophy in a New Key: A Study in the Symbolism of Reason, Rite, and Art.* New York: New American Library, 1948.

Larrimore, Mark. "Religion and the Promise of Happiness." *Social Research* 77, 2 (2010), 569–94.

Larson, Reed and Maryse H. Richards. *Divergent Realities: The Emotional Lives of Mothers, Fathers, and Adolescents.* New York: Basic Books, 1994.

Lasch, Christopher. *The Culture of Narcissism: American Life in an Age of Diminishing Expectations.* New York: Norton, 1979.

Latour, Bruno. "Where Are the Missing Masses? The Sociology of a Few Mundane Artifacts." In *Shaping Technology/Building Society: Studies in Sociotechnical Change*, edited by Wiebe E. Bijker and John Law, 151–80. Cambridge, MA: MIT Press, 1992.

———. *Reassembling the Social: An Introduction to Actor-Network Theory.* New York: Oxford University Press, 2005.

Lavers, Annette. *Roland Barthes: Structuralism and After.* London: Methuen, 1982.

LeDoux, Joseph. *The Emotional Brain: The Mysterious Underpinnings of Emotional Life.* New York: Simon & Schuster, 1996.

Leezenberg, Michiel. "The Structural Transformation of the Coffeehouse: Religion, Language, and the Public Sphere in the Modernizing Muslim World." In *Things: Religion and the Question of Materiality*, edited by Dick Houtman and Birgit Meyer, 267–81. New York: Fordham University Press, 2012.

Lefebvre, Henri. *The Production of Space*, trans. Donald Nicholson-Smith. Oxford: Basil Blackwell, 1991.

Lewis, George E. and Benjamin Piekut. "Introduction: On Critical Improvisation Studies." In *The Oxford Handbook of Critical Improvisation Studies, vol 1*, edited by George E. Lewis and Benjamin Piekut, 1–37. New York: Oxford University Press, 2016.

Leys, Ruth. "Affect and Intention: A Reply to William E. Connolly." *Critical Inquiry* 37, 4 (2011), 799–805.

———. "The Turn to Affect: A Critique." *Critical Inquiry* 37, 3 (2011), 434–72.

Lindsay, D. Michael. *Faith in the Halls of Power: How Evangelicals Joined the American Elite.* New York: Oxford University Press, 2007.

Lizardo, Omar and Michael Strand. "Skills, Toolkits, Contexts and Institutions: Clarifying the Relationship between Different Approaches to Cognition in Cultural Sociology." *Poetics* 38 (2010), 204–27.

Logan, Dana W. "The Lean Closet: Asceticism in Postindustrial Consumer Culture." *Journal of the American Academy of Religion* 85, 3 (2017), 600–28.

MacIntyre, Alasdair. *After Virtue: A Study in Moral Theory*, 2nd ed. Notre Dame, IN: University of Notre Dame Press, 1984.

Mahmood, Saba. *Politics of Piety: The Islamic Revival and the Feminist Subject.* Princeton, NJ: Princeton University Press, 2005.

———. "Religious Reason and Secular Affect: An Incommensurable Divide?" *Critical Inquiry* 35, 4 (2009), 836–62.

Mallapragada, Madhavi. *Virtual Homelands: Indian Immigrants and Online Cultures in the United States.* Champaign: University of Illinois Press, 2014.

Markovitz, Jonathan. "Art and Abu Ghraib." *Contexts* 8, 3 (2009), 62–64.

Marks, Stephen R. "Durkheim's Theory of Anomie." *American Journal of Sociology* 80 (September 1974), 329–63.

Marti, Gerardo and Gladys Ganiel. *The Deconstructed Church: Understanding Emerging Christianity*. New York: Oxford University Press, 2014.

Martin, David. *A General Theory of Secularization*. Oxford: Blackwell, 1978.

———. *Forbidden Revolutions: Pentecostalism in Latin America and Catholicism in Eastern Europe*. London: SPCK, 1996.

Mascia-Lees, Frances. "The Body and Embodiment in the History of Feminist Anthropology." In *Mapping Feminist Anthropology in the Twenty-First Century*, edited by Ellen Lewin and Leni M. Silverstein, 146–67. New Brunswick, NJ: Rutgers University Press, 2016.

Massey, Douglas S. *Categorically Unequal: The American Stratification System*. New York: Russell Sage Foundation, 2007.

Masuzawa, Tomoko. "The Sacred Difference in the *Elementary Forms*: On Durkheim's Last Quest." *Representations* 23 (Summer 1988), 25–50.

Mathisen, James A. "Reviving 'Muscular Christianity': Gil Dodds and the Institutionalization of Sport Evangelism." *Sociological Focus* 23, 3 (1990), 233–49.

Mauss, Marcel. "The Techniques of the Body." *Economy and Society* 2, 1 (1973), 70–88 [originally published 1935].

Mazumdar, Shampa and Sanjoy Mazumdar. "Place Identity and Religion: A Study of Hindu Immigrants in America." In *The Role of Place Identity in the Perception, Understanding, and Design of Built Environments*, edited by Casakin Hernan and Bernardo Fatima, 133–46. Danvers, MA: Bentham Books, 2012.

McGuire, Meredith. "Embodied Practices: Negotiation and Resistance." In *Everyday Religion Observing Modern Religious Lives*, edited by Nancy Tatom Ammerman, 187–200. New York: Oxford University Press, 2007.

McKinney, John C. "The Role of Constructive Typology in Scientific Sociological Analysis." *Social Forces* 28, 3 (1950), 235–40.

McRoberts, Omar M. *Streets of Glory: Church and Community in a Black Urban Neighborhood*. Chicago: University of Chicago Press, 2003.

Mele, Alfred R. *Springs of Action: Understanding Intentional Behavior*. New York: Oxford University Press, 1992.

Menard, Andrew. "Nationalism and the Nature of Thoreau's 'Walking.'" *New England Quarterly* 85, 4 (2012), 591–621.

Merleau-Ponty, Maurice. *Phenomenology of Perception*, trans. Donald Landes. London: Routledge, 2012, originally published 1945.

Mescoli, Elsa. "Islamic Food Practices in a Migration Context: An Ethnography Among Moroccan Women in Milan (Italy)." In *Everyday Life Practices of Muslims in Europe*, edited by Erkan Toguslu, 9–39. Leuven: Leuven University Press, 2015.

Meyer, Birgit. "Religious Sensations: Why Media, Aesthetics, and Power Matter in the Study of Contemporary Religion." In *Religion: Beyond a Concept*, edited by Hent de Vries, 704–23. New York: Fordham University Press, 2008.

———. "'There Is a Spirit in that Image': Mass-Produced Jesus Pictures and Protestant-Pentecostal Animation in Ghana." In *Things: Religion and the Question of Materiality*, edited by Dick Houtman and Birgit Meyer, 296–320. New York: Fordham University Press, 2012.

Milburn, Michael A. and Sheree D. Conrad. *Raised to Rage: The Politics of Anger and the Roots of Authoritarianism*. Cambridge, MA: MIT Press, 2016.

Miller, Daniel. *A Theory of Shopping*. Oxford: Berg, 1998.

Miller, Daniel and Sophie Woodward. *Blue Jeans: The Art of the Ordinary*. Berkeley and Los Angeles: University of California Press, 2012.

Miller, Stephen. *Walking New York: Reflections of American Writers from Walt Whitman to Teju Cole*. New York: Fordham University Press, 2015.

Mills, C. Wright. "Situated Action and Vocabularies of Motive." *American Sociological Review* 5, 6 (1940), 904–13.

Mishra, Sangay K. *Desis Divided: The Political Lives of South Asian Americans*. Minneapolis: University of Minnesota Press, 2016.

Mitchell, Nathan D. *The Mystery of the Rosary: Marian Devotion and the Reinvention of Catholicism*. New York: NYU Press, 2009.

Moors, Annelies. "The Affective Power of the Face Veil: Between Disgust and Fascination." In *Things: Religion and the Question of Materiality*, edited by Dick Houtman and Birgit Meyer, 282–95. New York: Fordham University Press, 2012.

———. "Wearing Gold, Owning Gold: The Multiple Meanings of Gold Jewelry." *Etnofoor* 25, 1 (2013), 78–89.

Moos, Felix. "Religion and Politics in Japan: The Case of Soka Gakkai." *Asian Survey* 13, 3 (1963), 136–42.

Morey, Peter and Amina Yaqin. *Framing Muslims: Stereotyping and Representation after 9/11*. Cambridge, MA: Harvard University Press, 2011.

Morgan, David. "Imaging Protestant Piety: The Icons of Warner Sallman." *Religion and American Culture* 3 (Winter 1993), 29–47.

———. "For Christ and the Republic: Protestant Illustration and the History of Literacy in Nineteenth-Century America." In *The Visual Culture of American Religions*, edited by David Morgan and Sally M. Promey, 49–67. Berkeley and Los Angeles: University of California Press, 2001.

———. *Sacred Gaze: Religious Visual Culture in Theory and Practice*. Berkeley and Los Angeles: University of California Press, 2005.

———, ed., *Religion and Material Culture: The Matter of Belief*. New York: Routledge, 2009.

———. "Rhetoric of the Heart: Figuring the Body in Devotion to the Sacred Heart of Jesus." In *Things: Religion and the Question of Materiality*, edited by Dick Houtman and Birgit Meyer, 90–111. New York: Fordham University Press, 2012.

———. *The Embodied Eye: Religious Visual Culture and the Social Life of Feeling*. Berkeley and Los Angeles: University of California Press, 2012.

———. *Images at Work: The Material Culture of Enchantment*. New York: Oxford University Press, 2018.

Morgan, David and Sally M. Promey, eds. *The Visual Culture of American Religions*. Berkeley and Los Angeles: University of California Press, 2001.

Morris, Brian. "What We Talk about When We Talk about 'Walking in the City.'" *Cultural Studies* 18, 5 (2004), 675–97.

Munson, Ziad. *The Making of Pro-life Activists: How Social Movement Mobilization Works*. Chicago: University of Chicago Press, 2009.

Murphy, Mary C., Claude M. Steele, and James J. Gross. "Signaling Threat: How Situational Cues Affect Women in Math, Science, and Engineering Settings." *Psychological Science* 18, 10 (2007), 879–85.

Naidu, Maheshvari. "Seeing (through) the Gaze: Marking Religious and Cultural Differences onto Muslim Female Bodies." *Journal for the Study of Religion* 22, 2 (2009), 23–42.

Neal, David T., Wendy Wood, and Aimee Drolet. "How Do People Adhere to Goals When Willpower Is Low? The Profits (And Pitfalls) of Strong Habits." *Journal of Personality and Social Psychology* 104, 6 (2013), 959–75.

Neal, David T., Wendy Wood, Jennifer S. Labrecque, and Phillippa Lally. "How Do Habits Guide Behavior? Perceived and Actual Triggers of Habits in Daily Life." *Journal of Experimental Social Psychology* 48, 2 (2012), 492–98.

Nelson, Timothy J. *Every Time I Feel the Spirit: Religious Experience and Ritual in an African American Church*. New York: NYU Press, 2005.

———. "At Ease with Our Own Kind: Worship Practices and Class Segregation in American Religion." In *Religion and Class in America: Culture, History, and Politics*, edited by Sean McCloud and William A. Mirola, 45–68. Boston: Brill. 2009.

———. "Transformations: The Social Construction of Religious Ritual." In *Understanding Religious Ritual: Theoretical Approaches and Innovations*, edited by John P. Hoffman, 9–31. New York: Routledge, 2012.

Ng, Veronica. "The Problem of *Place*: A Foucauldian and Discursive Analysis on *Place*." In *Space and Place, vol. 3: Exploring Critical Issues*, edited by Didem Kilickiran, Christina Alegria, and Carl Haddrell, 185–204. Oxford: Inter-Disciplinary Press, 2013.

Nicolaou, Corinna. *A None's Story: Searching for Meaning Inside Christianity, Judaism, Buddhism, and Islam*. New York: Columbia University Press, 2016.

Nicolini, David. *Practice Theory, Work, and Organization: An Introduction*. New York: Oxford University Press, 2012.

Nolan, James L., Jr. *The Therapeutic State: Justifying Government at Century's End*. New York: NYU Press, 1998.

Noland, Carrie. *Agency and Embodiment*. Cambridge, MA: Harvard University Press, 2009.

Noomen, Ineke, Stef Aupers, and Dick Houtman. "In Their Own Image? Catholic, Protestant, and Holistic Spiritual Appropriations of the Internet." In *Things: Religion and the Question of Materiality*, edited by Dick Houtman and Birgit Meyer, 379–92. New York: Fordham University Press, 2012.

Norton, Matthew. "Mechanisms and Meaning Structures." *Sociological Theory* 32, 2 (2014), 162–87.

Novak, Shannon A. "Corporeal Congregations and Asynchronous Lives: Unpacking the Pews at Spring Street." *American Anthropologist* 119, 2 (2017), 236–52.

Nussbaum, Martha C. *Upheavals of Thought: The Intelligence of Emotions*. New York: Cambridge University Press, 2001.

Ogien, Albert and Toby Matthews. "Pragmatisms and Sociologies." *Revue française de sociologie* 55, 3 (2014), 414–28.

Oliver, Kelly. *The Colonization of Psychic Space: A Psychoanalytic Social Theory of Oppression*. Minneapolis: University of Minnesota Press, 2004.

Olson, Ted. *Blue Ridge Folklife*. Jackson: University of Mississippi Press, 1998.

Orlin, Lena Cowen. *Locating Privacy in Tudor London*. New York: Oxford University Press, 2007.

Orsi, Robert A. "Everyday Miracles: The Study of Lived Religion." In *Lived Religion in America: Toward a History of Practice*, edited by David D. Hall, 3–21. Princeton, NJ: Princeton University Press, 1997.

———. *Between Heaven and Earth: The Religious Worlds People Make and the Scholars Who Study Them*. Princeton, NJ: Princeton University Press, 2005.

———. "The Problem of the Holy." In *Cambridge Companion to Religious Studies*, edited by Robert A. Orsi, 84–106. New York: Cambridge University Press, 2016.

Ortner, Sherry B. "Theory in Anthropology Since the Sixties." *Comparative Studies in Society and History* 26, 1 (1984), 126–66.

———. *Anthropology and Social Theory: Culture, Power, and the Acting Subject*. Durham, NC: Duke University Press, 2006.

———. "Dark Anthropology and Its Others: Theory Since the Eighties." *HAU: Journal of Ethnographic Theory* 6, 1 (2016), 47–73.

Ouelette, Judith A. and Wendy Wood. "Habit and Intention in Everyday Life: The Multiple Processes by Which Past Behavior Predicts Future Behavior." *Psychological Bulletin* 124, 1 (1998), 54–74.

Overton, Willis F. "Embodiment from a Relational Perspective." In *Developmental Perspectives on Embodiment and Consciousness*, edited by Willis F. Overton, Ulrich Müller, and Judith L. Newman, 1–18. New York: Lawrence Erlbaum, 2008.

Pagis, Michal. "From Abstract Concepts to Experiential Knowledge: Embodying Enlightenment in a Meditation Center." *Qualitative Sociology* 33 (2010), 469–89.

———. "Producing Intersubjectivity in Silence: An Ethnographic Study of Meditation Practice." *Ethnography* 11, 2 (2010), 309–28.

Palmer, Susan J. "Women's 'Cocoon Work' in New Religious Movements: Sexual Experimentation and Feminine Rites of Passage." *Journal for the Scientific Study of Religion* 32, 4 (1993), 343–55.

Paloutzian, Raymond F. "Psychology of Religious Conversion and Spiritual Transformation." In *The Oxford Handbook of Religious Conversion*, edited by Lewis R. Rambo and Charles E. Farhadian, 210–48. New York: Oxford University Press, 2014.

Parsons, Talcott. *The Social System*. New York: Free Press, 1951.

Pasulka, Diana. "Purgatory in the Carolinas: Catholic Devotionalism in Nineteenth-Century South Carolina." In *Southern Crossroads: Perspectives on Religion and Culture*, edited by Walter H. Cosner, Jr. and Rodger M. Payne, 275–302. Nashville: University Press of Kentucky, 2008.

Pattillo-McCoy, Mary. "Church Culture as a Strategy of Action in the Black Community." *American Sociological Review* 63, 6 (1998), 767–84.

Peabody, Norbert. "Disciplining the Body, Disciplining the Body-Politic: Physical Culture and Social Violence among North Indian Wrestlers." *Comparative Studies in Society and History* 52, 2 (2009), 372–400.

Peché, Linda Ho. "'I Would Pay Homage, Not Go All Bling': Vietnamese American Youth Reflect on Family and Religious Life." In *Sustaining Faith Traditions: Race, Ethnicity, and Religion among the Latino and Asian American Second Generation*, edited by Carolyn Chen and Russell Jeung, 222–40. New York: NYU Press, 2012.

Peelen, Janneke and Willy Jansen. "Emotive Movement on the Road to Santiago De Compostela." *Etnofoor* 20, 1 (2007), 75–96.

Peña, Elaine A. "Beyond Mexico: Guadalupan Sacred Space Production and Mobilization in a Chicago Suburb." *American Quarterly* 60, 3 (2008), 721–47.

———. *Performing Piety: Making Space Sacred with the Virgin of Guadalupe*. Berkeley and Los Angeles: University of California Press, 2011.

Perry, Samuel L. "She Works Hard(er) for the Money: Gender, Fundraising, and Employment in Evangelical Parachurch Organizations." *Sociology of Religion* 74, 3 (2013), 392–415.

Persson, Asha. "Embodied Worlds: A Semiotic Phenomenology of Satyananda Yoga." *Journal of the Royal Anthropological Institute* 16, 4 (2010), 797–815.

Pickering, Andrew. *The Mangle of Practice: Time, Agency, and Science*. Chicago: University of Chicago Press, 1995.

Pine, B. Joseph and James H. Gilmore. *The Experience Economy*, rev. ed. Boston: Harvard Business School Press, 2011.

Poloma, Margaret M. and George H. Gallup. *Varieties of Prayer: A Survey Report*. New York: Continuum, 1991.

Pope, Liston. *Millhands and Preachers: A Study of Gastonia*. New Haven, CT: Yale University Press, 1942.

Porpora, Douglas. "Heroes, Religion, and Transcendental Metanarratives." *Sociological Forum* 11, 2 (1996), 209–30.

Potter, Jonathan and Margaret Wetherell. *Discourse and Social Psychology: Beyond Attitudes and Behavior*. London: Sage, 1987.

Powers, Paul R. "Interiors, Intentions, and the 'Spirituality' of Islamic Ritual Practice." *Journal of the American Academy of Religion* 72, 2 (2004), 425–59.

Pressing, Jeff. "Improvisation: Methods and Models." In *Generative Processes in Music: The Psychology of Performance, Improvisation, and Composition*, edited by John Sloboda, 130–79. New York: Oxford University Press, 2001.

Prince, Stephen. "Beholding Blood Sacrifice in *The Passion of the Christ*." *Film Quarterly* 59, 4 (2006), 11–22.

Proudfoot, Wayne. *Religious Experience*. Berkeley and Los Angeles: University of California Press, 1985.

Purcell, Bridget. "The House Unbound: Refiguring Gender and Domestic Boundaries in Urbanizing Southeast Turkey." *City and Society* 29, 1 (2017), 14–34.

Purcell, Sarah J. *Sealed with Blood: War, Sacrifice, and Memory in Revolutionary America*. Philadelphia: University of Pennsylvania Press, 2002.

Putney, Clifford. *Muscular Christianity: Manhood and Sports in Protestant America, 1880–1920*. Cambridge, MA: Harvard University Press, 2001.

Quinn, Jeffrey M., Anthony Pascoe, Wendy Wood, and David T. Neal. "Can't Control Yourself? Monitor Those Bad Habits." *Personality and Social Psychology Bulletin* 36, 4 (2010), 499–511.

Rakow, Katja. "Therapeutic Culture and Religion in America." *Religion Compass* 7, 11 (2013), 485–97.

Rauthmann, John F., Esther M. Guillaume, Elysia Todd, Ryne A. Sherman, Ashley Bell Jones, David Gallardo-Pujol, Christopher S. Nave, Matthias Ziegler, and David C. Funder. "The

Situational Eight DIAMONDS: A Taxonomy of Major Dimensions of Situation Characteristics." *Journal of Personality and Social Psychology* 107, 4 (2014), 677–718.

Rauthmann, John F., Ryne A. Sherman, and David C. Funder. "Principles of Situation Research: Towards a Better Understanding of Psychological Situations." *European Journal of Personality* 29 (2015), 363–81.

Rawls, Ann Warfield. "Durkheim's Epistemology: The Neglected Argument." *American Journal of Sociology* 102, 2 (1996), 430–82.

———. "Durkheim's Epistemology: The Initial Critique, 1915–1924." *Sociological Quarterly* 38, 1 (1997), 111–45.

———. "Durkheim's Challenge to Philosophy: Human Reason Explained as a Product of Enacted Social Practice." *American Journal of Sociology* 104, 3 (1998), 887–901.

Read, John. *Catherine Booth: Laying the Foundations of a Radical Movement*. Cambridge, UK: Lutterworth Press, 2013.

Reckwitz, Andreas. "Toward a Theory of Social Practices: A Development in Culturalist Theorizing." *European Journal of Social Theory* 5, 2 (2002), 243–63.

Ricciardi, Gabriella. "Telling Stories, Building Altars: Mexican American Women's Altars in Oregon." *Oregon Historical Quarterly* 107, 4 (2006), 536–52.

Richardson, Herbert W. "Three Myths of Transcendence." In *Transcendence*, edited by Herbert W. Richardson and Donald R. Cutler, 98–113. Boston: Beacon Press, 1969.

Ricoeur, Paul. "The Metaphorical Process as Cognition, Imagination, and Feeling." *Critical Inquiry* 5, 1 (1978), 143–59.

Rieff, Philip. *The Triumph of the Therapeutic: Uses of Faith After Freud*. New York: Harper & Row, 1966.

Riess, Jana K. "Stripling Warriors Choose the Right: The Cultural Engagements of Contemporary Mormon Kitsch." *Sunstone* (June 1999), 36–47.

Riis, Ole and Linda Woodhead. *A Sociology of Religious Emotion*. New York: Oxford University Press, 2010.

Robbins, Joel. *Becoming Sinners: Christianity and Moral Torment in a Papua New Guinea Society*. Berkeley and Los Angeles: University of California Press, 2004.

———. "Pentecostal Networks and the Spirit of Globalization: On the Social Productivity of Ritual Forms." *Social Analysis* 53, 1 (2009), 55–66.

Roodenburg, Herman. "Pierre Bourdieu: Issues of Embodiment and Authenticity." *Etnofoor* 17, 1–2 (2004), 215–26.

Roof, Wade Clark. *Spiritual Marketplace: Baby Boomers and the Remaking of American Religion*. Princeton, NJ: Princeton University Press, 1999.

Rouse, Carolyn. *Engaged Surrender: African American Women and Islam*. Berkeley and Los Angeles: University of California Press, 2004.

Rouse, Carolyn and Janet Hoskins. "Purity, Soul Food, and Sunni Islam: Explorations at the Intersection of Consumption and Resistance." *Cultural Anthropology* 19 (May 2004), 226–49.

Rouse, Joseph. "Practice Theory." In *Philosophy of Anthropology and Sociology*, edited by Stephen P. Turner and Mark W. Risjord, 499–540. New York: Elsevier, 2007.

Rousseau, Jean-Jacques. *The Confessions*, trans. J. M. Cohen. New York: Penguin Books, 1953, originally published 1765.

Ryle, Gilbert. *The Concept of Mind*. London: Mayflower Press, 1949.
———. "Feelings." *Philosophical Quarterly* 1, 3 (1951), 193–205.
Samimian-Darash, Limor. "Rebuilding the Body through Violence and Control." *Ethnography* 14, 1 (2013), 46–63.
Sánchez, Rafael. "Channel Surfing: Media, Mediumship, and State Authority in the María Lionza Possession Cult (Venezuela)." In *Religion and Media*, edited by Hent de Vries and Samuel Weber, 388–434. Stanford, CA: Stanford University Press, 2001.
Sanderson, Catherine. *Social Psychology*. New York: John Wiley & Sons, 2010.
Sanderson, Eleanor. "Eschatology and Development: Embodying Messianic Spaces of Hope." *Space and Culture* 11, 2 (2008), 93–108.
Scarantino, Andrea. "Affordances Explained." *Philosophy of Science* 70, 5 (2003), 949–61.
Schaeffer, Frank. *Portofino: A Novel*. New York: Carroll & Graf, 1992.
Schatzki, Theodore R. "Practice Minded Orders." In *The Practice Turn in Contemporary Theory*, edited by Theodore R. Schatzki, Karin Knorr Cetina, and Eike von Savigny, 50–64. New York: Routledge, 2001.
Schatzki, Theodore R., Karin Knorr Cetina, and Eike von Savigny, eds. *The Practice Turn in Contemporary Theory*. New York: Routledge, 2001.
Scheer, Monique. "Are Emotions a Kind of Practice (And Is That What Makes Them Have a History)? A Bourdieuian Approach to Understanding Emotion." *History and Theory* 51, 2 (2012), 193–220.
Schladerbeck, Jessica. "Pregnant Maryland Teen Barred from Christian School Graduation." *New York Daily News*, May 24, 2017.
Schleiermacher, Friedrich. *On Religion: Speeches to Its Cultured Despisers*. Cambridge: Cambridge University Press, 1996 [1799].
Schmaus, Warren. "Rawls, Durkheim, and Causality: A Critical Discussion." *American Journal of Sociology* 104 (November 1998), 872–86.
———. *Rethinking Durkheim and His Tradition*. Cambridge, UK: Cambridge University Press, 2004.
Schmidt, Leigh Eric. *Hearing Things: Religion, Illusion, and the American Enlightenment*. Cambridge, MA: Harvard University Press, 2000.
———. *Village Atheists: How America's Unbelievers Made Their Way in a Godly Nation*. Princeton, NJ: Princeton University Press, 2016.
Scholem, Gershom G. *On the Kabbalah and Its Symbolism*. London: Routledge and Kegan Paul, 1965.
Schutz, Alfred. "On Multiple Realities." *Philosophy and Phenomenological Research* 5 (June 1945), 533–76.
———. "Common-Sense and Scientific Interpretation of Human Action." *Philosophy and Phenomenological Research* 14 (September 1953), 1–38.
———. *Life Forms and Meaning Structure*. London: Routledge, 1982.
———. *Collected Papers VI. Literary Reality and Relationships*, edited by Michael Barber. Dordrecht: Springer, 2013.
Searle, John R. *Speech Acts*. Cambridge, UK: Cambridge University Press, 1969.
———. *Making the Social World: The Structure of Human Civilization*. New York: Oxford University Press, 2015.

Seligman, Rebecca. "Distress, Dissociation, and Embodied Experience: Reconsidering the Pathways to Mediumship and Mental Health." *Ethos* 33, 1 (2005), 71–99.

———. "The Unmaking and Making of Self: Embodied Suffering and Mind-Body Healing in Brazilian Candomblé." *Ethos* 38, 3 (2010), 297–320.

Seligman, Rebecca and Laurence J. Kirmayer. "Dissociative Experience and Cultural Neuroscience: Narrative, Metaphor and Mechanism." *Culture, Medicine, Psychiatry* 32, 1 (2008), 31–64.

Sewell Jr., William H. "Geertz, Cultural Systems, and History: From Synchrony to Transformation." *Representations* 59 (Summer 1997), 35–55.

Sharma, Devika and Frederik Tygstrup, eds. *Structures of Feeling: Affectivity and the Study of Culture.* Berlin: De Gruyter, 2015.

Sharp, Shane. "How Does Prayer Help Manage Emotions?" *Social Psychology Quarterly* 73, 4 (2010), 417–37.

Shiffman, Saul. "Dynamic Influences on Smoking Relapse Process." *Journal of Personality* 73 (2005), 1715–48.

Shiffman, Saul, Arthur A. Stone, and Michael R. Hufford. "Ecological Momentary Assessment." *Annual Review of Clinical Psychology* 4 (2008), 1–32.

Shoaps, Robin A. "The Many Voices of Rush Limbaugh: The Use of Transposition in Constructing a Rhetoric of Common Sense." *Text* 19, 3 (1999), 399–437.

———. "'Pray Earnestly': The Textual Construction of Personal Involvement in Pentecostal Prayer and Song." *Journal of Linguistic Anthropology* 12, 1 (2002), 34–71.

Shteynberg, Garriy, Jacob B. Hirsh, Evan P. Apfelbaum, Jeff T. Larsen, Adam D. Galinsky, and Neal J. Roese. "Feeling More Together: Group Attention Intensifies Emotion." *Emotion* 14, 6 (2014), 1102–14.

Sijapati, Megan Adamson and Tina Harris. "From Heavy Beads to Safety Pins: Adornment and Religiosity in Hindu Women's Pote Practices." *Material Religion* 12, 1 (2016), 1–25.

Simpson, Brent and Robb Willer. "Altruism and Indirect Reciprocity: The Interaction of Person and Situation in Prosocial Behavior." *Social Psychology Quarterly* 71, 1 (2008), 37–52.

Smith, Christian. *American Evangelicalism: Embattled and Thriving.* Chicago: University of Chicago Press, 1998.

———. *Soul Searching: The Religious and Spiritual Lives of American Teenagers.* New York: Oxford University Press, 2005.

———. "Why Christianity Works: An Emotions-Focused Phenomenological Account." *Sociology of Religion* 68, 2 (2007), 165–78.

———. *What Is a Person? Rethinking Humanity, Social Life, and the Moral Good from the Person Up.* Chicago: University of Chicago Press, 2010.

Solnit, Rebecca. *Wanderlust: A History of Walking.* New York: Viking, 2000.

Sossa, Alexis. "'Yeah, and What's the Problem?' Embodiment, Cultural Practices and Working Out in a Dutch Gym." *Social Sciences* 6, 44 (2017), 1–15.

Soyer, Francois. "The Public Baptism of Muslims in Early Modern Spain and Portugal: Forging Communal Identity through Collective Emotional Display." *Journal of Religious History* 39, 4 (2015), 506–23.

Sparrow, Tom and Adam Hutchinson, eds. *A History of Habit: From Aristotle to Bourdieu.* New York: Lexington Books, 2013.

Spatz, Ben. *What a Body Can Do: Technique as Knowledge, Practice as Research.* New York: Routledge, 2015.

———. "Embodiment as First Affordance: Tinkering, Tuning, Tracking." *Performance Philosophy* 2, 2 (2017), 257–71.

Spiegel, Gabrielle M. "Introduction." In *Practicing History: New Directions in Historical Writing after the Linguistic Turn*, edited by Gabrielle M. Spiegel, 1–31. New York: Routledge, 2005.

Spillman, Lyn and Brian Conway. "Texts, Bodies, and the Memory of Bloody Sunday." *Symbolic Interaction* 30, 1 (2007), 79–103.

Spinosa, Charles. "Derridian Dispersion and Heideggerian Articulation: General Tendencies in the Practices that Govern Intelligibility." In *The Practice Turn in Contemporary Theory*, edited by Theodore R. Schatzki, Karin Knorr Cetina, and Eike von Savigny, 209–22. New York: Routledge, 2001.

Sponsler, Claire. *Drama and Resistance: Bodies, Goods, and Theatricality in Late Medieval England.* Minneapolis: University of Minnesota Press, 1997.

Springs, Jason A. "What Cultural Theorists of Religion Have to Learn from Wittgenstein; Or, How to Read Geertz as a Practice Theorist." *Journal of the American Academy of Religion* 76, 4 (2008), 934–69.

Starnes, Todd. *God Bless America: Real Stories from the Front Lines of the Attack on Traditional Values.* Lake Mary, FL: Charisma Media, 2014.

Stasch, Rupert. "Knowing Minds Is a Matter of Authority: Political Dimensions of Opacity Statements in Korowai Moral Psychology." *Anthropological Quarterly* 81, 2 (Spring 2008), 443–53.

Steele, Liza G. "'A Gift from God': Adolescent Motherhood and Religion in Brazilian Favelas." *Sociology of Religion* 72, 1 (2011), 4–27.

Stout, Jeffrey. *Democracy and Tradition.* Princeton, NJ: Princeton University Press, 2004.

Stout, Rowland. *The Inner Life of a Rational Agent: In Defence of Philosophical Behaviourism.* Edinburgh: Edinburgh University Press, 2006.

Strosser, Garrett L., Peter K. Jonason, Robert Lawson, Ashley N. Reid, and Alex W. Vittum-Jones. "When Private Reporting Is More Positive Than Public Reporting." *Social Psychology* 47, 3 (2016), 150–62.

Sullivan, Susan Crawford. *Living Faith: Everyday Religion and Mothers in Poverty.* Chicago: University of Chicago Press, 2011.

Supp-Montgomerie, Jenna. "Affect and the Study of Religion." *Religion Compass* 9/10 (2015), 335–45.

Swedberg, Richard. *The Art of Social Theory.* Princeton, NJ: Princeton University Press, 2014.

Swidler, Ann. "Culture in Action: Symbols and Strategies." *American Sociological Review* 51, 2 (1986), 273–86.

———. "What Anchors Cultural Practices?" In *The Practice Turn in Contemporary Theory*, edited by Theodore R. Schatzki, Karin Knorr Cetina, and Eike von Savigny, 83–101. New York: Routledge, 2001.

Tanney, Julia. "The Color Flows Back: Intention and Interpretation in Literature and in Everyday Life." *Journal of European Studies* 38, 3 (2008), 229–52.

Taves, Ann. *Religious Experience Reconsidered: A Building Block Approach to the Study of Religion and Other Special Things.* Princeton, NJ: Princeton University Press, 2009.

———. *Revelatory Events: Three Case Studies of the Emergence of New Spiritual Paths.* Princeton, NJ: Princeton University Press, 2016.

Tavory, Iddo and Daniel Winchester. "Experiential Careers: The Routinization and De-routinization of Religious Life." *Theory and Society* 41 (2012), 351–73.

Tesler, Michael. "Priming Predispositions and Changing Policy Positions: An Account of When Mass Opinion Is Primed or Changed." *American Journal of Political Science* 59, 4 (2015), 806–24.

Thompson, E. P. "Time, Work-Discipline, and Industrial Capitalism." *Past & Present* 38 (1967), 56–97.

Thoreau, Henry David. "Walking." *Atlantic Monthly* 9, 56 (June 1862), 657–74.

Thrift, Nigel. "Driving in the City." *Theory, Culture & Society* 21, 4/5 (2004), 41–59.

Throop, C. Jason. "Interpretation and the Limits of Interpretability: On Rethinking Clifford Geertz's Semiotics of Religious Experience." *Journal of North African Studies* 14, 3 (2009), 369–84.

Tilley, Charles. *Durable Inequality.* Berkeley and Los Angeles: University of California Press, 1998.

Tomasello, Michael. *A Natural History of Human Thinking.* Cambridge, MA: Harvard University Press, 2014.

Troeltsch, Ernst. *The Social Teachings of the Christian Churches.* New York: Free Press, 1931.

Tuan, Yi-Fu. *Space and Place: The Perspective of Experience.* Minneapolis: University of Minnesota Press, 1977.

Turner, Bryan S. *The Body and Society: Explorations in Social Theory.* New York: Oxford University Press, 1984.

Turner, Jonathan H. and Jan E. Stets. "Sociological Theories of Human Emotions." *Annual Review of Sociology* 32 (2006), 25–52.

Turner, Victor. *Forest of Symbols: Aspects of Ndembu Ritual.* Ithaca, NY: Cornell University Press, 1967.

Tweed, Thomas. *Crossing and Dwelling: A Theory of Religion.* Cambridge, MA: Harvard University Press, 2006.

Upton, Candace L. "Virtue Ethics and Moral Psychology: The Situationist Debate." *Journal of Ethics* 13, 2 (2009), 103–15.

Urban, Hugh B. "Secret Bodies." In *The Economics of Ecstasy: Tantra, Secrecy and Power in Colonial Bengal,* edited by Hugh B. Urban and Wendy Doniger, 138–60. New York: Oxford University Press, 2001.

Urry, John. *The Tourist Gaze: Leisure and Travel in Contemporary Societies.* London: Sage, 1990.

———. "The 'System' of Automobility." *Theory, Culture & Society* 21, 4/5 (2004), 25–39.

Vaisey, Stephen. "Motivation and Justification: A Dual-Process Model of Culture in Action." *American Journal of Sociology* 114, 6 (2009), 1675–1715.

Valentino, Nicholas A., Krysha Gregorowicz, and Eric W. Groenendyk. "Efficacy, Emotions, and the Habit of Participation." *Political Behavior* 31, 3 (2009), 307–30.

Van Beek, Walter E. A. *The Forge and the Funeral: The Smith in Kapsiki/Higi Culture.* East Lansing: Michigan State University Press, 2015.

Van Gent, Jacqueline and Spencer E. Young. "Introduction: Emotions and Conversion." *Journal of Religious History* 39, 4 (2015), 461–67.

Van Santen, José C. M. "The Tasbirwol (Prayer Beads) under Attack: How the Common Practice of Counting One's Beads Reveals Its Secrets in the Muslim Community of North Cameroon." In *Things: Religion and the Question of Materiality*, edited by Dick Houtman and Birgit Meyer, 180–97. New York: Fordham University Press, 2012.

Van Wolputte, Steven. "Hang on to Your Self: Of Bodies, Embodiment, and Selves." *Annual Review of Anthropology* 33 (2004), 252–69.

Velde, Paul. "Fear of the Sublime." *Antioch Review* 68 (Spring 2010), 217–31.

Verduyn, Phillippe, Iven Van Mechelen, and Francis Tuerlinckx. "The Relation Between Event Processing and the Duration of Emotional Experience." *Emotion* 11, 1 (2011), 20–28.

Vergunst, Jo. "Key Figure of Mobility: The Pedestrian." *Social Anthropology* 25, 1 (2017), 13–27.

Vickery, Amanda. *Behind Closed Doors: At Home in Gregorian England*. New Haven, CT: Yale University Press, 2009.

Vogel, Nina, Nilam Ram, David E. Conroy, Aaron L. Pincus, and Denis Gerstorf. "How the Social Ecology and Social Situation Shape Individuals' Affect Valence and Arousal." *Emotion* 17, 3 (2017), 509–27.

Wacker, Grant. *America's Pastor: Billy Graham and the Shaping of a Nation*. Cambridge, MA: Harvard University Press, 2014.

Wacquant, Loïc. *Body and Soul: Notebooks of an Apprentice Boxer*. New York: Oxford University Press, 2006.

Wagner, Helmut R. "The Bergsonian Period of Alfred Schutz." *Philosophy and Phenomenological Research* 38 (1977), 187–99.

Wallace, J. Warner. "Young Christians Are Leaving the Church—Here's Why." *Fox News*, September 9, 2018.

Wansink, Brian, Collin R. Payne, and Mitsuru Shimizu. "'Is This a Meal or Snack?': Situational Cues That Drive Perceptions." *Appetite* 54, 1 (2010), 214–16.

Waskul, Dennis S. and Phillip Vannini. "Introduction: The Body in Symbolic Interaction." In *Body/Embodiment: Symbolic Interaction and the Sociology of the Body*, edited by Dennis S. Waskul and Phillip Vannini, 1–20. New York: Routledge, 2006.

Weber, Max. *The Protestant Ethic and the Spirit of Capitalism*, trans. Talcott Parsons. New York: Charles Scribner's Sons, 1958, originally published 1920.

———. *Roscher and Knies: The Logical Problems of Historical Economics*, trans. Guy Oakes. New York: Free Press, 1975.

———. *Economy and Society*, edited by Guenther Roth ad Claus Wittich. Berkeley and Los Angeles: University of California Press, 1978.

White, Geoffrey M. "Emotive Institutions." In *A Companion to Psychological Anthropology: Modernity and Psychocultural Change*, edited by Conerly Casey and Robert B. Edgerton, 341–54. Oxford: Blackwell, 2005.

Whitehead, Andrew L. "Financial Commitment Within Federations of Small Groups: The Effect of Cell-Based Congregational Structure on Individual Giving." *Journal for the Scientific Study of Religion* 49, 4 (2010), 640–56.

Wicklund, Robert A. and Jostein Rise. "Intentions and Other Symbolic Contributions to Society." *Social Psychology* 39, 4 (2008), 205–12.

Wilcox, W. Bradford. "Conservative Protestant Child Rearing: Authoritarian or Authoritative?" *American Sociological Review* 63 (1998), 796–809.

———. *Soft Patriarchs, New Men: How Christianity Shapes Fathers and Husbands*. Chicago: University of Chicago Press, 2004.
Wilf, Eitan. "Semiotic Dimensions of Creativity." *Annual Review of Anthropology* 43 (2014), 397–412.
Wilson, Bryan R. *Religious Sects: A Sociological Study*. New York: McGraw Hill, 1970.
Wimberley, Ronald C., Thomas C. Hood, C. M. Lipsey, Donald Clelland, and Marguerite Hay. "Conversion in a Billy Graham Crusade: Spontaneous Event or Ritual Performance?" *Sociological Quarterly* 16, 2 (1975), 162–70.
Witten, Marsha. *All Is Forgiven: The Secular Message in American Protestantism*. Princeton, NJ: Princeton University Press, 1993.
Wittgenstein, Ludwig. *Philosophical Investigations*. London: Blackwell, 1953.
Wollschleger, Jason. "Interaction Ritual Chains and Religious Participation." *Sociological Forum* 27, 4 (2012), 896–912.
Wolpert Daniel M. and J. Randall Flanagan. "Motor Learning." *Current Biology* 20, 11 (2010), R467–R472.
Wood, Stacy L. and James R. Bettman. "Predicting Happiness: How Normative Feeling Rules Influence (and Even Reverse) Durability Bias." *Journal of Consumer Psychology* 17, 3 (2007), 188–201.
Wood, Wendy, Jeffrey M. Quinn, and Deborah A. Kashy. "Habits in Everyday Life: Thought, Emotion, and Action." *Journal of Personality and Social Psychology* 83.6 (2002): 1281–97.
Wood, Wendy and Dennis Rünger. "Psychology of Habit." *Annual Review of Psychology* 67 (2016), 289–314.
Woolf, Serena J. "The Nature of Habit: F. M. Alexander and John Dewey." *AmSAT Journal* 9 (Spring 2016), 46–56.
Wuthnow, Robert. *Acts of Compassion: Caring for Others and Helping Ourselves*. Princeton, NJ: Princeton University Press, 1991.
———. *Learning to Care: Elementary Kindness in an Age of Indifference*. New York: Oxford University Press, 1995.
———. *All in Sync: How Music and Art Are Revitalizing American Religion*. Berkeley and Los Angeles: University of California Press, 2003.
———. *America and the Challenges of Religious Diversity*. Princeton, NJ: Princeton University Press, 2005.
———. *Boundless Faith: The Global Outreach of American Churches*. Berkeley and Los Angeles: University of California Press, 2009.
———. *The God Problem: Expressing Faith and Being Reasonable*. Berkeley and Los Angeles: University of California Press, 2012.
———. *Small-Town America: Finding Community, Shaping the Future*. Princeton, NJ: Princeton University Press, 2013.
———. *Inventing American Religion: Polls, Surveys, and the Tenuous Quest for a Nation's Faith*. New York: Oxford University Press, 2015.
———. *American Misfits and the Making of Middle-Class Respectability*. Princeton, NJ: Princeton University Press, 2017.
Yang Yang. "Social Inequalities in the United States, 1972–2004: An Age-Period-Cohort Analysis." *American Sociological Review* 73, 2 (2008), 2004–26.

Young, Cristobal. "Model Uncertainty in Sociological Research: An Application to Religion and Economic Growth." *American Sociological Review* 74, 3 (2009), 380–97.

Young, Serinity. *Women Who Fly: Goddesses, Witches, Mystics, and Other Airborne Females.* New York: Oxford University Press, 2018.

Young, Spencer E. "Faith, Favour, and Fervour: Emotions and Conversion among the Early Dominicans." *Journal of Religious History* 39, 4 (2015), 468–83.

Yukich, Grace and Ruth Braunstein. "Encounters at the Religious Edge: Variation in Religious Expression Across Interfaith Advocacy and Social Movement Settings." *Journal for the Scientific Study of Religion* 53, 4 (2014), 791–807.

Zandbergen, Dorien. "Fulfilling the Sacred Potential of Technology: New Edge Technophilia, Consumerism, and Spirituality in Silicon Valley." In *Things: Religion and the Question of Materiality*, edited by Dick Houtman and Birgit Meyer, 356–78. New York: Fordham University Press, 2012.

Zondervan, Antonius A. W. *Sociology and the Sacred: An Introduction to Philip Rieff's Theory of Culture.* Toronto: University of Toronto Press, 2005.

INDEX

abstinence programs, 172
Abu Ghraib atrocities, news images of, 188–89
Abu-Lughod, Lila, 6
accordion effect, 87
actionable intentions, 99–100
actions: focus on, 84; intended meanings of, 81–82; strategies of, 35–36
actor network theory, 64
adjectival feelings, 107, 108
adornments: of religious practitioners, 159–61; subjective connotations of for devotees, 160
aesthetic practices, affordances in, 64
affect: feelings and intensity of, 107–9, 125; intention in action controlling, 96; motivations and, 81
affect theory, 107n.4
affective experience, marketing of, 143
affective forecasts, 140
affordances, 63–72; in aesthetic practices, 64; affective power of, 160; anthropomorphized, 67; bodily, 160; in control of sacred spaces, 64–65; definition of, 63; ethical, 69–71; facilitating and constraining power of, 65–66; feeling right, 69; fetishized, 68; interlocutors as, 68; ordering and arrangement of, 63–64; for religious practices, 65–66; situational capacity to deploy, 70–71; spiritual, 68; symbolizing status differences, 70–72; technology and, 67; as view of material culture's role in religious practices, 66–67

African American churches: call and response motif in, 132; styles of, 73–74
African American Muslims, food taboos among, 167–68
African American women, churchgoing attire of, 161
aggregative practices, 97
Ahmed, Sara, 124–25
al-Quaisi, Ali Shallal, 187
Alexander, Catherine, 54–55
Alexander, Jeffrey, 19n.17
alien, emotive rejection of, 124–25
alignment, 89–91
Alston, William P., 107
"American Covenant," 187
American evangelicals, subcultural identity of, 141
American pragmatism, 3n.1, 10, 84
America's Pastor, 93
Ammerman, Nancy Tatom, 153, 154
anger: controlling, 112, 124; impeding thought, 52; sinfulness of, 127
anti-Muslim violence, 186
Apollonian cultures, 16
Appadurai, Arjun, 65
Archer, Margaret S., 10n.5
Aristotle, on habitus, 148
art, as emotional authority, 131–32
Art Disrupts Religion (Francis), 131
Asad, Talal, 3, 6, 28–31
ascetic economic behavior, 169–70
assessment, 91–92
Astaire-Rogers dance movements, 99–100

230 INDEX

athletics, bodily discipline in, 176
attire: of African-American churchgoing women, 161; religious meaning of, 156–57
attuning, 177
Augustine, 98
authority, feelings and, 126–35
automobiles, as body routines, 156
awe, 143–44

Bachelard, Gaston, 58
bafflement, 30, 144
Bakhtin, Mikhail M., 102
Bandelj, Nina, 114
Barnes, Barry, 90
Barthes, Roland, 189
Becket, Thomas, murder of, 57
beliefs: background, 90, 101–2; as habit, 47, 48; as lived, 6n.2; situational cues triggering, 52–53. *See also* religious beliefs
Bell, Catherine, 30–31, 136
Bellah, Robert, 21; on enlightenment fundamentalism, 109; on feelings as moral guide, 106; on negative influences of religion, 39; on sacred as felt whole, 24–25, 26; on Sheila's story, 139
Bender, Courtney, 42, 50, 53, 115–16
Benedict, Ruth, 16
Bennett, Jane, 109
Berger, Peter: on bodily expressions, 148; on habit, 113; on intentions, 80; on intersubjectivity, 90; on motives, 87–88; on the sacred, 21, 23, 24–26; sacred canopy concept of, 38
Bergson, Henri, 147
Berryman, Phillip, 37
Bhagavad Gita, intention in, 77
Biehl, Joao, 9
Bivins, Jason, 141
Black Pentecostal preaching, absolute intentionality of, 77
Bloch, Maurice, 31
blood sacrifice/blood atonement, 187–88
Bloody Sunday, 183–84

bodies: exceptional, 150, 189–92; as focal point of experience, 148; in human personhood, 146n.1; metaphoric references to parts of, 182–83; mutilated, 188; need for research on, 194; as relational, 151; in religious practice, 147–51; as representations, 150, 179–89; role of, 8–9; as socially constructed, 150–51; tattooing and painting of, 146–47; techniques of, 147; as tool for communicating identity, 178; tuning or attuning, 177
bodily affordances, 160
bodily experience, 6, 31, 173
bodily expression, 147–48, 183
bodily movement, 156–57; coordinated in rituals, 176; as embodiment of habitus, 148; feelings and, 129; gendered and racialized, 159; showing intention, 98
bodily proximity, 136
bodily symbolism, 146–47
body building subculture, 171–72
body callusing, 173
body discipline, 150, 171, 176, 178–79; conceptual apparatus and, 172–73; in disciplined situations, 174–75; external imposition of, 169–70; extreme physical conditioning in, 173–74; highly regimented, 177; individualistic, 177; intense training for, 172–73; for self-improvement, 172
body memory, 157n.27, 159, 194
body practices, as habit, 158–59
body representations: discursive structuring of, 183–84; interacting with corporeal bodies, 185–86
body rituals, 150; norms of, 166; performance aspect of, 164–65; power expressed in, 167–68; staging of, 164; strictness of, 166–67; verbal instruction and interpretation of, 165
body routines, 150, 151–64; acquiring religious meaning, 157–58; affecting observers, 158; learned by mimicry, 157; rejection and setting aside of, 162; religion-based, 159–60; with religious meaning, 157–58; subversion

of, 161–62; unintentional disruptions of, 163–64
Boltanski, Luc, 185
Born Again Bodies (Griffith), 172
Borsch, Frederick, 62–63
Bourdieu, Pierre, 6; on embodiment of habitus, 148–49; on feelings, 117; on intention, 78; on practice as regulated improvisation, 12; on practice theory, 31–34, 88; on private motives, 83; on recurrent situations, 43; on rhetoric of intention, 102; situational dispositions of, 3
Bourke, Joanna, 133
bowing, 156, 159
boxers, mental discipline of, 173
Braunstein, Ruth, 97
Brazilian Pentecostals: in prisons, 42, 53; sexual prohibitions of, 167
Brazilian prisoners: body discipline of, 177–78; pentecostalism of, 42, 53
Bremer, Thomas, 62
The Broken Covenant (Bellah), 39
Brown, Bill, 64
Brown, Norman, 183
Buddhist home altars, 58
Buddhist meditation, 173, 175; walking, 153
Buffalo Creek flood, impact of on survivors, 163
Bunyan, John, 155
Burawoy, Michael, 43
Burke, Kenneth, 22
Burmese American home altars, 59
Butler, Judith: on conditioned emotions, 142n.94; on embodiment, 148; on feelings, 142; on stylized repetition of acts, 159; on subversion, 161–62
Bynum, Caroline, 178

Cacioppo, John T., 137n.79
call and response motif, 132
Calvinist conventicles, 169
Canterbury Cathedral, Becket's murder in, 57
Castañeda-Liles, María Del Socorro, 59
categories/categorization: conceptual, 7, 16; drawbacks of, 30–31; fourfold, 16; sociologists continued interest in, 40n.68
Catholic Charismatics, 115
Catholic cult of pain, 190
Catholic home altars, 58
Catholicism, intention in, 77
cemeteries, as catchment zones, 168
centering prayer practitioners, 94
Cetina, Karin Knorr, 9
Chen, Carolyn, 39
child abuse, religiously legitimated, 118
chosenness, 187
Christ: symbolic drinking of blood of, 181; symbolic representation of body of, 181, 182
"Christ at the Door" (Sallman), 66
Christianity: habit in tradition of, 10–11; muscular, 186–87
church: cultural authority of, 128; pollution of, 57
Cioffi, Frank, 98
classification: conceptual, 14, 18–19, 21, 22, 146; redirected toward "categories in practice," 38, 40n.68; of sacred and profane, 26, 37–38; of social facts, 16
Clawson, Laura, 99
Clinton, Hillary, 122
cocoon work, 175
cognitive processing, 10–11
collective effervescence, 15, 20, 135, 138
collective emotions, 136–37
collective representations, 17, 20, 181
collectivity: commitment to, 137–38; emotional power of, 135–36; power of, 167–68
Collins, Peter, 174
Collins, Randall, 43–44, 135–36, 137, 170
Comaroff, Jean, 126
commercialization, 142–43
commodification, 134–35
complex societies, unifying symbols and rituals in, 20–21

Comte, August, 16
concealment, 92–93
congregations: cultures of, 70; institutionalized, 97–98; intentional, 77, 78, 97–98; segregated, 78; supportive social relationships in, 117, 131, 191
consecration, 37, 55, 66
control, free-floating methods of, 171
controlled experimental-design studies, 9
conversion, 132–33
Conway, Brian, 183–84
Cooper, Amy, 170–71n.56
Corrigan, John, 128
Crawley, Ashon, 77
critical realism, 32n.50
cross-disciplinary interaction, 40
cross-fertilization, 2
Csordas, Thomas, 6, 96, 115
cultural distinctions, ritual in, 140–41
cultural logics, 19n.17
culture: feelings as, 142–45; focus on, 21–28; religious sphere in, 23; as strategies of action, 35–36

dance, as body ritual, 165
Dant, Tim, 171
dark anthropology, 37, 39
Davidman, Lynn, 162
Davidson, Donald, 88–89, 89
Day Reconstruction Method, 119
de Certeau, Michel, 6; on feeling tone, 54; on "pedestrian speech acts," 152; on practices in everyday life, 32–33; on space as practiced place, 44
degradation ceremonies, 166
Deleuze, Gilles, 171
DeLillo, Don, 152–53
DeNora, Tia, 64, 65
Depression era motion pictures, 99–100
Desmond, Matthew, 176
devoted bodies, 184
Dewey, John, 38; on habit, 10; on importance of action and structure, 84; on improvisation *vs.* habit, 11

digitally mediated bodily encounters, 179–80
Dionysian cultures, 16
"disappointing ports of call," 140
discipline: bodily, 169–79; of industrial society, 170; social support of, 169–70
discursive space, 55, 59
discursive structuring, 3m 183–84, 185
displacement dynamics, embracing, 123–24
dispositional-situational interaction, 44n.6
disruptive cues, 52–53
divine feminine, 185–86
divine voices, 68, 71
Dobson, James, 52
Dollard, John, 39
Dormer, Anne, 60
Dougherty, Beth, 141
Douglas, Mary: on affordances, 64–65; on conceptual categories, 37–38; on home as space under control, 59–62; on tidying as ritual, 174–75
drag (cross-dressing), 161–62
dread, 143–44
dream time, 189
Drescher, Elizabeth, 153
driving, as body routine, 155–56
dual information processing studies, 46
Dubler, Joshua, on inmates' religious practices, 177–78
durability bias, 140
Duranti, Alessandro, 100–101
Durkheim, Émile: classificatory approach of, 22–23; on collective effervescence, 138; collective representations of, 181; on collectivity's power, 167; on coordinated rituals, 176; on feelings in religion, 108; on purity of sacred space, 61; on ritual, 3, 113, 135, 137, 140–41; on ritual symbolization of power, 143; on sacred and profane, 15–17, 26–28; on sacred as set apart, 49–50; on social role of sacred, 14–21; structuralist applications of, 37–38; on tattooing and painting of bodies, 146–47
dwelt-in spaces, 54

Ecological Momentary Assessment method, 119
Elementary Forms of Religious Life (Durkheim), 14–15, 19, 26, 146
Eliade, Mircea, 152, 189
Elias, Norbert, 107n.4
Eliasoph, Nina, 55
Eliot, T. S., *Murder in the Cathedral* of, 57
Elisha, Omri, 165, 190–91
The Embodied Eye (Morgan), 131–32
embodiment: in human personhood, 146n.1; need for research on, 194; relational quality of, 148; in religious practice, 147–51. *See also* bodies
emerging church services, subverting traditional "Sunday" best attire, 161
Emirbayer, Mustafa, 19n.17
emoticons, 121–22
emotional authority, in collective religious practice, 128–29
emotional complicity, 132–34
emotional contagion, 137n.79
emotional experience, first- and second-order, 138
emotional labor, 131, 134
emotional pain, theodicies mitigating, 113
emotional states, 112
emotioneering, 127–28, 142
emotions: affect and, 107n.4; collective, 136–37; habit controlling, 111–12; interchangeable with feelings, 107n.4; as situational, 113; theoretical approaches to, 107n.4
emotive institutions, 129–30
empirical studies, 6
enacted practices, 20–21
enlightenment fundamentalism, 109
Episcopalians, intention in, 77
epistemological arguments, 3–4, 6, 36
Erikson, Kai T., 163
ethical affordance, 69–71
ethnographic research, 2, 8–9, 33, 37, 43, 56, 62, 100, 154, 155, 171
Eucharist, 181

evaluative assessments, 91–92
everyday life, 23–24; connection of with sacred, 29; fluidity of, 62; practices in, 32–33; sacred experience in, 61–62; separation of sacred from, 40–41
Everything in Its Path (Erikson), 163
ex-Orthodox Jewish women, loss of body routines in, 162
expressive entrepreneurship, 143
expressive individualism, 134–35

face-the-moment encounters, 175
face-to-face encounters, 175
face-to-place encounters, 175
Fanon, Frantz, 159
Feast of Immolation, 181
feeling rules, 120–26; authority and, 126–35; breaches in, 121; definition of, 120; explicitly taught, 120–21; gendering of, 122; implicitly learned, 121; public vs. private, 122; as relational norms, 125–26; restorative mechanisms in, 121; in workplace cultures, 121–22
"feeling thermometer" questions, 125
feeling states, 117
feeling tone, 54, 65
feelings, 8, 105, 194; cued by events, 109–10; as culture, 142–45; general condition, 107; habits shaping, 110, 111–16; intense extraordinary, habitual, 115–16; interchangeable with emotions, 107n.4; prayer as substitute for expressing, 123–24; privileged over thought, 108–9; reasons for increased interest in, 105–6; relationships' effects on, 119–20; in ritual, 135–41; self-reflexive, 107; situational, 113, 119–20; situational adaptability of, 123–24; situational variability of, 116–17; in studies about religion, 108–9; visceral manifestations of, 107; well-being and, 116–20. *See also* feeling rules
Fernandez-Kelly, Patricia, 143
flags, evoking feelings, 132
food taboos, 167

Forbidden Revolutions (Martin), 37
Foster, Susan Leigh, 178–79
Foucault, Michel, 3, 6, 29; on body discipline, 169, 170, 177
France, Lisa Respers, 55–56
Francis, Philip S., 131, 132
Freeman, David, 127
Freud, Sigmund, id-ego-superego conceptualization of, 16
funerary rites, 168

Gallagher, Sally K., 69–70
Ganiel, Gladys, 161
Garcia, Alfredo, 118
Garrett, Sarah, 134–35
gay friendly areas, 191
Geertz, Clifford, 3; Asad's critique of, 28–31; on bafflement, 144; functionalism of, 37; on moods and motivations, 78, 82, 89; on rituals, 38; on the sacred, 21–28, 108
gemeinschaft-gesellschaft distinction, 16
gender, constituted through styles of the flesh, 159
genuflecting, 156; habitually making, 158, 159
German Baptists, strictness of, 166–67
Getting to Church: Narratives of Gender and Joining (Gallagher), 69–70
Ghanaian Pentecostal churches, 138; Jesus pictures of, 68, 71
Ghaziani, Amin, 191
Gibson, James, 63
Gibson, Mel, *The Passion of the Christ* movie of, 52
Gilbert, Margaret, 137
Girard, René, 187
goals, 79; intentions as, 80–81; motives and, 80–82
Goffman, Erving, 54, 121–22, 166, 169–70
Gollwitzer, Peter, 94
Gorski, Philip, 169–70, 187
Graham, Billy, revivals of, 93
Grant, Don, 139
Graybiel, Ann M., 11n.9
Gregg, Melissa, 121–22

Griffith, Marie, 39, 172
Grosz, Elizabeth, 191
groups style, 55
Guadalupan immigrants, sacred space of, 56–57

habits, 10–11; bodily practices as, 158–59; body routines as, 157; deadening possibilities of, 10–11; facilitating emotional states, 112; good and bad, 47; guiding behavior in favorable directions, 75; intense feeling and, 115–16; as non-deliberative behavior, 111–12; of praying at meals, 49; in pursuing goals, 81; regulating emotions, 113–14; in religious practice, 94–96; shaping feeling, 110, 111–16; situationally cued, 46–48, 51, 94, 112–14; suppressing emotions, 111–12
Habits of the Heart (Bellah), 39, 106
habitus, 33–34n.52, 148; embodiment of, 148–49
Hackett, David G., 39
halal rules, 167
Handman, Courtney, 154–55
happiness: gospel of, 126; religion and, 116–20
Harding, Susan, 156
Harvey, David, 58
Hatfield, Elaine, 137n.79
Hayward, R. David, 136
hazardous situational cues, 52–53
healthy-minded religious experience, 18
heavenly beings, as emotional authorities, 130
hegemonic masculinity, 186–88
Heller, Agnes, 57–58
heresy, formation of, 29–30
Hervieu-Léger, Danièle, 6n.2
heteroglossia, 102–3
Higginbotham, Evelyn Brooks, 161
Hindu American home altars, 58
Hindu nationalism, 185–86
Hindu websites, 67

Hindu women: adornments of, 71–72; online forum for, 67
Hindu wrestlers, 185–86
historic studies, 2, 9, 12, 149
Hochschild, Arlie: on commercialization of feelings, 142–43; on feeling rules, 126, 134–35; flight attendant study of, 120–21
Holmes-Rodman, Paula Elizabeth, 97
home altars, 58–60
homeless women, bureaucratic control of, 170–71n.56
homes, as sacred spaces, 57–62
homophily/heterophily, cues signaling, 51
Hoskins, Janet, 167–68
human action/interaction, as purposive, 4
human behavior: embodied character of, 146–47; indeterminacy of, 13; situated character of, 4
Husserl, Edmund, 79, 86
Hutter, Michael, 45
hyperembodiment, 163–64

icons, evoking feelings, 132
identity, raising salience of, 50–51
imagined situations, 4, 36, 152
immigrant families, home altars among, 58
improvisation, 10, 11–12; need for in decision-makers, 114–15; regulated, 12–13, 88
India, Hindu nationalism and anti-Muslim violence in, 185–86
individual consciousness, sacred incarnating in, 20
individualism, 134–35
industrial age, bodily discipline in, 170–71
Inhorn, Marcia, 186–87
institutional disciplines, 170, 171
institutional power, 12, 170, 128, 178, 182
institutionalized situations, 47–48
Integral Yoga Institute, 172
integrative practices, 97
intentionality, 194; collective, 97–98; two kinds of, 78, 85–88
intentions, 8; actionable, 99–100; aligned, 89–91; assessing, 91–92; concealment of, 92–93; definition of, 77; expression of, 100, 104; in forming habit, 94–96; gathering information to interpret, 84–85; goal-oriented, 80–81; implicit communication of, 98–99; mistaken assumptions about, 100–101; as motives, 79–80; neglect of, 78; prior, 85–87, 95–96, 98; prior vs. in action, 78; questions regarding, 78; in religious practice, 93–104; rhetorics of, 100–104; sincerity of, 92; situational fungibility of, 88; in social theory, 78, 79–85; sustaining, aligning, and assessing, 78, 88–93
intentions in action, 78, 85–87; modulating behavior, 96; motives and, 88
interaction: between bodies and space, 191; bodily movement and, 148–49, 153; body rituals and, 164. *See also* social interaction
interfaith advocacy, 97
interlocutors, as affordances, 68
intersubjectivity, 90
inward experience, sacred space and, 56–57
Islam, comedic performances subverting misconceptions of, 162

Jackson, Michael, 182–83
Jaeger, Stephen, 99–100
James, William, 11, 38, 108; on nonhabitual "happenings," 115–16; on religious experience, 18, 144, 152; sub-universes of, 26
Jansen, Willy, 129–30
Jesus pictures, 68, 71
Jewish tradition, habit in, 10–11
jilbab, habit of wearing, 144
Joas, Hans, 45
Johnson, Andrew, 42, 53, 96–97
Johnston, Erin, 94, 172
Joselit, Jenna Weissman, 66
Juster, Susan, 187

Kahneman, Daniel, 116
Karelian Orthodox women, daily religious practices of, 158–59
Katz, Jack, 155–56
Keane, Webb, 69

Kermani, Zohreh, 100
Keys, Jennifer, 52–53
Kirsch, David, 63
Klassen, Pamela, 39, 139, 160
kneeling, 156, 159
know-how, 10
knowing subject, 33
Kormina, Jeanne, 70–71
Krause, Neal, 136
Kugelmass, Heather, 118
Kupari, Helena, 158
Kyttä, Marketta, 64

La Sainte-Baume cave, 74
L'Abri Christian training center, 69
labyrinths, walking, 155
Lakoff, George, 181–82
Langer, Suzanne, 22, 28
language, uses of, 38
Latino neo-Pentecostals, in New York Dance Parade, 165
Latour, Bruno, 64
Lefebvre, Henri, 6, 44, 53
Lenten blessing, 113, 114
Levi-Strauss, Claude, 16
Leviticus, body representations in, 181
Lichterman, Paul, 55
lifetime goal, religion as way of attaining, 117
lifting hands, 156
Lindsay, D. Michael, 114–15, 123
linguistic-physical movement homologies, 154
listening, as bodily practice, 158n.28
lived religion, 2, 36, 39
lived situations, 4
Lizardo, Omar, 70
Locke, Peter, 9
The Logic of Practice (Bourdieu), 33
Love's Body (Brown), 183
Luckmann, Thomas, 3; on bodily expressions, 148; on habit, 113; on intentions, 80; on intersubjectivity, 90; on motives, 87–88; on sacred, 21, 23–25
Luehrmann, Sonja, 70–71

MacIntyre, Alasdair, 169
Mahmood, Saba, 6, 126
manspreading, 155
María Lionza possession cult, 123–24
marketing, as profanation, 66
Marti, Gerardo, 161
Martin, David, 37
martyrs, as emotional authorities, 130
Marxism, emphasizing infrastructural determinants, 84
Mary Magdalene, as Mother Earth, 74–75
Maslow, Abraham, 24, 26
masquerades, 161–62
Masuzawa, Tomoko, 19–20n.18
material culture, as affordances in religion, 66–67
materialism, religious criticism of, 134
materiality, focus on, 2
Mauss, Marcel: on body routines, 151–52, 157; on embodied practices, 147; influence of on practice theory, 148; on sacred and profane, 15–16
McRoberts, Omar, 129
Mead, George Herbert, 23, 38
meals, situational cuing in, 49
meaning: intrinsic to practices, 34–35; making of, 25, 30; problem of, 21–23
meaninglessness, 21–22
meditation: bodily discipline in, 174; Buddhist, 173, 175; as source of divine assurance, 111
mental acts, evidence of, 82
mental discipline, 173
mental states, 17, 85, 104
Merleau-Ponty, Maurice, 6, 87, 147, 148
metaphoric communication, 181
metaphoric homologies, 154
metaphorization, 182–83
methodological situationism, 9
Mexican American home altars, 59
Mexican American immigrants, control of sacred spaces of, 72–73
Meyer, Birgit, 68, 138

military discipline, 171, 173
Miller, Daniel, 161
Millhands and Preachers (Pope), 74
Mills, C. Wright, 82–83, 102
mind-body dualism, transcending, 149
Mirza, Shazia, 162
mirror neuron research, 136–37
monastic regimen, 170
moods, long-lasting, 89
Moors, Annelies, 160
moral principles, conformity or deviation from, 92
Morey, Peter, 162
Morgan, David, 66–67, 69, 131–32, 180, 183
Morris, Brian, 191
Morton, Cathy, 115
Moses action figures, 66
motives/motivations, 79; goals and, 80–82; intentions as, 79–80; internalized, 80; long-lasting, 89; as strategies for action, 82–83; as vocabularies, 82
motor learning, 48–49
multivocality, 102–3
music, as emotional authority, 131–32
Muslim literature, connections between bodies and religious texts in, 156n.26
Muslim women, face veiling of, 160
Muslims: Feast of Immolation of, 181; hypermasculinized, 186
my particularity, 178
mystic states, techniques of body in, 147
myth of volitions, 82

Nelson, Timothy, 68, 138, 139
norms, relational, 125–26
Novak, Shannon A., 168
numinous, 130–31

Olson, Ted, 132–33
O'Neil, Kathleen, 139
ontological questions, 32
Orsi, Robert, 6, 39, 68, 130, 155, 190
orthodoxy, formation of, 29–30
Ortner, Sherry, 35, 37, 38n.64, 144

Otto, Rudolf, 108
Outline of a Theory of Practice (Bourdieu), 33–34

Pagis, Michal, 173, 174, 175
pain, cult of, 190
pair skating, bodily discipline in, 176
Palestinian women, gold jewelry of, 160
Papua New Guinea Christians, 154–55
paramount reality, 23
Parsons, Talcott, 16, 22–23, 80
The Passion of the Christ, 52
paternalistic bodily metaphors, 181–82
Pattillo-McCoy, Mary, 73–74
Peabody, Norbert, 185–86
peak experiences, 26
Peelen, Janneke, 129–30
Peirce, Charles, 38
Peña, Elaine A., 56
Pentecostal churches: absolute intentionality in, 77; Ghanaian, 68, 71, 138; South African, 126
pentecostalism: in Brazil's prisons, 42, 53; sexual prohibitions in, 167
Perry, Samuel, 101
persecuted church, 190–91
personal space, disciplined, 174–75
Persson, Asha, 182
phenomena: classification of, 16; perceived from actor's perspective, 23; perceived as reality, 34
phenomenological sociology, 23
phenomenology, in everyday reality, 24
pilgrimages, 129–30; as Catholic, 154; intentions and, 97
Pilgrim's Progress (Bunyan), 155
place, in situations, 44, 45
planning: in intentionality, 85–86; in pursuing goals, 81
plasticity, 9–10
polysymbolism, 183
Pope, Liston, 39, 74
possibility, conditions of, 33
pote, 71–72

power, 3, 10, 12; appropriation of, 74–75; enforcement of through body discipline, 178; of individuals in collectivity, 167–68; sacred as, 17; structure and action interplay with, 32n.50; transference of, 73–74
power differentials, 92; in feeling rules, 126–27
power dynamics, 29, 72–76; role of, 4; in sacred space, 59–62
practical competence, 70–71
practical wisdom, ritual and, 136
practice: anchored in certain situations, 47–48; bodies' role in, 8–9; as bundles of activities and discourses, 33–34n.52; categories in, 38; defining meanings of situation spaces, 54–55; definition of, 1; dynamics of, 10; embodied agents changing, 31–32; enacted, 20–21; in everyday life, 32–33; increasing focus on, 3, 31–41, 34–35; meanings intrinsic to, 34–35; noncognitive, 31; ontological status of, 34; plasticity of, 9–10; religion as, 193; situations shaping, 8; state and institutional power in, 12; structuring of, 34. *See also* religious practice
practice theory, 3; Bourdieu on, 33–34; as bundle of perspectives, 35; emphasizing complexity of social life, 3–4; habit in, 10–11; improvisation in, 11–12; multiplicity of interacting components in, 36–37; power in, 12; recasting of Durkheim's work in, 37–38; roots of, 3n.1; second generation, 4–5; situated beliefs in, 6n.2; Spiegel on, 32n.49
pragmatism, 3n.1, 10, 38–39, 84
prayer: as anti-anxiety device, 123–24; centering, 94, 119; expressing intentions, 103; habitual, 113–14; at meals, 49, 51; situational cues encouraging, 49–50; as source of divine assurance, 111
prayer closets, 60–61
priming, 53
Primitive Classification, 15–16
Prince, Stephen, 52

Prince concert, in sacred space, 55–56
Princeton University chapel building, multi-faith services in, 62–63
prior intentions, 85–87, 98; habit and, 95–96
prisoners: body discipline of, 177–78; pentecostalism among, 42, 53
problem-solving behavior, 78
profane: practices in, 32–33; sacred and, 15–21
Promey, Sally M., 66–67
Proudfoot, Wayne, 105–6, 107
public situational spaces, 54
Purcell, Bridget, 62
Purcell, Sarah, 187

Quaker discipline, 174
Quaker Faith and Practice (Collins), 174
qualitative research, 2, 78, 108, 120, 125, 194–95
quantitative research, 2, 9, 37, 78, 108, 194–95
Qur'an, intention in, 77

racialized bodily movements, 159
rape, as tool of subjugation and control, 178
Rapson, Richard L., 137n.79
rational-choice theory, 39, 95
Rawls, Ann Warfield, 20–21
reality: cultural construction of, 147–48; everyday, 23–24; how phenomena come to be perceived as, 34; multiple, 25–26; ontological questions about, 32; social construction of, 3
Reckwitz, Andreas, 35n.54
recurrent cues, 46
relationality of feelings, 125–26
religion: authority of to define feelings, 127–35; broadening scope of scholarship on, 2–3; challenges for study of, 193–95; as culturally constructed, 5; divisions in study of, 1–2; dominating national and international events, 6; drawback of categorizations of, 30–31; feelings and, 113–14; long-lasting moods and motivations of, 89; negative cultural influences

of, 39; as practice, 1, 45, 84; in services of power structures, 74–75; social life interaction with, 39–40; as therapeutic, 131. *See also* religious practice

Religion of Fear (Bivins), 141

religious beliefs, 84, 144; ethical affordances and, 70–71; practiced, 149; stylized, 110

religious experience: body routines in, 152–53; building blocks in, 108

religious practice: affordances for, 65–66; appropriation of, 74; bodies and embodiment in, 147–51; in concrete situations, 194; disparate manifestations of, 195; fluidity and variability of, 76; habit in, 94–96; informing people's thinking about feelings, 110; intention in, 93–104; justifying improvisations, 114–15; rewards of, 93–94; situations in, 42–43, 45–46; social interaction in, 96–100; in spaces where cues prompt habitual responses, 48–49; transferability of, to dissimilar situations, 73–74; as voluntaristic, 73; well-being and, 117–20

Religious Roots of Rebellion (Berryman), 37

religious self-help literature, 123–24

repetitive chants, 28

representations, bodies as, 179–89

respect, collective feeling of, 17

revival meetings, 93, 125

rewards, 93–94

Richardson, Samuel, 60

Rise, Jostein, 103

ritual attention theory, 99–100

ritual manipulations, 28

ritual weeping, 139

rituals: affirming theodicies, 113; body, 164–68; coordinated bodily movements in, 176; in drawing cultural distinctions, 140–41; emphasis on, 18–19; evoking intense emotion, 139–40; feelings in, 8, 135–41; mental and emotional characteristics of, 17; role of bodies in, 149; sacred, 3; as symbol, 25. *See also* body rituals

river baptisms, 132–33

Robbins, Joel, 129

Rodney King case, 185

Roof, Wade Clark, 106

Rouse, Carolyn, 167–68

Rousseau, Jean-Jacques, 152

Russian Orthodox prayer, 70–71

Ryle, Gilbert, 82, 89, 95, 107

sacred, 14–21; attributes of, 17; conflicting views of, 30–31; emotional aspect of, 17; emotional power of, 108; everyday life and, 29; as felt whole, 24; Geertz on, 21–28; grounded in social constructionism, 26–27; mental distinction of, 17; as ritual symbolization of power, 143; as separate from profane, 15–21, 24, 40–41; as set apart, 49–50; as symbol of power, 14–16, 17; as tool for understanding social arrangements, 17–18; as totality and as constituent parts, 19–20n.18

Sacred Canopy (Berger), 23

sacred canopy concept, 7, 38

Sacred Harp singing, 99

sacred heart, 180–81, 183

sacred-profane dualism, 15–21, 24, 40–41

sacred space, 55–56; control of, 59–62; differing from inward experience, 56–57; in homes, 57–58; murder in, 57; power dynamics in, 72–76; power to control uses of, 62–63; purity of, 61–62; regulations of, 57

sacred symbols, 27–28

saints, as emotional authorities, 130

Sallman, Warner, 66

San Antonio missions, preservation of, 62

Sánchez, Rafael, 123–24

Sanderson, Eleanor, 165

Satyananda Yoga, 182

Schaeffer, Edith and Francis, 69

Schaeffer, Frank, 69

Schleiermacher, Friedrich, 108, 111

Schmaus, Warren, 19n.18

Schmidt, Leigh, 68

Schutz, Alfred: on bodily expressions, 147–48; on fear of insignificance, 143–44; on intentions, 79; on multiple realities, 25–26; phenomenological sociology of, 23
Searle, John, 85–87, 90, 101–2
Second Tepeyac, 56–57
segmentation practices, 66
self, decentering of, 4–5
self-improvement, 172
self-perceptions, in rituals, 17
Seligman, Rebecca, 163
sensory ritual entrainment, 141
sermons, discursive structures in, 3
Set in Stone: America's Embrace of the Ten Commandments (Joselit), 66
sexual identities, 191
Shakta tantrism, 185–86
Sharp, Shane, 123
Sheila story, 139
sick-soul, 18
sign of the cross. *See* genuflecting
signaling threat, 50–51
sitting, as body routine, 156
situated temporal action, 4
situational cues, 46–53; activating habits, 46–47; affecting behavior, 51; disruptive, 52–53; hazardous, 52–53; for meals, 49; raising salience of person's identity, 50–51
situational dispositions, 3, 4
situational spaces: examples of, 53–54; practices defining meaning of, 54–55
situations: definition of, 44, 45; disciplining, 175–76; influencing religious practices, 42–43; as performative moments of valuation, 45n.10; power dynamics in, 72–76; practices anchored in, 47–48; in religious practices, 45–46; renewed interest in, 43–44; shaping religious activities and experiences, 8; synthetic, 67
skill, 70–71
Smith, Christian, 77, 128, 141
Smith, Wilfred Cantwell, 24
social assemblage, 45

social construction/constructionism, 3, 5, 26–27, 30, 36; of categories, 19n.18; enacted practices of, 20–21
Social Construction of Reality, 23
social interaction, 1, 4, 18, 23, 31–32; bodily engaged, 3, 6; digital, 179–80; governed by feeling rules, 144–45; in religious practice, 96–100; situated, 8, 11–12, 45, 194–95
social life: classification of, 16; religion interaction with, 39–40
social order, symbolism and, 14–15
social practices literature, late-20th-century, 3
social situations, feelings of well-being in, 116–17
social structure, 4–5; ambiguities in, 19n.18
social theory, intention in, 79–85
societal power, rituals as representations of, 181–82
Soka Gakkai, 59–60
somatic nationalism, 185, 186n.95
somatopoesis, 182
Sossa, Alexis, 171–72
South African Pentecostal churches, 126
space, 53–63; discursive, 55; dwelt-in, 54; multiple uses of, 62–63; as practiced place, 44; sacred, 55–57; where cues prompt habitual responses, 48–49
space under control, 59–60, 62–63; affordances in, 64–65
spatial Sunday, 54–55
Spencer, Herbert, 16
Spiegel, Gabrielle M., 32n.49
Spillman, Lyn, 183–84
Spiral Winds Coven, 100
spiritual affordances, 73
Spiritual Marketplace (Roof), 106
spiritual struggles, 118–19
Sponsler, Claire, 184
Springs, Jason A., 22n.24
Stark, David, 45
Starnes, Todd, 123
state, exercising discipline, 169; power of, 57, 178; role of in religious practice, 12

status distinctions, 3; affordances symbolizing, 70–72
Steele, Liza, 167
Stephens, Laura, 139
Stets, Jan E., 107n.4
Steven, Wallace, 24
Stout, Rowland, 87
Strand, Michael, 70
strictness, as practice, 166–67
structures: power and action interplay with, 32n.50; of practices, 34
structuring processes, 8, 14
styles of the flesh, 159–60
stylized beliefs, 110
subcultures, body discipline in, 171–72
sub-universes, 26
subversion, 161–62
Sullivan, Susan Crawford, 115
"Sunday best" attire, 161
supportive social relationships, 117
surveys, 9, 53, 66, 70, 84, 108, 113, 119, 125–26
Swaggart, Jimmy, 122
Swidler, Ann, 35–36, 83
symbol systems, 22; human need for, 28–29
symbolic codes, 19n.17
symbolic contributions, 103
symbolic universe, 23
symbolism, social order and, 14–15
symbols: body as, 180–81; in cultural system, 23; epistemological reality of, 24–25; transcendent, 25–26
synthetic situations, 67

Tam Giáo, intention in, 77
Tarde, Gabriel, 16
tattoos, 178
Taves, Ann, 108
Tavory, Iddo, 133
"Techniques of the Body" (Mauss), 147
technological affordances, 67
theodicies, 3, 21–22, 113
theoretical works, value of, 194
Thoreau, Henry David, 151
Thrift, Nigel, 155–56

Throop, C. Jason, 38n.63
Tilley, Charles, 91
Tillich, Paul, 24
tinkering, 177
Tomasello, Michael, 94–95
Tönnies, Ferdinand, 16
totalitarian states, body discipline in, 178
transcendence, 25–26
transcendent symbols, 25–26
tribal rituals, as representations of societal power, 181
Troeltsch, Ernst, 18
truth/falsehood, as institutional practices, 29–30
Turner, Jonathan H., 107n.4
Turner, Victor, 136
typifications, 88
typological demarcation, precariousness of, 19–20

uncertainty, 13
Unfinished: The Anthropology of Becoming (Biehl, Locke), 9
unreality, ontological questions about, 32
Upton, Candace, 47
Urapmin, spirit women of, 129
Urdank, Albion M., 39
Urry, John, 175

Van Beek, Walter E. A., 54
Varieties of Religious Experience (James), 152
Velde, Paul, 143
verbal alignment, 90–91
Vickery, Amanda, 60
Vietnamese American home altars, 58
violence, collective responses to, 188–89
Vipassana Buddhist meditation, 173, 175
virtual communication, 67

Wacker, Grant, 93
Wacquant, Loïc, 173
walking, 151–52; in religious practice accounts, 152–53; as spiritual practice, 153–55

"we-ness," 124–25

Weber, Max, 18, 23; on intention, 81–82; on meaning, 3, 25; on meaninglessness and theodicy, 21–22; on rationally ascetic economic behavior, 169–70; on religion as "switchman," 78

wedding rituals, 166

well-being, 116–20; situational variability in, 119–20

Wheaton, Belinda, 171

White, Geoffrey, 129, 130

White Christian nationalism, 124–25

White Noise (DeLillo), 152–53

Whitehead, Andrew L., 97–98

wholeness, symbols of, 25–26

Wicklund, Robert A., 103

Wilhelm Meister's Years of Travel (Goethe), 143–44

Winchester, Daniel, 133

windsurfing subculture, 171

Wittgenstein, Ludwig, 22; on intentionality, 87, 98–99, 100; on uses of language, 38

Woodward, Sophie, 161

workplace cultures, feeling rules in, 121–22

Wuthnow, Robert, 102

Yaqin, Amina, 162

Yiddish New Year's postcards, 67

yoga: body discipline of, 172, 178–79; rewards of, 94; Satyananda, 182

Yukich, Grace, 97

zeitgeist, culture as, 142

A NOTE ON THE TYPE

This book has been composed in Arno, an Old-style serif typeface in the classic Venetian tradition, designed by Robert Slimbach at Adobe.

GPSR Authorized Representative: Easy Access System Europe - Mustamäe tee
50, 10621 Tallinn, Estonia, gpsr.requests@easproject.com

www.ingramcontent.com/pod-product-compliance
Lightning Source LLC
Chambersburg PA
CBHW030618230426
43661CB00053B/2051